Hollow Victory

Hollow Victory

THE WHITE RIVER EXPEDITION OF 1879 AND THE BATTLE OF MILK CREEK

MARK E. MILLER

University Press of Colorado

© 1997 by the University Press of Colorado
Published by the University Press of Colorado
P.O. Box 849
Niwot, Colorado 80544
Tel. (303) 530-5337

All Rights reserved. Printed in the United States of America.

The University Press of Colorado is a cooperative publishing enterprise supported, in part, by Adams State College, Colorado State University, Fort Lewis College, Mesa State College, Metropolitan State College of Denver, University of Colorado, University of Northern Colorado, University of Southern Colorado, and Western State College of Denver.

Library of Congress Cataloging-in-Publication Data

Miller, Mark E., 1951–
    Hollow Victory: the White River Expedition of 1879 and the Battle of Milk Creek / Mark E. Miller.
    p. cm.
    Includes bibliographical references and index.
    ISBN 0-87081-463-X (hardcover : alk. paper)
    1. Milk Creek (Rio Blanco County and Moffat County, Colo.), Battle of, 1879. 2. Ute Indians–Wars, 1879. 3. Ute Indians–Government relations. 4. United States. Army. Cavalry, 5th. 5. Meeker, Nathan Cook, 1814-1879. I title.

E83.879.M56 1997   97-22971
973.8 ' 3--dc21   CIP

The paper used in this publication meets the minimum requirements of the American National Standard for Information Sciences—Permanence of Paper for Printed Library Materials. ANSI Z39.48-1948

10 9 8 7 6 5 4 3 2 1

*This book is dedicated to my parents,
Frank and Betty Rose,
and to the memory of the Fort Fred Steele garrison
June 1868–November 1886*

Contents

Preface		ix
Acknowledgments		xv
Chapter 1	Seeds of Discord	1
Chapter 2	The White River Expedition	11
Chapter 3	March to Milk Creek	27
Chapter 4	September 29, 1879	53
Chapter 5	Entrenchment at Milk Creek	85
Chapter 6	The Whitest Black Men in the Cavalry	95
Chapter 7	Merritt's Lightning March	125
Chapter 8	Aftermath	145
Appendix A	Roster of Expeditionary Troops and Civilians	161
Appendix B	Casualties at Milk Creek September 29–October 5, 1879	171
Appendix C	Citations for Bravery at the Battle of Milk Creek	181
Appendix D	Official Reports and Selected Correspondence Regarding the Milk Creek Battle	193
Notes		211
Bibliography		231
Index		241

Preface

. . . one wonders how we learn from our past if our historical legacy is little more than a series of inaccuracies passed from one generation to the next.
—Christian J. Buys, 1986[1]

National attention riveted on northwestern Colorado in the fall of 1879 when U.S. troops from Fort Fred Steele in Wyoming Territory fought a pitched battle with Ute Indians in an isolated Rocky Mountain valley in Colorado. Called the White River Expedition, the military detail led by Major Thomas T. Thornburgh was sent to arrest insurgent Ute Indian leaders at the White River Agency, Colorado. The expedition marched over one hundred fifty miles in nine days, September 21 to September 29, 1879, before it reached Milk Creek, twenty-two miles short of its destination on the Ute Reservation. There, just inside the northern border of the reservation, troops met armed resistance from a Ute force; a quiet valley erupted in prolonged and bloody conflict. On the same day that engagement began, Utes killed all of the male employees at the agency and took women and children hostage. Details of the outbreak at the agency, known as the Meeker Massacre, and subsequent changes in Indian policy have been covered in a number of publications, but I focus on the drama of the hardships endured and courage of the members of the expedition.

This brief episode in Western history is important for several reasons. First, it is an excellent example of how disparate Indian policies were between the Department of the Interior and War Department, and how the lack of open dialog with Native Americans produced brutal consequences in the West. A complex series of events precipitated the engagement at Milk Creek and carved an indelible mark on Western history. The causes and the effects testify to the serious problem of communication that so often blocks peaceful exchange between nations in conflict.

Second, the Milk Creek battle lasted 142 hours and thus became one of the longest sustained fights between the U. S. Cavalry and Native Americans during decades of the 1850s through the 1890s, the years of the Indian wars. The Apache War (1881–1886)and the Nez Perce migration in 1877 were composed of a series of briefer battles and skirmishes over longer periods of time. Rescue of combatants in 1868 at Beecher Island, in what is now eastern Colorado, took longer, but the battle was between the Cheyenne and volunteers rather than army regulars.

Third, some Utes and soldiers at Milk Creek were former allies in the Sioux war and had actually become friends during the Big Horn and Yellowstone Expedition of 1876. Consequently, they might have been able to negotiate through their differences and reach a peaceful resolution to the problems at the agency. Instead the incident became a costly lesson in failed diplomacy.

Fourth, although many good primary and secondary references cover these events, there remains considerable ambiguity about specific circumstances. A clear need exists for a synthesis of the evidence and development of an explanatory model for what occurred as a guide for future interdisciplinary research.

No one won the battle of Milk Creek. Although the Utes controlled the battlefield for 138 hours, they ultimately lost when they were forced from reservation lands in Colorado and sent to a new reservation in Utah. The soldiers likewise failed to protect agency personnel from a few Indians. Indian agent Nathan C. Meeker, who more than anyone precipitated the confrontation, lost his life. Perhaps the only benefactors were settlers who moved onto what had been Ute Reservation lands in Colorado. Any gain at the expense of an entire culture is, at best, a hollow victory.

In some ways the final outcome of the conflict is less provocative than the obscure but revealing details of the White River Expedition itself. Accurate contemporary written records are sparse; there were no newspaper correspondents at the battle; the first correspondent arrived with the relief column led by Colonel Wesley Merritt, and few eyewitness accounts are available except in official records and congressional testimony. Yet there are many secondary references, reminiscences, and analyses that were written several years, if not decades, after the incident. Researchers who compare and contrast these versions quickly discover contradictions, misquotes, and blind alleys. Scholar Christian J. Buys pointed out at least eighteen discrepancies in primary and secondary accounts. He characterized the expedition history as a "complex labyrinth of conflicting historical reports," and claimed that, because of a lack of consensus about particular aspects, researchers can raise legitimate concerns "about reliably describing this historical event."[2]

Buys is so critical of the literature about the battle that he concluded researchers cannot establish major events of the attack because there is insufficient agreement among authors.[3] He is correct in his assessment of numerous discrepancies, but I disagree that the discrepancies prevent researchers from reconstructing details. While conflicting interpretations do exist, a careful screening of primary sources exposes probable event sequences and tactical maneuvers that help to re-create this fateful engagement.

Even so, the recognition of inaccurate recording and the perception of ambiguities pervade the entire history of the incident. Controversy over the accuracy of newspaper accounts developed as soon as the battle ended; a controversy even raged within the ranks of the United States Army. Captain J. S. Payne, who commanded the besieged troops, declared that, while some of the events chronicled in the daily and illustrated press were true, many stories were the purest fiction. He wrote his account of the battle in *The United Service*, published in 1880, because he realized that he could not disabuse "the public mind of the many erroneous impressions of that affair," a task he considered useless.[4] General George Crook, on the other hand, who had orchestrated the relief forces and eventually coordinated reinforcement efforts from Fort Fred Steele and Rawlins, proclaimed in his annual report that "the public journals gave such exhaustive and accurate narrations" that it was unnecessary for him to go into detail about the Ute outbreak.[5]

These opposing opinions probably stem from the fact that there were two story lines related to the White River Expedition of 1879: the first was about the battle and the second was the account of the relief force. When correspondents arrived in Rawlins and at Milk Creek, the battle was no longer a hot story. Several correspondents, including John C. Dyer of the *New York World* and *Chicago Tribune*, Jerome B. Stillson of the *New York Herald*, John F. Finerty of the *Chicago Times*, and W. P. Boardman of the *Denver Tribune*, wrote what they could although none saw any combat at Milk Creek.[6]

Because no correspondents rode with Major Thomas Thornburgh's expedition, there were no journalists who were eyewitnesses; all of their information was secondhand. This opened the door for misquotes and embellishment of details when reporters interviewed combatants or tried to reconstruct events from official records. Captain Payne's criticism centers specifically on coverage of the battle. Reporters who wanted stories with firsthand facts were compelled to chronicle the relief force, the march to the agency, and subsequent activities of the peace commission rather than the battle. These eyewitness, follow-up stories were probably more accurate and may be what General Crook praised so highly.

Of those who took part in the battle, some obviously were better positioned than others to see certain aspects of the engagement. The accuracy of individual recollections, therefore, varies dramatically even when an impartial correspondent takes the interview. The range of observations from among the participants is so broad that this factor alone gives rise to some of the confusion that permeates the historical record.

All of these limitations were clear when I wrote this book. Like many other sources, this is a secondary historical account. While I cite many of the familiar, often ambiguous references, as well as additional sources, my goal is not to be the final word on the White River Expedition. Rather the events chronicled are offered as a basis for future studies that may apply expertise from fields other than history. The sequence and detail of many specific incidents should be scrutinized with a search for new and independent data, particularly through interdisciplinary research. Indeed, current thinking in battlefield studies virtually requires that researchers integrate the written record and archaeological evidence to develop more holistic explanations of combat behavior.[7]

The Milk Creek battle site is now on the National Register of Historic Places, and some of its archaeological record remains intact even though substantial quantities of battle relics have been removed without detailed documentation.⁸ This record at the site and at sites related to the expedition, if ever subjected to systematic archaeological research, may clarify some of the lingering historical questions that have frustrated researchers for so long. For instance, what was the actual route of the expedition between Rawlins and Milk Creek? Exactly where were the field camps located which were used during the march? How did the order of battle unfold? Detailed study of the terrain may reveal the old agency road tracks, debris at the camps along the route, Lieutenant Butler D. Price's entrenchments at the Fortification Creek supply camp, and artifacts from initial battle positions and subsequent tactical maneuvers by both forces. The historic landscape of the White River Expedition has undergone a series of changes in land ownership. Federal, state, and private lands now encompass what was the arena for Major Thornburgh, Agent Meeker, and the Ute Nation in 1879. Careful and deliberate negotiations between scholars and landowners are required to adequately research and preserve the remaining delicate historical evidence.

Lacking an archaeological record, I have delved deeper into historical records to establish relevant facets of the White River Expedition. I used archival documents such as post returns and muster rolls found at the National Archives to resolve questions of troop strength and composition. Some veterans even recalled specific battle scenes in a few obscure newspaper interviews. Hopefully these accounts will prove useful if investigators conduct on-site research to identify any patterning in the distribution of material remains.

Some inconsistencies, however, will always remain. I have tried to include each significant incident mentioned by every author I encountered, although I am sure I may have missed some. Many incidents cannot be verified because they are not corroborated in separate accounts by other authors.

When two or more authors mention the same event but disagree on the details, I tried to use the version most often corroborated in multiple sources. Of the primary sources, those documents written shortly after the battle are generally more convincing than those written by and about participants decades later. The passage of time seems to have clouded the facts and inflated the exploits.

Misspellings occur throughout many of the references I quote. I included most of the text as it was written, rather than make extensive use of the word sic, and made spelling corrections only to reduce confusion. Finally, any omissions or lingering inaccuracies remain my responsibility.

Mark E. Miller
Laramie, Wyoming
April 16, 1997

Acknowledgments

Dozens of people and organizations deserve special acknowledgment for their assistance in helping me to prepare this manuscript. Many benefactors are mentioned here, but for those whom I may have missed, you have an equal share of my gratitude for all that you have done. Several individuals and agencies provided photographs and illustrations to accompany the text. Their courtesy is acknowledged in each figure caption.

The research could not have been completed without the assistance of many individuals. These include George Brox of Rawlins, Wyoming; William Jayne of the National Cemetery System, Department of Veterans Affairs, Washington, D.C.; Daniel Y. Meschter of Wenatchee, Washington; Kevin Black, Colorado State Archaeologist's Office; Dale Wedel of the Wyoming State Archaeologist's Office; and Anne Bond of the Colorado Historical Society, who sent information on Buffalo Soldiers in Colorado. Also helpful were the staffs of several research facilities, including the American Heritage Center at the University of Wyoming, the State Archives and Historical Section of the Department of Commerce in Cheyenne, Coe Library at the University of Wyoming, the Albany County, Wyoming, Public Library, and the Military Reference Branch of the National Archives in Washington, D.C. Rod Miller, Dr. Dave Kathka, Dr. Phil Roberts, Leona Miller, and two reviewers for the University Press of Colorado, John Monnett and David Halaas, read all or portions of earlier versions of this manuscript and helped me correct the obvious errors. I extend my warm personal gratitude to Clifford Duncan, former Northern Ute tribal historian, for helping me keep perspective on the different ways the U.S. government and Ute Nation recognized leadership and authority within the tribe.

I would like to thank four individuals at the University Press of Colorado for their help and encouragement during this project: Luther Wilson, director; Jody Berman, former managing editor; Amy H. Sorrells, editorial and production manager; and Laura Furney, acquisitions editor. Thanks also to Sallie M. Greenwood for sharing her editorial skills. Finally, thanks to my wife, Leona, and son, Joshua, for their patient endurance while I spent endless hours on this manuscript.

Thanks to all of you whose help made this book possible.

Hollow Victory

1
Seeds of Discord

. . . awe these savages, so that they will stay at home.
—Nathan C. Meeker, August 11, 1879[1]

Native culture in North America had maintained a successful Stone Age existence for over eleven thousand years before cross-cultural contact with Euroamericans beginning in the sixteenth century brought unprecedented change. After centuries of contact, the 1870s were particularly troubled years for native people in the American West because peaceful coexistence with immigrants and settlers finally ceased on the High Plains and in the Rocky Mountains. By the close of the decade, the end of their free roaming, indigenous culture was profound, and the land and the people who lived there were changed forever.

The foundations for trouble at the White River Agency, one of three agencies on the Ute Reservation in Colorado, were building for the decade prior to the 1879 battle on Milk Creek. By 1870, the Union Pacific Railroad, which, with the Central Pacific, completed the first transcontinental railroad just the year before, helped open public access to traditional Indian homelands. Just as the Oregon and Bozeman Trails had affected the Sioux and Cheyenne only a few years earlier, the railroad now stimulated settlement and enhanced commercial development in territories recently occupied only by Ute equestrian hunters and gatherers. The resulting demographic, economic, and social changes developed more quickly than did comprehension of their impact. These changes set the Ute Nation on a collision course with the frenzied charge of Manifest Destiny. Regular contacts had occurred between the Utes and immigrants from the United States in the 1850s and 1860s and even earlier, primarily in regions south and east of White River country.[2] There had even been a brief conflict in 1854–1855 when the army retaliated against marauding

Utes. But those exchanges were inconclusive and cultural differences remained in a tenuous balance. To alleviate problems of extensive contact between Utes and settlers, a reservation was established in 1868 in western Colorado. Even though the region encompassed about 15 million acres, the Utes faced growing sedentism unfamiliar to their traditional way of life.

In 1878 the Yampa and Grand River Ute bands were affiliated with the White River Agency in the remote northern part of the Ute Reservation. Other bands occupied the southern reaches of the reservation, at Ignacio and at Los Piños; some lived under the capable leadership of Ouray, perhaps the most diplomatic of all Ute leaders. Although free to roam throughout the region, eight hundred men, women, and children enrolled that year at White River.[3]

A rough estimate is that six hundred of them were women and children and there were perhaps two hundred adult males. On the other hand, General of the Army William Tecumseh Sherman calculated that the Ute population for the combined bands in 1879 was 4,164, of whom about eight hundred were warriors. Using Sherman's numbers, the warriors, then, composed 19 percent of the 4,164 Ute population. Applying the 19 percent figure to the eight hundred Utes enrolled at the White River Agency suggests that about 152 band members could have been skilled and battle-tested fighters at the time of the Milk Creek engagement.[4]

At least three principals had assumed leadership roles in the White River bands by the late 1870s: Chief Jack, whose Indian name was Nicaagat; Colorow, a Comanche; and Douglas, who was also known as Quinkent. Each man was a powerful personality in his own right and would figure prominently in the events of September and October 1879.

The Ute people had lived in the western part of North America for millennia. Generations had called the area now known as Colorado home. But with the encroachment of Euroamerican settlers, the country did not seem as big as it once was, and in 1879 the Utes faced a host of festering troubles.

Western Colorado is a rugged country. Geological forces had long since shaped the Rocky Mountain landscape and created high elevations and undulating topography that supported diverse ecosystems and

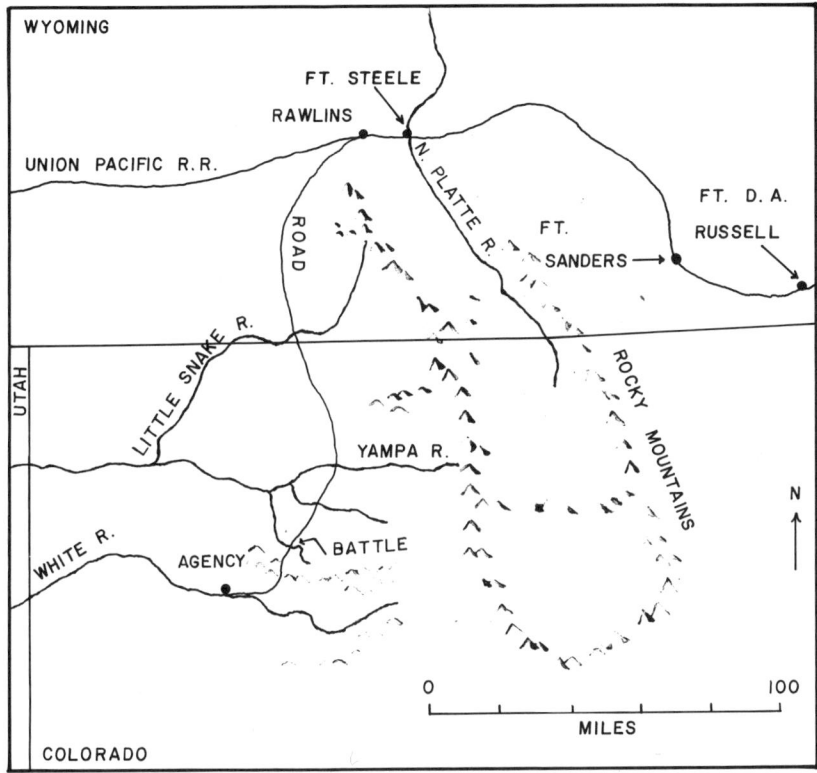

Map 1.1 The scene of the 1879 White River Expedition and Ute homeland.

contained a rich variety of natural resources. But a bountiful country was a mixed blessing in the late nineteenth century. While some bedrock formations contained high-quality chert and quartzite ideal for making arrowheads and tools, other strata held minerals and precious metals that were almost useless to native populations but valued greatly by the advancing white culture. In 1873 the encroaching Euroamericans got the minerals and precious metals that they wanted so desperately through peaceful, if not coercive, negotiation when the Utes signed the Brunot Treaty and relinquished the silver-rich San Juan Mountains of southern Colorado Territory to the United States.[5]

The economy of the United States was suffering in the early 1870s even though the post–Civil War West presented a huge frontier for expansion. Eager efforts to exploit the West and conspicuous post-war consumption combined to shake the nation's economic stability. American culture had over-expanded, citizens had over-consumed, industry over-produced, and unscrupulous financiers had misused credit.[6] The result was the economic crisis of 1873 that was fueled in part by uncertainty over how to deal with rich yields from newly discovered silver lodes in the West.

Demand for silver was low because the gold standard for coinage was more widely accepted, yet the bullion supply was growing thanks to the Western mines. Also, Congress had dropped the standard silver dollar from the list of United States coins in 1873. A year later, in an unsuccessful effort to furnish more money to the economy without using silver, the federal government, under pressure from bankers, manufacturers, and farmers, inflated currency by issuing paper money even though it was not backed up by large amounts of gold in the treasury. Within five years, politicians returned to silver coinage as a partial solution to the cash-flow problem. The United States renewed silver dollars as legal tender on February 28, 1878 under the Bland-Allison Act.[7]

Silver speculators now had a major market that encouraged mineral exploration farther into remote regions of western Colorado. In 1878 and 1879 the United States minted over fifty million new coins, called Morgan dollars for their designer, George T. Morgan, at facilities in Philadelphia, New Orleans, San Francisco, and Carson City. Each coin contained 90 percent silver and 10 percent copper, with an individual net weight of .77344 ounces of pure silver.[8]

Demand for minerals was not the only or even the most important concern to Utes, who may have tolerated mining if other problems hadn't followed so closely. For example, when Colorado became a state in 1876, many citizens mounted a campaign to urge the federal government to remove the tribe to Indian Territory, the region that later became Oklahoma. Forcing the Indians to leave would free the entire reservation for economic development and white settlement.[9] Residents even tried to expedite removal by discrediting the Utes by blaming them for unsolved crimes and for crimes that had never occurred.

Northwestern Colorado was becoming a political maelstrom in which the White River Utes struggled to survive. Adding fuel to the growing turmoil was the arrival of an inexperienced Indian agent at White River in the spring of 1878, a replacement for the Reverend E. H. Danforth, who had been there since 1874. Nathan C. Meeker, an "elderly eccentric who had dabbled in several of the unorthodox intellectual and social movements of the period," had just come from a shaky attempt to form a utopian colony north of Denver named for his longtime acquaintance, Horace Greeley.[10] The project adversely affected Meeker personally and financially.

Meeker was determined to regain his financial standing and to rekindle his preoccupation with social reform at White River. He worked diligently to compel the Utes to abandon their traditional lifestyle in favor of agricultural self-sufficiency and urged them to comply with his idealized model of civilization. In contrast to his work at the Greeley community, Meeker's naive and uncompromising demands would yield more than a failed social experiment.

Meeker's problems with the Utes began as soon as he moved the agency to the fertile Powell Valley, downriver from Danforth's original location. The new site, chosen in the summer of 1878, was a dozen or so miles to the southwest, at a lower elevation, and better suited to Meeker's agricultural objectives. The relocation angered many Utes because they grazed their pony herds on the lush grasses of the Powell Valley and often held horse races there. Meeker ignored traditional land uses when he selected the new site and encouraged Utes to become farmers; he wanted them to dig irrigation ditches, plow up the sod, and farm the land. Douglas and a few other Utes fiddled a bit with farming, but most of the Indians were extremely reluctant and would not farm unless compelled to do so. Jack and Colorow led the strongest resistance.

Tension between the Indians and the reformer grew. By the summer of 1879 Meeker concluded that he couldn't accomplish his utopian goals without military assistance from the War Department. His efforts to obtain armed support from the War Department began a confusing dialogue with his agency, the Deparment of the Interior, which had no military function, and the War Department regarding jurisdiction over reservation Utes in northwestern Colorado.

Part of the problem in requesting military intervention was the manner in which the War Department administered the West. Fourteen Western states and territories composed the Military Division of the Missouri, which was then subdivided into four departments. The area of northern Colorado was in the Department of the Missouri and administered from Fort Leavenworth, Kansas, while the nearest military outpost, Fort Fred Steele, north of the agency and in Wyoming Territory, was in the Department of the Platte and administered from Omaha Barracks in Nebraska. Meeker's initial efforts to involve the army were to write two letters to the post commander at Fort Fred Steele, Major Thomas T. Thornburgh, the first in November 1878 and the second in June 1879. The second letter caused Thornburgh to try to ascertain the validity of some of Meeker's accusations regarding Ute behavior off of the reservation. Meeker thought that Utes were leaving the reservation and heading north to buy ammunition from stores along the rivers and to conduct raids. It is equally possible, however, that they were going to Wyoming to trade with the Shoshone for buffalo robes.

Utes leaving the reservation was only one of the agent's concerns. The summer of 1879 brought drought conditions to much of the Colorado mountain country. Streams were low on the western slope, and many drainages were reduced to trickles. Brush and grass were tinder dry and Meeker suspected the Utes of having set numerous fires that were raging in nearby hills. Meeker made that particular accusation in a letter to Thornburgh in June, and that precipitated Thornburgh's inquiries. He sent his findings to Brigadier General George Crook, commander of the Department of the Platte headquartered at Omaha Barracks:

> Headquarters Fort Fred Steele, Wyo.,
> July 27, 1879
>
> SIR: I have the honor to submit the following report of the recent visit of the Ute Indians from the White River Agency to this vicinity:
> About the 25th of June a band of some 100 Indians from the White River Agency made their appearance at a mining camp on the divide near the head of Jack and Savoy Creeks, some 60 miles south of this post and engaged in hunting and trading in this vicinity for about one week, when they departed (as they said) for their agency.

I did not learn of the presence of these Indians until after their departure, nor was I notified by the agent at White River that they had left their agency until June 11, when I received a communication from him dated June 7, stating that a considerable number of the Indians had left their reservation and were burning timber and wantonly destroying game along Bear and Snake Rivers, also warning all miners and ranchmen, and requesting me to cause them to return to their reservation. Upon receiving this letter I made inquiries and could not find such a state of affairs to exist, but did find that the Indians had killed a great deal of game and used the skins for trade. The miners they visited in this section were not molested, but on the contrary were presented with an abundance of game. No stock was molested, and so far as I can learn no one attributes the burning of timber to these Indians.

Since I have been in command of this post (one year) Agent Meeker, of the White River agency, has written me two letters, dated November 11, 1878, and June 7, 1879. These letters have usually come to me after the Indians had paid a flying but peaceable visit to this country and departed (as they always say) to their agency. The White River Agency is situated some 200 miles from this post, and there are very few settlers in the country between Fort Fred Steele and the agency, consequently I am not informed as soon as I should be of the movements of these Indians. Bear and Snake Rivers are about 100 miles from this post, and to reach them by travelling this distance would require the trip to be made through a very rough country, impracticable for wagons, the only transportation available. I have never received any orders from my superior to cause these Indians to remain on their reservation at the request of the agent, but am ready to attempt anything required of me. I have been able to communicate with nearly every ranchman residing within 100 miles of this post in reference to the late visit of these Indians, and forward herewith letters received from them. Both the letters mentioned above as having been received from Agent Meeker were forwarded to higher authority, and instructions have been asked to guide me in this matter.

> I am, very respectfully, your obedient servant,
> T. T. Thornburgh, Major Fourth Infantry,
> Commanding Post[11]

The correspondence from ranchers that Major Thornburgh mentioned came from several reputable men in the territory. Among them were Taylor Pennock, B. T. Ryan, W. B. Hugus, and J. W. Hugus. Not one of these men believed that any brushfires had been started by the Utes. In fact, the letter from W. B. Hugus mentioned that tie-men, workmen associated with the Union Pacific Railroad, admitted that fires on Brush and French Creeks had caught from their own campfires.[12] Even though the Indian agent had told Commissioner of Indian Affairs E. A. Hayt, in July, that the Utes had set the fires, the person responsible for starting the biggest "brushfire" may have been Nathan Meeker himself.[13]

The major and Agent Meeker met by chance on a railroad car a few days after Thornburgh had sent his message to General Crook. Meeker asked about the military's position on the Ute troubles, and Thornburgh answered that he had forwarded all of the agent's correspondence to higher authority but had not yet received any orders. Thornburgh then suggested that if Meeker requested the secretary of war to command him to keep the Indians on their reservation, then he could start a company of fifty cavalry with a day's notice. He would not advance, however, until commanded by his superiors to do so.[14]

By August 4 General Crook had written an endorsement memo to be attached to a growing file of correspondence relating to Meeker's complaints. Crook wrote that, "unless troops are stationed at the agencies they cannot know, in time, when Indians are absent by authority; nor can they prevent the occurrence of troubles, for which they are frequently, and most unjustly held responsible."[15] Crook's position was based in part on information from Thornburgh's July 27 report.

Meeker, in a July 7 letter to Commissioner Hayt, criticized Thornburgh for disregarding his requests for military intervention during the early summer. In another letter to Hayt, dated August 11, Meeker characterized the Utes and their lifeways in contemptuous terms and wrote that, "what I want is sufficient military force to be sent hither to awe these savages, so that they will stay at home. When this shall be done, the Indians will be in a condition to improve, but now it is simply impossible, indeed I fear they are already so demoralized that years upon years will be required to make anything out of them."[16]

Meeker detailed three requirements that would facilitate his job at the White River Agency. First, the military must end the sale and distribution of ammunition, liquor, and annuity goods (products due annually to the Indians as a condition of a treaty) at stores off the reservation. Second, military intervention at these stores would help end the hunting lifestyle and force Indians to trap or work other ways to get money. Third, he would establish a store for the Utes at the White River Agency and would have the military keep Indians on the reservation and other white men off.[17] Meeker obviously would have been satisfied if these requirements were met. Coincidentally, he could also monopolize all commerce available to the Yampa and Grand River bands, who stayed at White River.

Annuity goods, an element in Meeker's first requirement, were important to the Utes because they were legally entitled to them as enrolled members of a reservation. The reservation system, however, made Utes dependent on the U.S. government for basic food items, yet they were almost powerless to ensure their delivery. What Meeker didn't mention was that some annuities had *not been delivered* for two years. James France, a Rawlins, Wyoming, businessman had held some twenty-five thousand pounds of flour, oats, and other supplies destined for the reservation because D. J. McCann, a contractor, hadn't paid a railroad freight bill. McCann, later charged with stealing government Indian agency supplies, spent a year at the Territorial Penitentiary in Laramie but was eventually found innocent.[18] Of course, Meeker might have wanted to control all annuity outlets to ensure that crucial commodities reached legitimate recipients on time.

Neither the Department of the Interior nor the War Department responded to Meeker's requests in ways that would have eased the tension. Tempers finally flared at White River on Monday, September 8, when Agent Meeker and Johnson, a Ute medicine man whose Indian name was Canalla or Canavish, argued over racehorses and the irrigation ditch. Strong words precipitated a brief fistfight, which ended when Johnson threw Meeker against a hitching post. Meeker's ego was bruised more than his body, and on September 10 he wrote Colorado governor F. W. Pitkin that the lives of his family and agency personnel were in danger and called once again for military assistance. He telegraphed the same message on September 13 to Commissioner of Indian Affairs E. A. Hayt at the Department of the Interior in Washington, DC.[19] Meeker's request for help set in motion events that precipitated the battle of Milk Creek. On September 15, 1879, a week after the fight, Acting Secretary of the Interior A. Bell wrote to Secretary of War George McCrary to request military support at White River from the nearest post. Responsibility soon passed down the chain of command when Secretary of War McCrary contacted General of the Army William Tecumseh Sherman, who contacted Lieutenant General Philip Sheridan, commander of the Military Division of the Missouri, whose office contacted General Crook at Omaha Barracks.[20] Utopia now seemed very far away.

2
The White River Expedition

. . . you will enforce obedience to the requirements of Agent Meeker.
—General George Crook, September 16, 1879[1]

Thomas Tipton Thornburgh was born on December 26, 1843 in New Market, in eastern Tennessee. He saw his first military action as a teenage volunteer private in the Union army during the Civil War. His regiment was the Sixth East Tennessee Infantry, which fought under Colonel Joseph A. Cooper in the Stones River campaign during the winter of 1862–1863.[2]

Thomas Thornburgh entered the U.S. Military Academy at West Point on July 1, 1863, the first day of the decisive Civil War battle at Gettysburg. He was commissioned a second lieutenant of artillery on June 17, 1867 and became a first lieutenant on April 21, 1870. Thornburgh's relatively rapid promotion to major and paymaster on April 26, 1875 was due in part to solid political connections through his brother, J. M. Thornburgh, former member of Congress from Tennessee.[3]

Thornburgh tired of paymaster duty by the spring of 1878. He yearned for a field commission and took the opportunity to transfer when General Crook in Omaha offered him a chance to switch positions with Major Henry G. Thomas, post commander at Fort Fred Steele in Wyoming Territory. Major Thornburgh grabbed the offer and transferred to the Fourth Infantry Regiment on May 23, 1878. He took command of the Wyoming post that had been established in 1868 to protect Union Pacific Railroad workers, and he became the only major in the regiment.[4]

Thornburgh did not have to wait long for a field command. On September 13, 1878, orders from the Department of the Platte sent him with a detachment of thirty-seven enlisted men of Company H, Fourth Infantry under First Lieutenant James H. Spencer into Nebraska to help stop the Cheyenne exodus from Indian Territory. Thornburgh believed that a successful campaign would repay General Crook for helping him secure his new post assignment, but this was not to be.

He was to patrol sixty miles of the Platte River and to intercept the Cheyennes if they attempted a crossing on their way north to their old homelands on the plains. The major requested pack mules and Indian scouts to expedite his search. Instead he was issued wagons that slowed him down and sent cattlemen whose tracking capabilities were limited. The Cheyennes crossed the river with Thornburgh in pursuit, but his wagons bogged down in quicksand, and the cattlemen lost interest in tracking the Indians when the Indians were no longer a threat to the cattlemen's livestock. Amid decoy trails, false accounts of Indian depredations, and faced with dwindling provisions, Thornburgh failed to stop the Cheyenne migration. He felt that he had let General Crook down, even though his detail, one of many in the region, had given the Indians their hottest chase.[5]

In spite of his failure, the major made a name for himself during an encounter at Camp Sheridan in Nebraska with Red Cloud and Young Man Afraid of His Horse, two Sioux leaders, during a council that provided a temporary respite from the harsh expedition. Red Cloud ridiculed the quality of the army's Springfield .45-70 rifles in front of Thornburgh, and the major took issue with the aging chief. Reportedly Thornburgh picked up a "Long Tom" and shot half dollars out of the air. The Sioux were so impressed with his marksmanship that they named Thornburgh "Chief Who Shoots The Stars."[6] Thornburgh returned to Fort Fred Steele with a solid reputation as a marksman.

Shortly after his return, he faced an even greater personal tragedy than the Nebraska mission. His three-year-old son, George W., died on March 5, 1879.[7] Infant George was buried at his father's lonely outpost along the banks of the North Platte River. The major and his wife, Lida, barely had time to mourn before events at White River escalated and duty beckoned once more.

General Crook sent a telegram to Thornburgh on September 16; the text bore a remarkable similarity to a September 15 letter from Commissioner of Indian Affairs Hayt to Secretary of the Interior Carl

Schurz. Meeker clearly was winning the battle of intimidation; Ute unrest had become a War Department matter:

> Headquarters Dept. of the Platte
> Asst. Adjutant General's Office
> Fort Omaha, Neb., September 16, 1879
>
> Commanding Officer
> Fort Fred Steele, Wyo.
>
> Under orders from the General of the Army, you will at once move with sufficient number of troops to arrest such Indian chiefs belonging to White River Agency as are insubordinate, and you will enforce obedience to the requirements of Agent Meeker. You will afford him such protection as the exigency of the case requires and hold the ringleaders as prisoners until an investigation can be had. You are authorized to suspend orders for movement of "E" Company, Third Cavalry, and to use this Company if necessary. Report receipt of this by telegraph and if you require additional troops.
>
> By Command of General Crook
> (Signed) R. Williams
> A. A. General[8]

Thornburgh acted quickly and decisively, determined that this time he would not let Crook down. He hardly slept the next two nights while making preparations, pondering troop strength, securing field provisions, and ordering transportation. He consulted with Captain William H. Bisbee, Fourth Infantry, who had just finished an inspection report at Fort Fred Steele on September 1, 1879.[9]

Bisbee's report, completed just two weeks before, shows that the troops available to Thornburgh were Companies E and H of the Fourth Infantry, and Company E of the Third Cavalry.

Company E, Fourth Infantry comprised three officers and forty-six enlisted men of whom sixteen were on special extra or daily duty, two were sick, and one was in arrest or confinement. One of the sick men, Sergeant William Keon, died on September 8, a week after Bisbee's inspection report.[10] One officer and three enlisted men were on detached service, and a second officer was absent with leave. Consequently, the field operating strength at the fort on the first of the month was limited to one officer and twenty-four enlisted men present for duty.

Company E, Third Cavalry was a different story. The need for mounted troops at Fort Fred Steele had diminished following the end of the Sioux war of 1876 and 1877, so the army had ordered Companies E, K, and M, Third Cavalry to Rock Creek, Wyoming, about fifty miles east of the fort on the Union Pacific Railroad, and then they were to proceed north to Fort McKinney, near present-day Buffalo, Wyoming. The Quartermaster's Department was furnishing the necessary transportation for the transfer when tempers flared at White River.

Company E consisted of one commanding officer and thirty-six cavalrymen present for duty on September 1. Seventeen other enlisted men were on special extra or daily duty and three were sick. Two officers were absent with leave and one enlisted man was absent without authority.

Captain Bisbee and nineteen enlisted men from Company H of the Fourth Infantry completed the Fort Fred Steele garrison present for duty and not assigned to other service. There simply were not enough men at the fort. Thornburgh would have to juggle his small command and request additional cavalry to assemble an effective expedition.

Troop strength was only one consideration since the expedition also needed supplies for extended duty. Bisbee's report listed ample supplies of good quality medical and hospital stores, and many of these would be needed. Animals on hand were in good condition and none had been used for unauthorized purposes such as personal trips or as draft animals. As of September 1, the stables contained ten serviceable draft horses and twenty-four serviceable mules. These animals and the cavalry mounts had been regularly fed with contract forage. Equipage was a bigger problem, however. Wagons and harnesses were in poor to fair condition and only two ambulances, three spring wagons, seven army wagons, and three carts were on hand. Thornburgh needed more vehicles to transport men and supplies.

The Fort Fred Steele magazine housed quantities of ordnance. Bisbee reported two field pieces (most likely twelve-pounder mountain howitzers), 132 rifles and carbines (by now these were the Springfield .45-70 Trap-Doors), and seventeen revolvers. Ammunition included 590 field-piece rounds, 11,000 rifle and carbine rounds, and 4,764 revolver rounds. Major Thornburgh would not need a howitzer since his orders were for a police action rather than warfare; a cannon would hardly convince the Utes of the military's peaceful intentions should any sensitive negotiations develop.

While these supplies were sufficient for a downsized garrison or a field command not expecting resistance, they probably were inadequate for a prolonged campaign against a well-equipped enemy. General Crook's troops, for example, used 25,000 rounds during a six-hour battle with a thousand to fifteen hundred Sioux on the Rosebud River in Montana Territory on June 17, 1876.[11] While Crook had a larger command than Thornburgh's and therefore would have expended more rounds, there is no doubt that soldiers wasted cartridges during that encounter. An expedition without adequate firepower while facing a potentially hostile adversary was taking a great risk.

The Fort Fred Steele garrison was well aware of the volatile situation at White River. An almost prophetic note in Bisbee's September 1, 1879 report portrayed the military's perspective on the disposition of Indians in the vicinity. He characterized the Utes at White River as treacherous and suggested that they bore watching.[12]

Major Thornburgh completed his appraisal of men, equipment, and supplies and sent a telegram to Omaha Barracks on the same day he had received his orders: "Your telegram received. I will make my arrangements to move as soon as possible. I don't believe it safe or prudent to go to the White River Agency with the troops at my disposal. I could not take more than eighty (80) men and it is evident the Utes mean mischief. I want fifteen wagons now at Rock Creek."[13] Perhaps anticipating difficulty in getting enough wagons, Thornburgh also sent a message to a Colonel Bronson in Rawlins, inquiring about the cost of getting immediate horse and mule transportation to move 50,000 pounds of expedition supplies.[14]

In a second telegram to Crook, Thornburgh reiterated the need for wagons: "With cavalry I can march to White River Agency in seven or eight days and with three companies I believe there will be but little risk. There are twenty-five wagons at Rock Creek and I should have them for forage and rations. In case I take all cavalry or for my infantry to ride distance to White River Agency two hundred miles. I have sufficient supplies at the post."[15] The wagons at Rock Creek probably were those supplied by the Quartermaster's Department to transport the Third Cavalry companies to Fort McKinney. Now a greater need loomed; Thornburgh ordered them to Fort Fred Steele.

The major then considered a command staff, and in one message he asked Lieutenant John Bourke, aide-de-camp at Omaha Barracks, to accompany the White River Expedition. Bourke could not go, so the major made alternative arrangements by assigning expedition responsibilities to other officers.

Wednesday, September 17 dawned with the continuation of furious planning; time was short. Thornburgh completed troop assignments to the expedition by adding two Fifth Cavalry companies from Fort D. A. Russell near Cheyenne. Omaha sent another telegram to Thornburgh; this one at 11:15 A.M.:

> Headquarters Dept. of the Platte
> Ass't. Adjutant General's Office
> Fort Omaha Neb. September, 17, 1879
>
> Commanding Officer
> Fort Fred Steele Wyo.
>
> Your telegrams of yesterday received. Commanding Officer Fort Russell ordered to send you two companies Fifth Cav. from his command. Train from Rock Creek has also been ordered to report to you. You will please organize

your command as soon as possible and proceed to carry out instructions contained in telegram of yesterday.

> By command of General Crook
> (sgd) R. Williams, A. A. General[16]

The Cheyenne post recorded the receipt of official notice to move companies on September 20.[17]

When the orders arrived, Captain J. Scott Payne was in command of Company F, Fifth Cavalry, and Captain William J. Volkmar was in command of Company D, Fifth Cavalry.[18] Their companies were ordered to proceed to Fort Fred Steele with Payne in general command. Second lieutenants Samuel A. Cherry, Company F, and James V. S. Paddock, Company D would accompany the detachment. The trip would be a homecoming of sorts for Payne and Cherry, who had been at Fort Fred Steele in 1878.

Thornburgh telegraphed Colonel Wesley Merritt, Fifth Cavalry, the commanding officer at D. A. Russell, to request that shelter tents be sent with the two cavalry companies and warned him that transportation was short.[19] Shelter tents were small enough to lighten the load and expedite travel.

Many of the men who prepared for action at Fort D. A. Russell had campaigned before. Captain Payne was an experienced veteran from Virginia, but a chronic sinus infection troubled him whenever he rode the dusty campaign trail, and the trip to White River would exacerbate his condition.[20] Payne, a West Point graduate with the class of 1866, was promoted to first lieutenant on May 23, 1867, but he resigned sixteen months later under a cloud of uncertainty concerning his political activities while serving as an officer. The clouds cleared by February 1873, when President Ulysses S. Grant appointed Payne a second lieutenant in the Sixth Cavalry. He was promoted to first lieutenant in the Fifth Cavalry a year and a half later and became a captain on June 4, 1875.[21] In 1876 Payne was part of the counsel for Captain Alexander Moore in court martial hearings related to charges of disobeying orders and misbehavior before the enemy during the Reynolds Campaign on the Powder River in March of that year.[22] He also participated with Company F in the Slim Buttes battle later that fall as Crook's Big Horn and Yellowstone Expedition drew to a close.[23]

An Indiana native, Samuel A. Cherry had graduated from West Point in 1875, five years after he entered, and was commissioned a second lieutenant in the Twenty-Third Infantry. Cherry voluntarily transferred to the Fifth Cavalry on July 28, 1876, scarcely a month after the Seventh Cavalry's defeat at the battle of the Little Bighorn.

A fellow West Point classmate, Fred A. Colby, described Cherry and explained why he took an extra year to graduate from the military academy. Cherry was

> . . . over six feet in height and full of spirit. I remember one thing about him which shows the brave, indomitable spirit of the man. We were performing an exercise in artillery drill, in which a gun taken all to pieces was to be put in working order and fired. The men were arranged on each side of the gun, and at a signal they put it together and fire it off. Lieut. Cherry was upon the one side of the gun and a young fellow by the name of Tyler, if I remember correctly, upon the other. Tyler was a small man, and, as I have said, Cherry was a large and powerful fellow. When the signal was given to place the gun in position, Cherry took hold of his end of the handspike with such force that the gun was slipping over onto Tyler, and Cherry, perceiving this, and in order to save his comrade, at once seized the gun, weighing over 1,000 pounds, by the cascabel, the round knob at the breech of the cannon, and strove to stay it by main strength. The gun was partially lifted and then fell on Cherry, breaking his thigh, and pressing the limb into the ground. Cherry lay there under the heavy gun without a murmur, and never made a moan when he was taken to the hospital with his mangled limb.
>
> He was confined in the hospital for some time and when he was declared convelescent [*sic*] he was granted a furlough of one year and therefore joined the class of 1875.[24]

As the Fort D. A. Russell troops made ready, Thornburgh continued to organize the White River Expedition from Fort Fred Steele. The twenty-five wagons at Rock Creek, and possibly some supplied either from the fort or Rawlins, were reserved for Thornburgh. The exact number of wagons used by the expedition is still a question that might be determined through a more detailed review of quartermaster records in the National Archives. Once Thornburgh secured these field vehicles, he sent a telegram on September 17 to Colonel Bronson in Rawlins notifying him that transportation had been arranged.[25]

Meanwhile, a steady stream of commerce flowed toward White River from Rawlins in spite of the alleged troubles at the agency. Civilian contract wagons laden with supplies snaked along the agency road, which was the best access to the White River country from the north.

Businessman James France accounted for each of the wagons en route from Rawlins. On Sunday, September 14, Carl Goldstein and Julius Moore headed toward the agency with two four-mule wagons carrying flour and other supplies. On the sixteenth, the same day Thornburgh received his orders, John Gordon went south with ten wagons, twenty-eight yoke of oxen (fifty-six animals), and three bullwhackers. His wagons were loaded with cooking utensils and other agency supplies. This was the same John Gordon who, in 1874, violated the 1868 Treaty of Fort Laramie between the Sioux and the U.S. government when he took a party of miners into the Black Hills, an act that helped precipitate the Sioux war two years later.[26]

John's brother, George Gordon, left Rawlins the next day with two drivers and three four-horse wagons hauling a threshing machine and parts for Meeker. Finally, on September 18, Al McCargar and his son left town in a wagon loaded with fencing wire and hardware.

Thornburgh waited at Fort Fred Steele for the elements of his command to form. On Friday, September 19, he telegraphed Omaha Barracks with an update:

Adjutant General
Department of Platte
Omaha Barracks, Omaha

Have no further reliable information, rumor of agency buildings burned and that Utes will certainly fight, also that Uintahs are crossing to Utes. Wagons expected tomorrow night when I will proceed to load & expect to camp at Rawlins on twenty-first. Command will consist of three (3) companies of cavalry and one (1) of infantry.

Thornburgh
Comd'g[27]

His telegram illustrates the effect created by the spread of rumors throughout the country between Rawlins and White River since Johnson's fight with Meeker. Like earlier complaints about brushfires, false reports trickling in from citizens tainted accurate information. There was no direct proof that either the agency had been burned or that Utes were amassing a large fighting force. Unlike the tons of contract supplies that teamsters were hauling south toward the agency, reliable information headed north was a much scarcer commodity.

Late on September 19 or early on September 20, Companies D and F of the Fifth Cavalry left Fort D. A. Russell for Fort Fred Steele aboard a Union Pacific train.[28] Some of the men made a few enemies along the way. At Laramie, one or more unnamed cavalrymen cut a Mr. Polchow's head open with an ax. A newspaper correspondent concluded that the soldiers were spoiling for a fight and just couldn't wait until they reached Indian country.[29]

The two Fort D. A. Russell companies arrived at Fort Fred Steele on September 20. The day before, Major Thornburgh had received a telegram from the headquarters of the Department of the Platte ordering Captain Volkmar back to Cheyenne. Thornburgh answered the telegram on September 20 saying that the captain would be relieved from duty at Fort Fred Steele and would return to Fort D. A. Russell.[30] Volkmar was under separate orders from the Division of the Missouri. He had been assigned as recorder of the board of officers at Chicago, Illinois, and was needed by the Department of the Platte for general court martial duty at Fort D. A. Russell. Volkmar's loss placed the young, unseasoned Lieutenant James V. S. Paddock in command of Company D, Fifth Cavalry.

Paddock was born in Illinois and, like Thornburgh, Payne, and Cherry, was a military academy graduate. He had entered West Point as a cadet on September 1, 1873 and was commissioned a second lieutenant assigned to the Fifth Cavalry on June 15, 1877.[31]

Major Thornburgh telegraphed General Crook to advise him of their status and to say that no medical officer had yet reported for duty.[32] The Assistant Adjutant General (AAG) at Omaha Barracks answered the same day, informing Thornburgh that Dr. Robert Grimes would arrive from Fort Laramie. The AAG had received a telegram from Colonel Albert G. Brackett, the commanding officer at Fort Laramie, on September 19 confirming that Dr. Grimes was under orders to report at Fort Fred Steele for duty with the White River Expedition.[33]

Acting assistant surgeon Robert B. Grimes, an Ohio native, had also seen service during Crook's Big Horn and Yellowstone Expedition. He would catch up with Thornburgh at 1:00 P.M. on September 22.[34]

The rest of the Fort Fred Steele units assembled. Captain Joseph J. Lawson commanded forty-nine enlisted men from Company E, Third Cavalry, and First Lieutenant Butler D. Price commanded twenty-nine enlisted men in Company E, Fourth Infantry.[35]

Lawson, while not a West Point graduate, was a savvy Irishman, an adept Indian fighter, and an excellent horseman. He had fought in the Eleventh Kentucky Cavalry Volunteers during the Civil War and had reached the rank of major.[36] His campaign experience in the regular army was seasoned by service during the Reynolds battle, the battle of Rosebud, Crook's "starvation" march of 1876, and the battle of Slim Buttes, when he was a first lieutenant with Company A, Third Cavalry. His cool mettle would serve Thornburgh's expedition well. Many of Lawson's Company E, Third Cavalry were also veterans of the Sioux war of 1876, and several others had enlisted as a result of the panic that the war had caused in the eastern states.

Lieutenant Butler Price was appointed to service from his native state of Pennsylvania. Price began his military career as a second lieutenant in the Pennsylvania Cavalry on January 4, 1862. He became a first lieutenant thirteen months later, then mustered out on January 5, 1865. He accepted the rank of second lieutenant during the fall of 1866 and was commissioned first lieutenant in the Fourth Infantry on November 25, 1873. Price now found himself in charge of an infantry company in the

Table 2.1 White River Expedition of 1879 Recap of Approximate Distances[37]

Date	From	To	Miles
Sun. Sept. 21	Fort Fred Steele	Rawlins	15.0
Mon. Sept. 22	Rawlins	Willows	18.0
Tue. Sept. 23	Willows	Soldier Wells	20.6
Wed. Sept. 24	Soldier Wells	Snake River	25.5
Thu. Sept. 25	Snake River	Fortification Creek	24.0
Fri. Sept. 26	Fortification Creek	Yampa River	19.0
Sat. Sept. 27	Yampa River	Williams Fork	15.3
Sun. Sept. 28	Williams Fork	Deer Creek Camp	9.8
Mon. Sept. 29	Deer Creek Camp	Milk Creek	11.5
		Total Distance:	158.7
	Milk Creek	White River Agency	21.6
		Total:	180.3

field because its captain, Charles John Von Herrmann, was away on recruiting service for the Department of the Army.[38]

Preparations were nearly complete. Thornburgh sent a brief and final telegram on September 21 from Fort Steele to Omaha Barracks. It simply stated that, "My command will camp at Rawlins tonight. No news."[39]

Thornburgh's White River Expedition left Fort Fred Steele on Sunday morning, September 21, 1879, trailing twenty-five or more wagons loaded with thirty days' rations, fifteen days of forage, and other equipage.[40] The column marched along the road south of the Union Pacific Railroad tracks, across fifteen miles of dusty hills and alkali flats, toward the growing community of Rawlins. Cavalrymen had left their sabres behind because neither a cavalry charge nor a full-dress parade were anticipated; the infantry rode in wagons. The quiet of the fall day was broken by clattering canteens, the shaking of haversacks and nosebags, barking dogs, and the monotonous rumble of iron-rimmed wheels cutting into the shallow topsoil. A listener could hear scores of muffled hoofbeats and detect an occasional snort from a horse chafing at its bit. Troopers

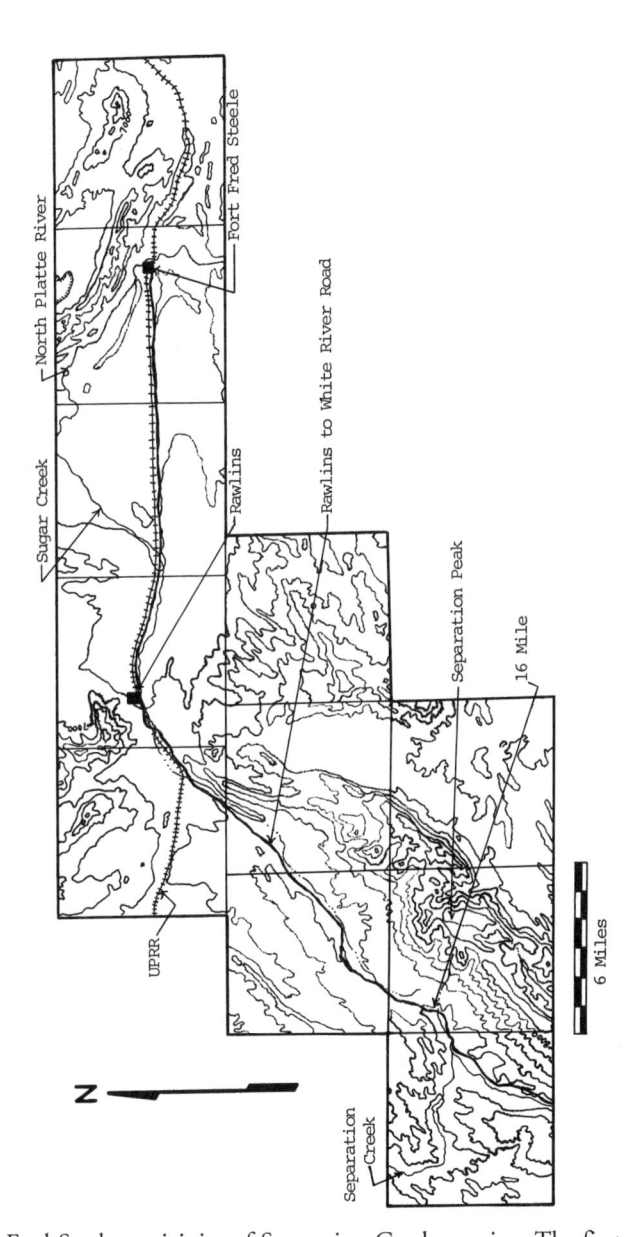

Map 2.1 Fort Fred Steele to vicinity of Separation Creek crossing. The first segment of the White River Expedition led by Major Thomas T. Thornburgh left Fort Fred Steele, on the North Platte River, Sept. 21, 1879 and made the crossing at Separation Creek, Sept. 23, 1879. Sources for this and subsequent maps include two U.S. Geological Survey 1:250,000 (Rawlins, Wyoming; Colorado; Craig, Colorado; Wyoming). Photocopies of the original General Land Office (GLO) Plats were extremely valuable for plotting the route. The Coe Library at the University of Wyoming in Laramie has GLO maps on microfiche, and the Bureau of Land Management supplied GLO maps of Colorado.

themselves contributed an "undercurrent of low laughter and soldier chaff which mark the freedom of a prairie march, or, as they say in the infantry, 'the route step.'"[41]

The command staff from Fort Fred Steele was composed of Thornburgh, Second Lieutenant Silas A. Wolf, Fourth Infantry acting assistant quartermaster (AAQM), Private Samuel W. Hagerman, an ambulance driver from Company H, Fourth Infantry, and Private William LaParle of Company E, Third Cavalry, hospital steward second class. Some sources also mention a Private O'Malley from the Fourth Infantry on staff, but I did not find his name in the primary sources I consulted.[42] Dr. Grimes from Fort Laramie was the medical officer and Second Lieutenant Samuel Cherry of Company F, Fifth Cavalry from Fort D. A. Russell was appointed battalion adjutant.

Pennsylvanian Silas Wolf, second lieutenant in the Fourth Infantry, was the most recent of the military academy graduates to participate in the expedition. He had been a cadet between July 1, 1874 and June 14, 1878 and had only been commissioned for fifteen months. Milk Creek would be an enlightening experience for this greenhorn.

The combined strength of the expedition has been a major point of debate. Captain Payne listed the total military fighting strength of the White River Expedition at about 180 men.[43] General Sherman, Lieutenant General Philip H. Sheridan, and the *Cheyenne Daily Leader* calculated it at about two hundred officers and men.[44] Other accounts total only the cavalry detachment. Of these, a 1910 source mentions six officers and 155 enlisted men, while two contemporary newsmen estimated 160 men in the three cavalry companies.[45] When either of these two cavalry totals is added to the troop strength of Company E, Fourth Infantry, each sum compares more favorably with Payne's, Sherman's, and Sheridan's accounting of a force of about two hundred men.

The importance of these figures emerges when they are compared to a comprehensive study of the incident published by Marshall Sprague in 1957, *Massacre: The Tragedy at White River*. He claimed that 153 officers and men and twenty-five civilians composed the expedition that left Rawlins on September 22. His count includes Thornburgh, Wolf, O'Malley, forty-three men of Company F, Fifth Cavalry, thirty men of Company E, Fourth Infantry, twenty-seven men of Company D, Fifth Cavalry, and fifty men of Company E, Third Cavalry.[46]

Sprague seems to have underestimated the size of the two Fort D. A. Russell companies, whose individual troop strength was not listed in post returns.[47] His low estimate is particularly evident when it is scaled against the 110 horses that were lost in the battle by the two Fifth Cavalry companies and the fact that post returns did mention that four officers and 114 enlisted men were on detached duty from D. A. Russell in late September 1879. Presumably, these men were in the White River Expedition. Each enlisted cavalryman probably would have had only a single mount, suggesting a total D. A. Russell contingent of about 110 to 114 men. Officers, however, may have brought additional mounts, which would upset the correlation between the number of horses and men.

Company muster rolls for the period of August 31 to October 31, 1879 also indicate that considerably more than Sprague's count of seventy men were detached to the White River Expedition from Fort D. A. Russell. A figure of more than one hundred is much more likely (Appendix A). Adding about 100 men from Fort D. A. Russell to eighty men from Fort Fred Steele yields Payne's fighting force of 180. If twenty-five civilians also went along (a figure that may be somewhat high unless each wagon was driven by a civilian), then the expedition would total about 205 men (216 if the muster roll total is used). One veteran, Private John Costigan of Company D, Fifth Cavalry, recalled that about 170 soldiers and civilians fought at Milk Creek, which reinforces this higher estimate because Price's thirty infantry had been left at Fortification Creek as a supply camp by the time the battle began.[48] Troop strength, by any of these measures, should have been sufficient because Meeker had only asked for one hundred total.[49]

Captain William Bisbee remained behind as post commander when the expeditionary force left Fort Fred Steele. He had at his disposal five officers and sixty-one enlisted men of Company H, Fourth Infantry.[50] Most of the garrison had gone with Major Thornburgh.

Thornburgh's command made good time, reaching Rawlins in the early afternoon of September 21, and camped about a half mile from town. Shortly after troopers arrived in the community, an incident reminiscent of the attack on Mr. Polchow the day before occurred. One of the soldiers threw a rock and struck a Mr. Murphy in the forehead. The missile inflicted a serious and potentially fatal wound. People speculated that, at the very least, the injury would disfigure the poor man for life. The Polchow and Murphy encounters left a bitter taste in Rawlins and Laramie, and at least one newspaper suggested such rowdyism should be summarily punished.[51] To many citizens, it was good riddance when the troopers marched south.

3
March to Milk Creek

Do not anticipate trouble.
—Major Thomas T. Thornburgh, September 26, 1879[1]

In 1879, Rawlins was a growing railroad community nestled between hills and near a cool, flowing spring. The town, established during construction of the Union Pacific Railroad, was named Rawlins Springs after the U.S. Army's chief of staff, Brigadier General John A. Rawlins, who drank from the spring in 1868. The name eventually was shortened to Rawlins.

Late September found the valleys and hills colored with aspen changing to red, orange, and yellow, the groves dotting grassy meadows like pools of paint on an artist's palette. Leaves drifted lazily to the ground, accumulating in dry creek channels.

A segment of the old freight road between the railroad depot at Rawlins and the White River Agency in Colorado south of the Union Pacific tracks snakes through narrow valleys carved by Separation Creek and other streams. The White River Expedition camped near the road south of Rawlins on Sunday night, September 21.

Major Thornburgh knew that he was responding to a vague complaint at White River registered by Nathan Meeker, a naive idealist, whom the major knew to be inflexible when it came to dealing with the Utes. He had many questions about how to proceed once he arrived at the agency, but for now he focused on the logistics of moving the large force over 160 miles of dry and rugged terrain between Rawlins and the agency. The upcoming march would be difficult physically, and Thornburgh decided to wait until his force was under way before he would begin to formulate a strategy.

At Rawlins, Thornburgh had hired local pioneer and livery-stable operator Joe Rankin to guide the expedition; initially he had tried to hire

Taylor Pennock, but Thornburgh's brother, who was visiting from Tennessee, would not excuse Pennock from guiding a hunting trip. Had Lieutenant C.A.H. McCauley of Company E, Third Cavalry not been on leave, the major may not have needed a civilian guide at all, because McCauley had traveled major portions of the trail to the White River Agency in 1878. He had mapped and documented much of the terrain, noting road conditions and describing natural resources along the way. The United States Government Printing Office published McCauley's detailed report early in 1879, and Thornburgh may have had a copy with him.[2]

The column headed toward the agency shortly after sunup on Monday morning, September 22, with enough supplies and grain to last a month.[3] Thornburgh's first decision was which route to choose: either follow the mountain route through the Sierra Madre directly south of Rawlins and cross over the Continental Divide at Bridger's Pass, or take the somewhat longer, less steep route that angled southwest across the Great Divide Basin toward the valley of Muddy Creek. The mountain route would be too rough for the loaded wagons, so Thornburgh selected the basin road.

The command trailed up the north bank of Sugar Creek and pointed toward the foot of Separation Peak, visible in the distance. The road snaked along the foot of a south-facing hogback where, in the fall and early winter, the sun would quickly melt off any snow that might drift on the trail. The pungent odor of sagebrush along the road permeated the air. Troopers followed the gradual incline southwest to the Willows, about eighteen miles beyond Rawlins. The campaign trail had begun in earnest and had already taken a toll. A Third Cavalry horse collapsed before they found water and meadow grass. Undaunted, several men later took out some cards and enjoyed a game of whist.[4]

Tuesday the battalion left the Willows and continued southwest on a course through the upper reaches of Separation Creek, crossing that stream and the Continental Divide, which separates it from the Muddy Creek drainage basin.

From here troopers rode down Alamosa Gulch, crossed the Overland Trail and Muddy Creek at Sulphur Springs Stage Station, then continued to Soldier Wells between Cow Creek and Dry Cow Creek,

Map 3.1

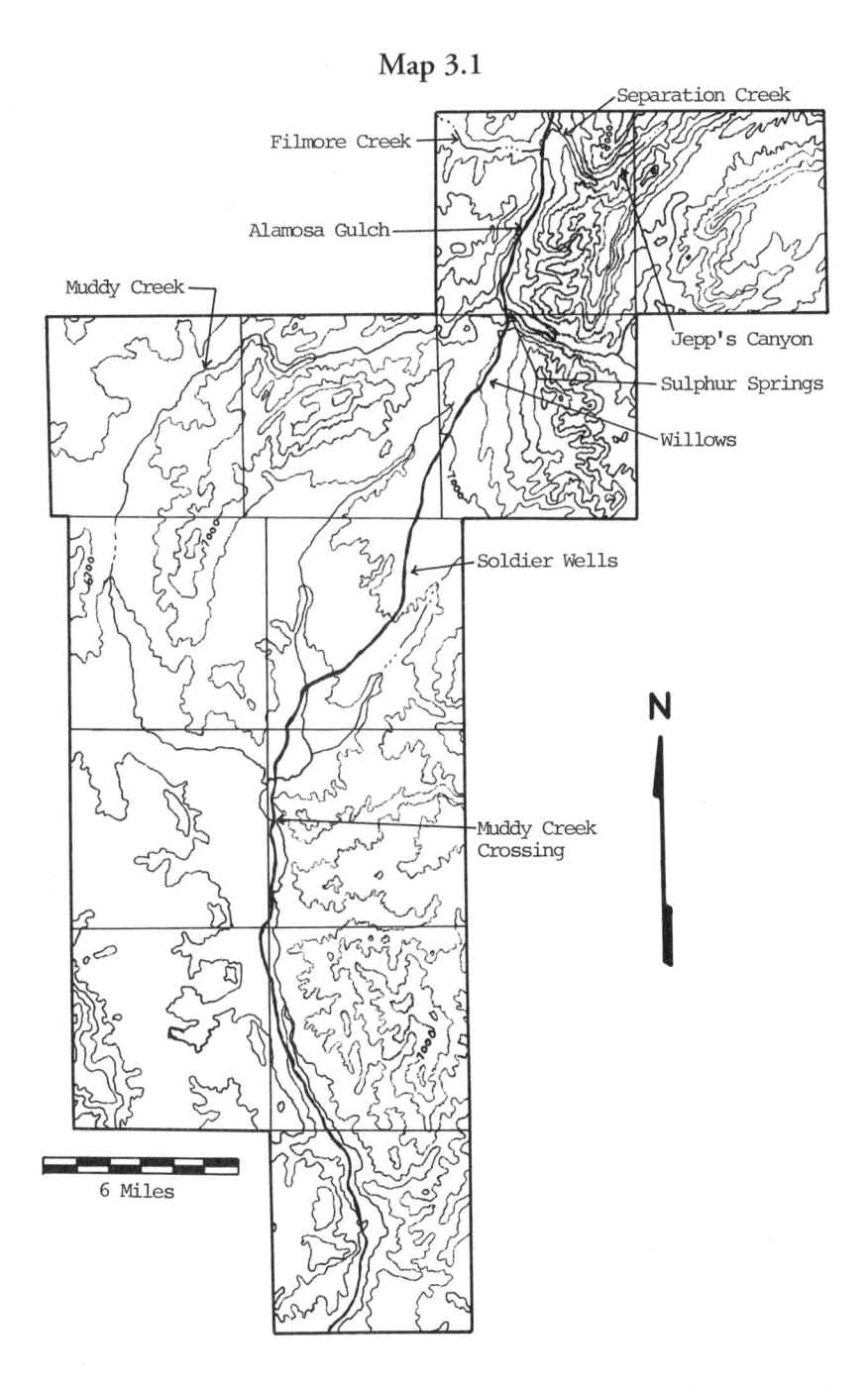

Map 3.1 Expedition route from Separation Creek crossing to north of Baggs's Ranch, in Wyoming

where they bedded down. They had traveled nearly twenty-one miles that day.[5]

Thornburgh's command marched from Soldier Wells to Snake River Crossing on Wednesday, September 24. Their route crossed Dry Cow Creek, then Muddy Creek again, and followed the valley south along the west bank of the stream. About this time, Thornburgh ordered a headquarters squad, including five men from Company E, Third Cavalry, to ride out in front of the command and stay a half to three-quarters of a mile ahead. Private Amandes M. Startzell, a member of this group, recalled years later that the headquarters party was fortunate because it was able to avoid the billowing dust that encircled the main column during the march.[6]

The journey on Thursday, September 25 covered about twenty to twenty-five miles, passing from Snake River Crossing into Colorado to a point on Fortification Creek, probably just south of Fortification Rocks, where they made camp. During this leg of the journey, the expedition noticed heavy smoke clouds drifting up from fires burning in the mountains to the east. Abandoned teepee sites and debris also had been seen during the day, signaling that the column was entering Indian country.[7]

Just the year before the White River Expedition, Lieutenant C.A.H. McCauley, then of the Third Artillery but soon to be reassigned to the Third Cavalry, was ordered to proceed to the White River Agency with Mr. W. S. Stickney, secretary of the Ute Commission.[8] McCauley traveled by buckboard, took notes, and prepared maps of the route through Wyoming and Colorado to the agency. Because they were traveling light, his group was able to take the mountain cut-off south of Rawlins, which followed relatively rugged, elevated terrain clear to the Snake River. McCauley's route tied in with the wagon road from Rawlins in a valley between Fourmile Creek and Fortification Creek, about twelve miles south of Snake River. From this junction south, the lieutenant's notes provide a detailed description of the same route used by the White River Expedition. This road, in September 1879, was the only established route to the agency from the north, and it was often closed more than six months a year due to inclement weather.[9]

A few miles past the junction of the mountain and basin routes is a series of hogbacks creating a mesa formation to the south. From here,

March to Milk Creek 31

Map 3.2

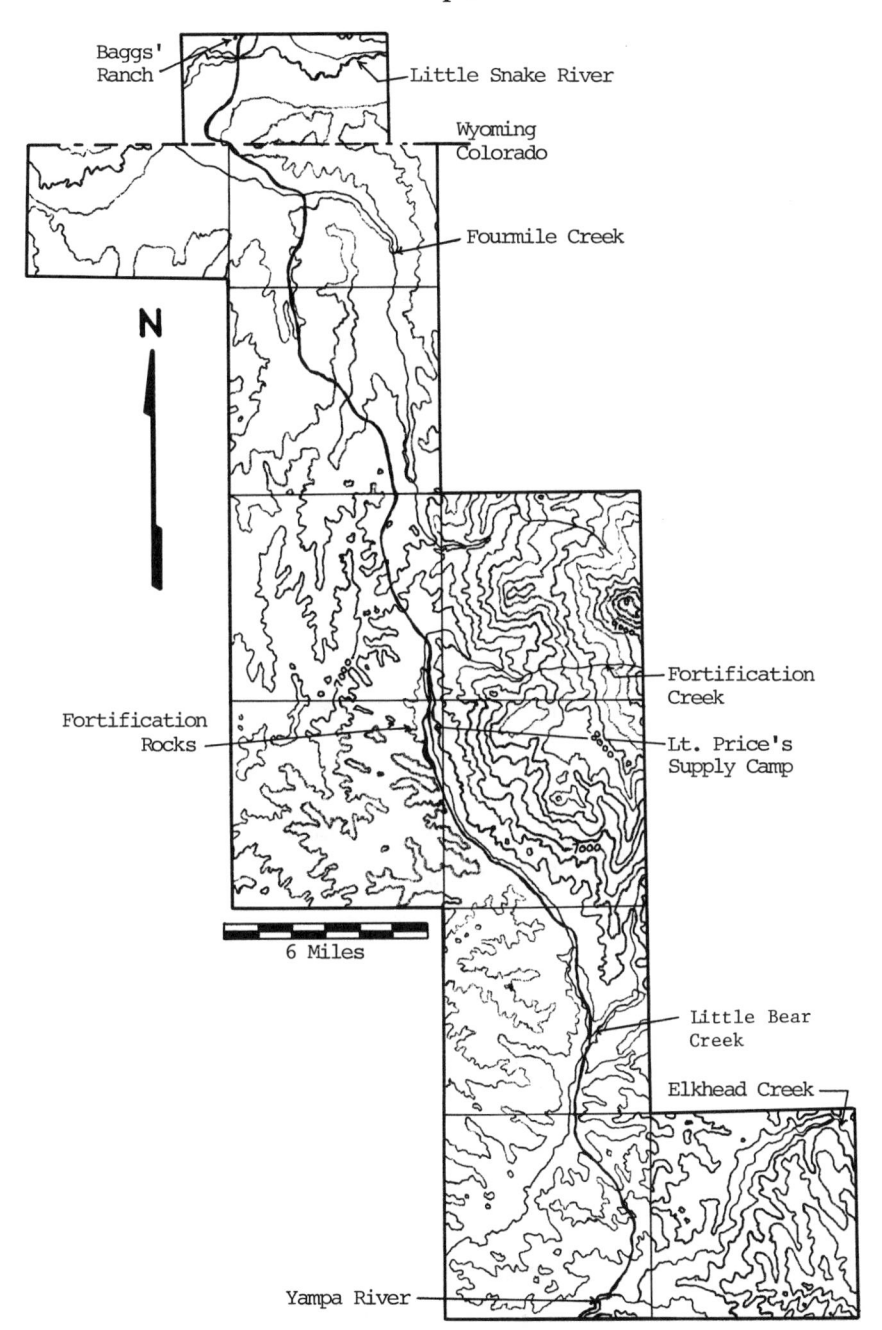

Map 3.2 Expedition route from Baggs's Ranch in Wyoming, into Colorado, and to the Yampa River

travelers turn due east for a mile and then head southeast toward the first crossing of Fortification Creek. Lieutenant McCauley describes the creek as changing

> from the clear and beautiful water at the road crossing to a muddy one, with alkaline constituents, below—its course becoming winding and sluggish, with deep banks, its timber but a few cottonwoods of small size.
>
> Bowlders [sic] of vesicular lava were observed . . . borne down from the hills to the left.
>
> About five miles south of the road-crossing exists a dike of porphyry, the direction of the wall east and west, distinct for over a mile, terminating abruptly not far distant from the creek . . . , the road passing close by its eastern end, which is known as the "Point of Rocks."
>
> The dike is at this end 5 feet thick and 12 feet above ground, not many yards back, being 30 feet vertically on the south side and 35 feet on the north, both bare of debris, while still farther west detached portions, with irregular profiles almost like castellated towers, rise 100 feet above the base of the general slope. . . .
>
> Ignorant of the origin of its name, on descending the creek one would naturally presume that it was derived from the appearance of a fortified wall in the distance. It is said, however, to have been so named from an actual fight there occurring between several Indian tribes or whites and Indians, who made use of this line of nature, and upon its top small piles of rocks near the road were pointed out by our guide as having been there placed by one of the contending bands or parties. . . .
>
> On the bank of the creek where it makes a large bend . . . opposite the Point of Rocks, a cabin was observed in the midst of a grassy bottom, where there was in all nearly ten acres of fine grazing; this, a deserted ranch, being the only one seen upon the stream.[10]

The White River Expedition probably camped at the abandoned cabin area on Thursday night, September 25.[11] Thornburgh assigned Lieutenant Butler D. Price and Company E, Fourth Infantry to remain there as a supply camp while the cavalry units continued on toward the agency. Eight wagons remained with Lieutenant Price's command and would eventually return to Rawlins for additional forage and supplies. These wagons presumably required that eight teamsters and forty-eight mules be left behind, thus reducing the size of the expedition. Night settled on the relaxed soldiers, who camped below the jagged profile of Fortification Rocks.

Major Thornburgh had been pondering the agency situation ever since he had received his initial orders on September 16. He had been told to enforce obedience to the requirements of the Indian agent, but what exactly were those requirements? Thornburgh had been on the road for five days and had not heard a word from Meeker. Finally he decided to prepare his first written communication to White River. Adjutant Cherry recorded his dictation in a letter that their courier, Charles Grafton Lowry, would carry to White River Agency:

> Headquarters White River Expedition
> Camp on Fortification Creek, Sept. 25, 1879
>
> Mr. Meeker
> Indian Agent, White River Agency, Colo.:
>
> Sir:
> In obedience to instructions from the General of the Army, I am now en route to your agency, and expect to arrive there on the 29th instant, for the purpose of affording you any assistance in my power in regulating your affairs, and to make arrests at your suggestion, and to hold as prisoners such of your Indians as you desire until investigations are made by your department. I have heard nothing definite from your agency for ten days and do not know what state of affairs exists, whether the Indians will leave at my approach or show hostilities. I send this letter

by Mr. Lowry, one of my guides, and desire you to communicate with me as soon as possible, giving me all the information in your power, in order that I may know what course I am to pursue. If practicable, meet me on the road at the earliest moment.

> Very respectfully, your obedient servant,
> T. T. Thornburgh
> Major 4th Infantry,
> Command'g Expedition[12]

Thornburgh's careful wording reveals his concern over the lack of communication from Meeker and his caution in executing his orders. Apparently, he considered his expedition as a sort of police force sent to quell unrest and restore peace, while Meeker's Department of the Interior had to resolve any disputes. The major's duties were unlike the standard warfare tactics of the Sioux war three years earlier or even of his chase of the Cheyenne in 1878. Thornburgh was not commanded to return hostiles to a reservation but to enter a reservation and arrest malcontents. He made it clear to Meeker that he would do what he was ordered by the army but that the Interior Department was responsible for any investigations into alleged Indian misconduct. Thornburgh's request for Meeker to meet him on the road demonstrates that he wanted to define better the role of the military expedition before they arrived at the agency. He was compelled to keep his actions rather vague and ambiguous until he had more specific input from Meeker, and this behavior certainly helped precipitate subsequent events.

Marshall Sprague wrote in *Massacre* that it also was on the evening of September 25 at Fortification Creek supply camp that the command first became aware of Ute Indians from the White River Agency. According to Sprague, Chief Jack's band had left White River for their fall hunt the same day that Thornburgh had left Fort Fred Steele and had found Thornburgh's troops on the Little Snake in Wyoming. Chief Jack "was furious at the invasion and canceled his hunt to watch it. He sent his band back to White River and shadowed the soldiers with his subchief Sowerwick and a few others." This scenario, however, does not coincide with participant testimony.[13]

The three cavalry companies and command staff left Price and the infantry behind at Fortification Creek Friday morning, September 26. Total fighting strength of the expedition was now about 150 troopers. The remaining wagons, teamsters, and mules continued on toward the agency, still over seventy-five miles to the south-southwest, beyond a rugged, dissected country.

The road passed down the valley on the east side of the stream, crossing the creek now and again during the descent toward the Yampa River cutoff. Several miles above the confluence with the Yampa River the creek banks were cut into nearly vertical walls rising twenty to forty feet above the water, necessitating detours.

The command rode up out of the valley, leaving Fortification Creek behind as they followed a shortcut trail to the southeast. They crossed a drainage divide and trailed down into the Yampa River Valley. Thornburgh turned the column upriver a short distance, then called a halt at 2:00 P.M., stopping at a point below Thomas Iles's ranch near the mouth of Elk Head Creek. They camped along the riverbanks, more than eighteen miles beyond Price's supply camp.[14]

Lieutenant Cherry and guide Joe Rankin rode across the Yampa to Peck's store to check the mail delivery schedule while several troopers took the opportunity to go fishing.

The Yampa River shows up on some early maps as the Bear because of confusion over what *yampa,* a Ute word, means. Some thought it meant bear, but it is the Ute name for *Carcum gairdneri*, an herb.[15] Here the river forms a beautiful valley; its headwaters are in the Derby Peak area of the Flattop Mountains. From there the river meanders west 170 miles to its confluence with the Green River.

While Thornburgh was heading south toward the agency, Chief Jack spoke with Agent Meeker about the difficulties at the agency, and Meeker informed Jack that troops were coming to enforce his policies. Jack opposed the use of military intervention and decided to ride north toward Fort Fred Steele to meet with military authorities. His party included Sowawick (Sowerwick), Unque, and at least two other Utes. Sowawick was affiliated with the White River Utes and Unque was an Uncompahgre from Los Piños Agency. These Indians arrived at Peck's store ahead of the expedition on September 26, and, according to

Marshall Sprague, they purchased ten thousand rounds of ammunition. Jack's own account says the Indians were buying sugar.[16]

If the Indians did buy cartridges, Jack must have sent them south to White River with two of his men shortly before he encountered Lieutenant Cherry and Joe Rankin at Peck's store. Cherry rode up to check on the mail and asked Mrs. Peck if she had any fixed—metallic cartridge—ammunition. She answered that she had sold her supply to the Utes for their fall hunt in Wyoming. Cherry may just have been curious, or he may have been seeking to add to the expedition's supply. He reported to Thornburgh that the Utes had purchased ammunition.

Jack was concealed in a back room of the store while Cherry talked with Mrs. Peck, and his companions waited outside and out of sight. Jack recognized Rankin as a deputy sheriff from Snake River and must have wondered if he had come to make arrests; Jack approached Cherry and Rankin to inquire why the soldiers were coming south. Cherry was noncommittal and convinced Jack to accompany them back to camp to discuss the expedition with Thornburgh.

That afternoon Jack and Sowawick rode back with Cherry and Rankin to meet with the major. Unque, the Uncompahgre with a visitation pass from the Los Piños agent in southern Colorado, followed with the other Indians. One of the soldiers who was fishing hollered out "Jack!" as the riders passed by, apparently recognizing him from a previous acquaintance.[17]

The Indians met Thornburgh in front of the major's big tent, and the commanding officer offered each of his guests some tobacco for a smoke. Jack accepted the offer of a Reina Victoria cigar and took the entire, and only, box the expedition possessed. The other officers milled about inside the tent as the Ute leader shook hands with everyone. Jack had learned to speak English during visits to cities back East and from previous scouting jobs with the army. He asked, "What is up? What are you going to do?"[18] The major replied that he wanted to talk about the business at the agency that had prompted his orders and that his orders were based on reports from Agent Meeker that the Utes might be wanting to go on the warpath. He added that he had received two orders and had not moved toward the reservation until the second notice. Jack emphatically denied the rumor of war and described their problems with Meeker's management at the agency. Jack complained about Meeker forcing the Utes to farm and plow and requiring all Indians to move to Powell Valley. He also said that they had to abandon their new homes so they could plow the area, and then he emphasized broken promises involving a new, red wagon.[19]

Major Thornburgh sympathized and conveyed to Jack that his intentions were peaceful and that he was only going to the agency to see what the problem was and to investigate the claim that Meeker had been beaten up.[20] He was firm, however, that his orders were to proceed to the agency. Thornburgh also indicated that he was after bad men, three in particular, who had been identified in a previous order as Glasseye, Chinaman, and Johnson. Chinaman was suspected of having set fires that allegedly destroyed a cabin, and Glasseye also may have been implicated; Johnson was accused of beating up Meeker. After hearing these accusations, Jack got the distinct impression that the major thought that all of the men, women, and children at the agency were bad Indians.[21]

Jack asked how many soldiers Thornburgh had brought with him but made no effort to walk through the camp to count for himself. Thornburgh calmly gave him an accurate total.[22] Jack then said that he had never expected soldiers to come because they were brothers and friends to one another. He was a particular friend of General Crook's, and the Utes had broken no treaty laws. Then he pointed to a soldier riding up to the group and commented, "Look how lean the government horses are; they go backward and forward carrying lies."[23]

The discussion of agency difficulties evolved toward slightly more friendly conversation. When asked how he had liked New York, Jack replied, "New York pretty good; pretty good theatre in New York."[24]

But Jack would not be diverted from his mission, and he steered the discussion back to the purpose of the military expedition, "Why you come for? What's the matter? What soldiers going to do?"

Thornburgh elaborated on the report that the Utes had beaten up Meeker when Jack suggested that Thornburgh leave the soldiers where they were and see for himself whether the agent had been beaten or not. The major answered that they were still a long way from the agency, but that if they found good grass closer to White River, perhaps at Milk Creek, he might go as Jack suggested.[25]

Thornburgh repeated that his orders from General Sherman were to investigate the rumors at the agency, and then he asked if Jack would accompany him, perhaps even meet the column the next morning down at the ford. The major had to be very careful in discussing the mission since he had not yet received more details from Meeker.

Jack was noncommittal and decided to spend the night at Peck's. Thornburgh looked at Cherry as Jack rode off and said,

> If I had the power, or if I thought it expedient under the circumstances, I should take Jack and these fellows in with me; but if I should do so the whole country would be aroused and would say that I brought on the trouble. These fellows have come here to spy, and it would be a good move to take them and hold them as hostages, but if I should do it I would be blamed by everybody all over the country, and my orders are such that I have to obey the commands of Mr. Meeker, so I would not feel justified in doing it.[26]

Thornburgh prepared a message after the meeting and sent it to Rawlins to be telegraphed to his departmental commander: "Have met some Utes here. They seem friendly and promise to go with me to agency. Say Utes don't understand why we have come. Have tried to explain satisfactorily. Do not anticipate trouble."[27]

This first discussion with the Utes hinted at the problems blocking a successful resolution to the conflict at White River. A huge obstacle was the incredible lack of communication between the reservation Utes and the Indian agent. History shows that policy disputes cannot be resolved amicably unless an open dialog exists between factions. In this case, initial discussions should have involved the Ute leaders residing at White River and Meeker's superiors in the Interior Department. But instead of pursuing new avenues of arbitration, Meeker sought coercion through a show of strength from the War Department. Now the fate of many were in the hands of three individuals: Meeker, Chief Jack, and Thornburgh, men who had not yet met collectively to negotiate a resolution. Each player was developing a different perspective on the situation without the benefit of face-to-face deliberation.

Map 3.3

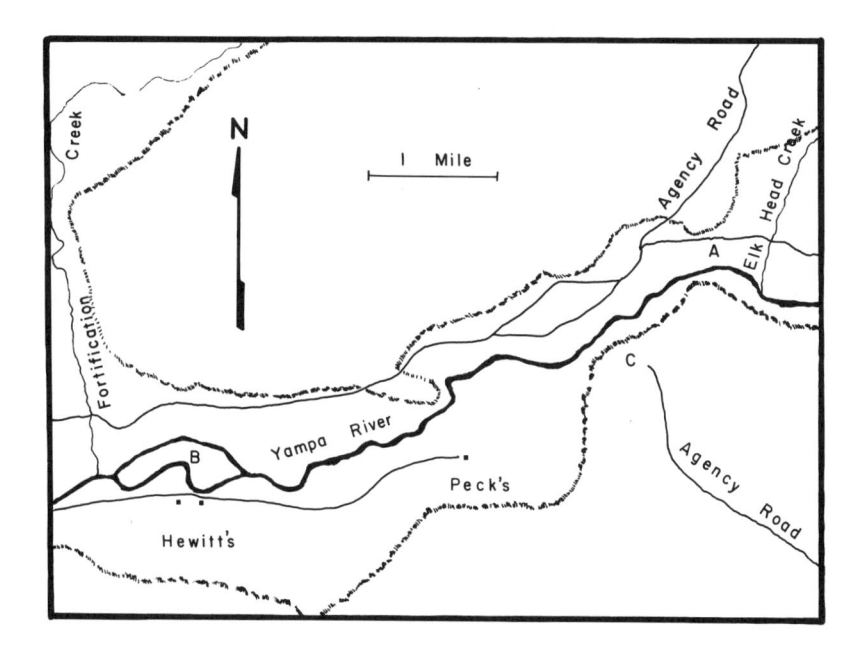

Map 3.3 Yampa River Valley and the crossing of the Rawlins to White River Agency road. This map depicts the relationships among the White River Agency Road, other trails, dwellings, and the Yampa River in Colorado. It is adapted from the General Land Office (GLO) plats in the Surveyor General's Office for Township Seven North, Range Ninety West; and Township Six North, Range Ninety West, which were made in 1878. Lieutenant McCauley's 1878 survey also was useful, particularly for establishing the position of Hewitt's (Hulett's) ranch and Peck's store. Position **A** is the likely spot for the expedition camp on the night of September 26, 1879, below Isles's ranch, which is not pictured. Position **B** is about four miles downriver and is the area McCauley describes as the river ford. Position **C** is where the White River Road leaves the valley and heads south toward Williams Fork.

Cherry and ten men went down to the ford from the soldier camp on Saturday morning, September 27 to see if Jack was waiting for the coumn. He was not there, so Cherry went to Peck's ranch, where he found Jack with two other Indians, probably Sowawick and Unque. He asked Jack to accompany the expedition but Jack refused, saying that he was going on ahead to the agency with the other Indians.[28]

Communication among the principals was so limited that nobody viewed the expedition in the same context. At the same time Thornburgh was writing Meeker to request more information on the purpose of the military advance, Chief Jack was interpreting the expedition as an armed invasion. If Meeker or anyone had been hoping to surprise the Utes with the arrival of troops, the ruse was discovered. The agent now had some explaining to do, both to the army and to the Indians.

The agency road crossed the Yampa River at the ford near Hewitt's ranch, where the river flowed in two channels four hundred yards apart (Map 3.3).[29] Each channel snaked along the mile-wide valley floor through areas heavily timbered with cottonwoods. Willow thickets and tangled undergrowth restricted access along the stream banks. One branch of the road south of the river headed about two miles upriver to Mr. Peck's ranch and store, where Jack, Cherry, and Rankin had met the day before. Where the road left the Yampa River was nearly sixty miles from the agency. It passes around steep hills and slopes, courses south for a few miles, then turns west toward the top of the divide between the Yampa River and Williams Fork (Map 3.4).

Before reaching the crest of the Williams Fork Mountains, the soldiers overtook George Gordon and the wagon train carrying Meeker's threshing machine. Al McCarger's wagon was near there, too. William McKinstry, Thornburgh's wagon master, spent two hours fixing one of Gordon's wagons that had broken down. The march continued across the divide after repairs were completed.[30]

The agency road left the divide in the Williams Fork Mountains and entered the head of a draw, probably one leading down into Jeffway Gulch. From there the descent to Williams Fork, as Lieutenant McCauley described in his 1878 report,

> . . . is between steep hills, with projecting sandstones of cretaceous age, their sides covered with scrub oak.

Map 3.4

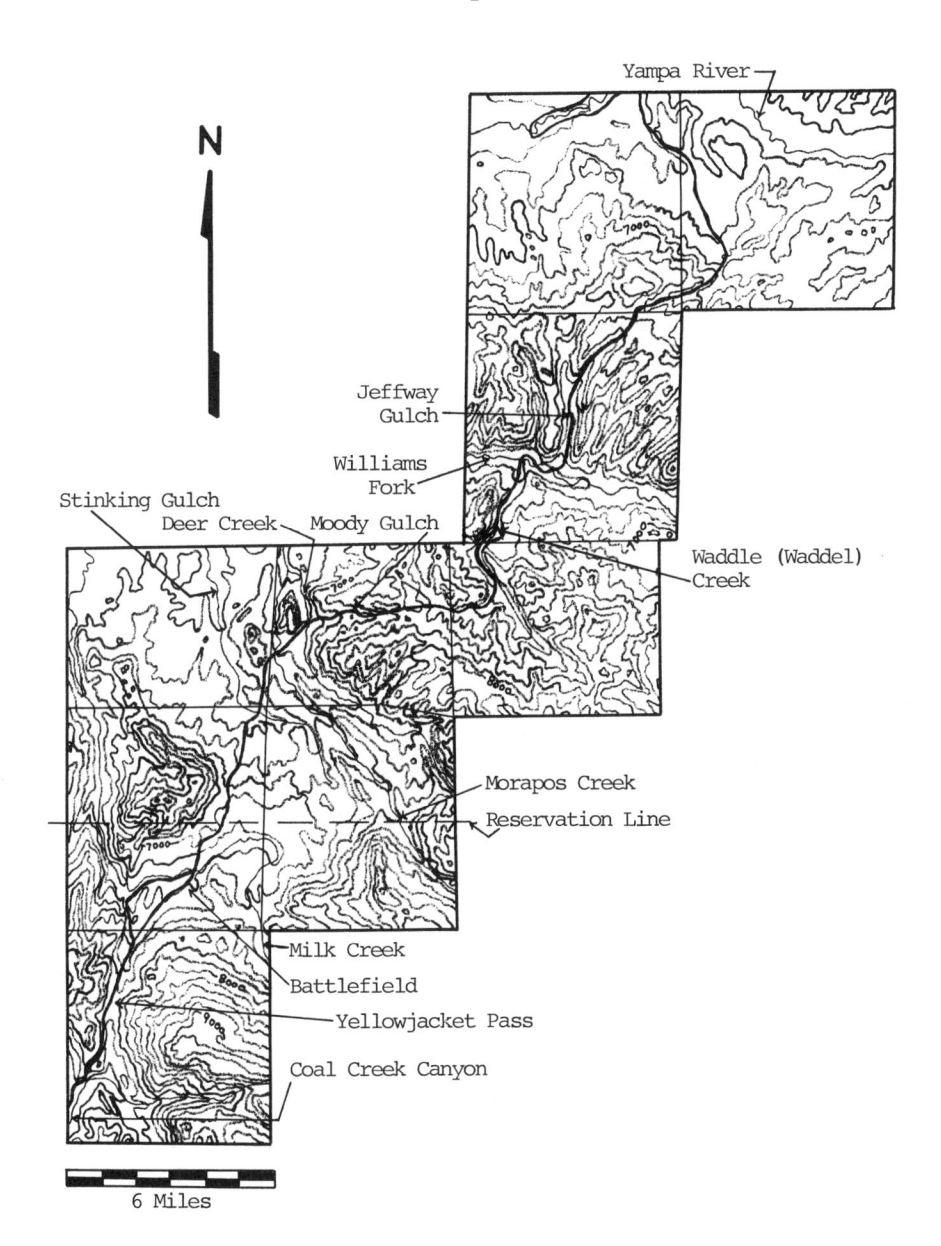

Map 3.4 Expedition route from Yampa River crossing to Coal Creek Canyon, north of the White River. The expedition was stopped at Milk Creek by Utes.

The road follows down a brook called Deer Creek, and between hills . . . Here the sandstone on the right dipped to the north about 15 degrees, and at one point an outcropping ledge with overhanging rock furnished fantastic forms of water sculpture. From frost and rain, a huge mass near the road was honey-combed throughout, being known locally as "The Wasp's Nest."[31]

The expedition passed through the mouth of Jeffway Gulch, reached Williams Fork Valley about fifteen miles by road from the Yampa River, and camped. It was Saturday, September 27, the seventh day of the march.

Fall scenery along the Williams Fork was a sight to behold. Rugged mountains embraced the rich, fertile valley. Hills to the north rose abruptly one thousand feet above the stream while those to the south rose about half that distance but were equally spectacular.[32] As the soldiers settled into camp, they noticed several riders coming from the hills to the south. They were representatives sent from the agency.

Chief Jack had been busy all that day, Saturday, September 27. He returned to White River and then sent a dozen Utes up Coal Creek to prepare a guard camp near the lakes and springs at the head of Beaver Creek, about four or five miles south of the reservation line. This vantage point overlooked the Milk Creek Valley and the agency road coming in from the north.[33] Then Jack dispatched a representative to accompany a contingent from the agency that passed through Milk Creek Valley and headed north to meet with the soldiers at Williams Fork.

The riders from the agency entered Thornburgh's camp at dusk. Among them were agency employee Wilmer Eskridge; Henry Jim, an agency interpreter; a Ute guide; and old Chief Colorow, who was Chief Jack's representative.[34] A man named Bummer Jim was present and may have been the Ute guide. One source mentions that Tonwah, Innayuirque, and Pourtave accompanied the riders, but these may be Indian names for some of those Utes already mentioned, or for some of the three other Utes who also had fallen in with the agency contingent. One of these other Utes was Freiscatte.[35]

Colorow was a husky figure with dark, penetrating eyes. He had a sense of resolve that gave the impression that he was a force to be reckoned with. His suspiciousness was obvious. He was surly and insincere but shook hands with his soldier counterparts and saluted. Someone offered him a smoke to break the ice.

"Big chief, no sabe smoke pipe," Colorow replied. Payne interpreted this refusal as a show of distrust and a rebuke of their hospitality, but Colorow simply may have wanted one of the high-quality Reina Victoria's that Chief Jack had been offered the night before.[36]

The Indians were noticeably impressed with Cherry's height and that of two other officers. Henry Jim was over six feet himself and Bummer Jim also was rather tall. Together, they asked the three officers to stand up to compare statures.[37] This innocent diversion, however, did little to ease the tension of the moment.

Eskridge had accompanied the group in order to bring Thornburgh a message from Meeker, possibly a reply to Thornburgh's request for information.[38] Meeker's message reads:

White River Agency, Col.
Sept. 27, 1879

To Major Thornburgh
or commander of U.S. Troops
between Bear and White Rivers, Colorado

Sir. Understanding that you are on the way hither with U. S. troops, I send a messenger, Mr. Eskridge, and two Indians, Henry (interpreter) and John Augisley, to inform you that the Indians are greatly excited, and wish you to stop at some convenient camping place, and then that you and five soldiers of your command come in to the agency, where a talk and a better understanding can be had. This I agree to, but I do not propose to order your movements; but it seems for the best. The Indians seem to consider the advance of troops as a declaration of real war; in this I am laboring to undeceive them, and at the same time convince them they cannot do whatever they please. The first object now is to allay apprehension.

Respectfully,
N. C. Meeker
Indian Agent[39]

Meeker had added fuel to the fires of discontent by involving the military. On the one hand, he knew specific details about the agency trouble but was clearly uncomfortable in directing troop movements. On the other, Thornburgh commanded the armed forces but was not privy to adequate information about the state of affairs at White River. This indecision and lack of coordination between representatives of the Department of the Interior and the War Department probably did little to alleviate the stress or clear the confusion felt by the White River Utes. Even Meeker's belated attempt to set up a council to negotiate the dispute was poorly timed. How could he be sincere if his call for a conference was initiated after his call for troops, and simultaneously with the advance of armed soldiers toward the reservation? Why hadn't a commission been appointed to arbitrate the dispute before the soldiers were called in? Utes could legitimately ask these questions. Thornburgh could wonder that if Meeker had read his letter of September 25, why had the agent not consented to meet the expedition on the road to White River?

Thornburgh finished reading the message, then explained again to Colorow why the soldiers had come, reiterating much of what had been said the night before at the Yampa River. He added that he had left two companies of infantry (an exaggeration) behind and then asked Colorow if he had anything to say.

Colorow apparently did all of the talking for the Utes, with Henry interpreting for him. He answered that there was no trouble at the agency and added that Chief Jack had authorized him to guarantee Thornburgh's safety at the agency.[40] He also suggested that there was plenty of water at Williams Fork and at a grassy spot on Deer Creek a few miles farther south, either of which would be a fine spot to use as a camp for the soldiers and stock while Thornburgh proceeded on with five men for discussions at White River.[41] According to Colorow, a tall officer (perhaps Cherry) said that he agreed with the Ute. Thornburgh quickly rebuked the officer and began to cite a list of depredations allegedly perpetrated by the Utes. Then a white-bearded officer (probably Lawson) added that it was his business to go about settling differences.[42]

Initially, the major argued that, "I cannot stop until I come to the agency, as my orders are to go there."[43] Then he conferred with his officers. According to Sprague, Thornburgh, Cherry, and Lawson ultimately favored sending a small detachment to the agency as per Meeker's most recent request and then moving the main force only far enough south until they reached good grass and a strategic camp location. Joe Rankin and Payne opposed their plan emphatically. Payne argued that the military was supposed to settle Indian troubles, not mediate them.[44] Exactly what were Thornburgh's orders?

Herein lies the dilemma. General Sherman had ordered Thornburgh to arrest malcontents and to hold them until an investigation was conducted, but the major was not ordered to conduct the investigation because that was the province of the Interior Department. Now Meeker was asking Thornburgh to open up negotiations at the agency before any other actions were implemented. The Indians did not want an armed military force to enter their reservation, yet Meeker had not yet agreed to meet Thornburgh en route. While most everyone wanted to negotiate to avoid conflict, no one had yet agreed as to where negotiations should occur. All sides, the soldiers, agency personnel, and the Indians, were frightened and suspicious of treachery.

After further deliberation, Thornburgh stood by the opinion of veteran Indian fighter Joseph Lawson. He prepared a return message:

> Headquarters White River Expedition
> Camp on Williams Fork, September 27, 1879
> Mr. Meeker, U. S. Ind. Agent, White River Agency.
>
> Sir:
>
> Your letter of this date just received. I will move to-morrow with part of my command to Milk River [*sic*]

or some good location for camp, or possibly may leave my entire command at this point, and will come in, as desired, with five men and a guide. Mr. Eskridge will remain to guide me to the agency. I will reach your agency some time on the 29th instant.

> Very respectfully, your obedient servant,
> T. T. Thornburgh
> Major, 4th Infantry, Commanding
> Expedition[45]

Payne tried unsuccessfully to catch Thornburgh's attention to prevent him from committing to leaving troops behind.[46] Lieutenant Cherry handed the letter to Henry Jim for delivery to Meeker. The interpreter apparently was a bit confused because he later testified that he understood Thornburgh to say that he would move his entire command.[47]

The expedition finally settled in for the night. Elsewhere the Utes were so intent on gathering ammunition that two settlers, Black Wilson and Joe Collum, buried rifles and cartridges at Perkin's store on Spring Gulch to keep them from falling into Indian hands.[48]

The column grew more tense and wary when they moved out Sunday morning, September 28. Troops crossed Williams Fork repeatedly as they followed the road downstream about a mile and a half below camp. From there the road headed south, up Waddel Creek about four miles, then west up to the head of Hart Gulch, then crossed over a divide and down Moody Gulch to Deer Creek, where the expedition camped for the night. The distance traveled on September 28 was roughly ten miles.[49]

Captain Payne looked down into Deer Creek from the divide and was impressed with the scenery. The Indians had suggested this spot for the main force to remain during the negotiations at the agency. Payne later described their campground as having

> several sweet springs overhung by masses of red sandstone, in some places eroded by the action of wind and water into forms of fantastic beauty; in others piled, rock upon rock, in inextricable confusion, as if the Titans had been

playing at bowls in the long, long ago. On our right a mountain, grim, brown, bare, rose to an altitude of three thousand feet; on the left the peaks shot skyward, their crests wearing the foliated aspect of cathedral spires . . .

The "divide" was crossed at an altitude of eight thousand feet, and we camped two miles from the top in a fine canyon, where good water and grass were found for our animals.[50]

The grandeur of majestic mountain scenery did little to subdue a cloud of growing apprehension. Each player was becoming more nervous as the hours passed. Rumors spread anxiety through the ranks and fueled rampant speculation. Events began to take on a life of their own.

What little information reached Thornburgh did nothing to ease tensions. Several worried travelers passed through the camp on Deer Creek.[51] Eugene Taylor came in from his sutler's tent on Milk Creek, a stream located near the northern edge of the reservation, and said Indians had confiscated his ammunition. Utes who had purchased cartridges only three days earlier were now stealing them.

Columbus Henry, one of John Gordon's bullwhackers, came in next. He said Chief Colorow told him that the Utes would fight if the soldiers crossed Milk Creek. Then he produced a crumpled piece of paper found on the road with a pencil sketch of four army officers riddled with bullet holes. Late that evening Charles G. Lowry returned from his trip to the agency to deliver Thornburgh's September 25 message.[52] He apparently carried a written message from Meeker that has since disappeared from official records, and he reported that conditions at White River were extremely unsettled.[53] Lowry hadn't delivered Thornburgh's dispatch to Meeker until the previous evening because Lowry had stopped to play monte and party with some men along the way. This delay added to the confusion about agency conditions and prevented timely assessment of the situation.[54] Lowry apparently was not disciplined for his casual behavior, but he would pay the ultimate price at the battle of Milk Creek.

These ominous accounts deeply troubled the expedition commander, and the entire command grew despondent. Thornburgh was particularly concerned about the apparently deteriorating situation at the agency, so he called another staff meeting to discuss the issues and reconsider their options. While many expedition members believed reinforcements were needed before further advance, the major first asked for Payne's ideas since he was second in command. Due to the growing tension, he concluded that Captain Payne's more aggressive stance had been the correct one after all, so he reversed his earlier opinion. Thornburgh decided not to leave the bulk of his command at Deer Creek or to go to the agency with only five men, or to wait for reinforcements.[55] It simply was too dangerous to separate his command considering the growing Ute threat. Several of the men were clearly nervous because they sat down that night to write letters home or to make out their wills.[56]

During the officers' meeting about planned movements for September 29, the discussion centered on how far the entire command should go before making camp and sending Thornburgh ahead with his small contingent toward the agency. Cherry later recalled that the decision was to make camp on the top of the ridge just north of Coal Creek Canyon, then move the cavalry through the canyon at night to position the troopers about twelve miles from the agency on the morning of September 30. This maneuver would have placed the expedition camp several miles into the Ute Reservation on September 29. Payne, on the other hand, later testified that his understanding was that they would march the command to Milk Creek and go into camp, then he would take the cavalry column through Coal Creek Canyon under cover of darkness.[57] Unfortunately, careful examination of these two testimonies does not clarify whether the decision at Deer Creek was to advance either to or well beyond Milk Creek on September 29, a judgment that bears directly on military efforts to minimize a show of force on the Ute Reservation. Historical records remain ambiguous, but I've chosen Payne's recollection because, as second in command and as the officer responsible for the planned advance, he would have been most familiar with strategic maneuvers.

Captain Payne outlined his alternative plan. He suspected an Indian ambush and argued that the steep-sided Coal Creek Canyon leading down to the White River south of Yellowjacket Pass was the most likely spot for one. A large column trapped in that canyon could not defend itself. He suggested that the troops should reach the northern edge of the reservation at Milk Creek the next day and make camp there. Then Thornburgh, Lowry, and five cavalrymen would leave through Yellowjacket Pass and ride down Coal Creek Canyon to the agency as originally planned. Payne would wait with the rest of the troops at Milk Creek until well after dark, then he would lead them out of the valley, over the pass, and down through Coal Creek Canyon by dawn on September 30. The entire force would then be in a strategic response position if they were needed at the agency.[58]

Thornburgh approved this new tactic, even though it was deceitful and could be easily misconstrued as an offensive maneuver. He probably reversed his policy because Meeker had not come out to meet him and there seemed to be a real threat to the civilians at White River.

But the Utes' veiled threats of violence were predicated on the fact that the expedition would first have to enter the reservation in force. A peaceful resolution probably could have been achieved if the troops had stayed north of Milk Creek and if they had respected the Indians' desire to protect their reservation from armed encroachment by the United States Army. In retrospect, Thornburgh probably had not given his first efforts to negotiate enough of a chance to succeed. Instead, he sent Wilmer Eskridge south into the night with a message to Meeker:

> Headquarters White River Expedition
> Camp on Deer Creek, Sept. 28, 1879

Mr. Meeker
U.S. Indian Agent, White River Agency, Col.:

Sir:
I have, after due deliberations, decided to modify my plans, as communicated in my letter of 27th inst., in the following particulars:
I shall move with my entire command to some convenient camp near and within striking distance of your agency, reaching such point during the 29th. I shall then halt and encamp the troops, and proceed to the agency with my guide and five soldiers, as communicated in my

letter of the 27th inst. Then and there I will be ready to have a conference with you and the Indians, so that an understanding may be arrived at and my course of action determined.

I have carefully considered whether or not it would be advisable to have my command at a point as distant as that desired by the Indians who were in my camp last night, and have reached the conclusion that under my orders, which require me to march this command to the agency, I am not at liberty to leave it at a point where it would not be available in case of trouble. You are authorized to say for me to the Indians that my course of conduct is entirely dependent on them.

Our desire is to avoid trouble, and we have not come for war. I requested you in my letter of the *26th* [italics added, it was actually the 25th] to meet me on the road before I reached the agency. I renew my request that you do so, and further desire that you bring such chiefs as may wish to accompany you.

I am, very respectfully, your obedient servant.

T. T. Thornburgh
Major, 4th Infantry, Com'd'g Expedition[59]

Thornburgh was still making every effort to avoid an armed confrontation with the Indians. He proposed two options. First, he still clearly preferred to meet with Meeker and the chiefs at some point along the road and to do so as soon as possible. The second option would be initiated if Meeker did not meet him on the road. Thornburgh would continue to the agency satisfied that his command was not far behind.

The first option was preferable for several reasons. Thornburgh could parley, avoid advancing his column, and still have troops nearby if they were needed. This meeting actually might have been possible north of the reservation, which would have reassured the Utes that the troops weren't going to invade. It is unclear why Meeker never responded in writing to Thornburgh's first invitation. Perhaps, had Lowry been more conscientious, Eskridge may have been able to bring a favorable response. Or Meeker simply may have been either unwilling or unable to leave the confines of the agency.

With this final letter sent by courier to the agency, Thornburgh settled into his bedroll. It would be a quiet, eerie night at Deer Creek and at White River Agency, where the Indians planned a war dance.[60] Tomorrow, Major Thomas Tipton Thornburgh would ride over the divide, down Milk Creek Valley, and into American history.

4
September 29, 1879

. . . after a desperate fight since 12 o'clock N. We hold our position at this hour.
—Captain J. Scott Payne, September 29, 1879[1]

Thornburgh's White River Expedition left Deer Creek camp shortly after dawn, between 6:15 A.M. and 6:30 A.M., September 29, 1879. Captain Payne recalled, "the first pencils of sunlight were gilding a lofty pinnacle, surmounted with a leaning rock so strikingly resembling a woman's form that one could almost fancy it an Olympian Venus bending down to kiss an earthly lover lying in the quaint, tender shadows at her feet."[2]

The column formed with Company E, Third Cavalry and Company F, Fifth Cavalry joined by Major Thornburgh in advance, and Lieutenant Paddock's Company D, Fifth Cavalry stayed to the rear guarding the wagon train. Each soldier was issued forty rounds of ammunition because neither an offensive action was planned nor a tactical defense anticipated. Usually cavalry units entering combat would have had several times that amount on their persons and in saddlebags.[3]

Quartermaster Wolf took charge of the government teams while John C. Davis drove a separate wagon owned by J. W. Hugus, the post sutler at Fort Fred Steele. Hugus had sent Davis along with some supplies for the expedition, and F. E. Blake accompanied him.[4] Each mule string tugged at its harnesses in answer to the snap of reins.

The long line of riders and wagons scaled the ridge between Deer Creek and Morapos Creek, crossed Morapos Creek and Stinking Gulch, then headed toward the divide above Milk Creek. About six miles from Deer Creek the expedition passed burning and smoldering grass. Thornburgh realized that Indians may have set the fire and moved the two advance cavalry companies about two miles ahead of the wagons.

Cavalrymen and teamsters trotted their animals over the hot ground quickly to prevent injury.[5]

Soon the advance companies reached the northern boundary of the Ute Reservation, the official boundary established by the Treaty of 1868, which put the line fifteen miles north of the fortieth parallel and about a half mile north of Milk Creek.[6] This is the present-day boundary line between Colorado's Moffat and Rio Blanco Counties. Travelers in the late nineteenth century generally ignored the official line and used Milk Creek as the boundary since it was easier to identify than a line on a map.

Emil Weber, a civilian, was uneasy about moving any closer to the agency. He, like some other expedition members, felt that the major should have taken Jack, Colorow, and the other Indians who had visited them on September 26 and 27 hostage as insurance against attack. He thought that Thornburgh was too concerned about exceeding his orders and suggested that they not advance. Thornburgh answered rather scornfully that Emil should go back if he was afraid; Weber did just that and later heard the outbreak of the battle from a safe distance.[7]

Thornburgh directed his advance companies forward, maintaining their distance ahead of the wagon train. The cavalry column topped the divide into Milk Creek at 9:30 A.M.; troopers dismounted and led their horses down into the valley.[8] Every officer and enlisted man was alert because Indians who may have set the grass fire might still be near.

Payne described Milk Creek:

> . . . a small stream running softly down a narrow valley; on the right hand, a mile off, a line of bluffs continuous and inaccessible, with broken ridges nearer the creek; on the left rounded knolls and what our English friends call "downs," furrowed with arroyos and running back to the high hills which form the advance guard of the White River Mountains. The air was soft and balmy as with the breath of the sweet south, and the bright sunshine shooting in broad flashes across the hilltops filled the valley as with liquid gold. Save in the long column which, dismounted, was winding its way down the hill, not a living

creature was in sight. Earth and sky were fair to behold, and the pictured calm seemed the very symbol of peace.[9]

Milk Creek was low and flowed through a meandering channel running northwest out of the forest and past the towering Three Points Mountain. Then it turned southwest through a mile-wide valley at the base of a steep mountain that rose twelve hundred feet above the stream. Milk Creek maintains this southwesterly course for about five miles until the valley narrows as it passes Little Beaver Creek. Below this juncture, the waters carve a steep canyon into the bedrock of the Danforth Hills, flow north, and eventually empty into the Yampa River.

Soldiers could see the agency road stretch ahead as it snaked along the bench north of Milk Creek, paralleling the stream for more than a mile. The road then turned south, crossed Milk Creek, and wound along the south bank for a couple of miles through the narrowing valley to the foot of the Danforth Hills. Beyond that and out of sight, the agency road turned south at the foot of the Danforth Hills and headed up Little Beaver Creek toward Yellowjacket Pass at the entrance to Coal Creek Canyon. Coal Creek flowed into the White River.

The two cavalry companies caught up with John Gordon's wagons, oxen, and three bullwhackers on the bench north of Milk Creek. Gordon's teamsters told Thornburgh that Utes had passed them earlier and told them to keep out of the way because there was going to be a fight with the soldiers.[10]

Thornburgh ignored Gordon's warning and the command passed the wagons, rode down to Milk Creek, and halted to water their stock. Officers and noncommissioned officers had already scouted the best watering spots and signaled troopers to them. Soldiers marched out from the column on both flanks for nearly a hundred yards to accommodate each thirsty horse. This was standard procedure for a stream that was a trickle due to drought.[11] About 10:15 A.M. the column rested one thousand yards upstream from where the agency road crossed Milk Creek.[12]

Thornburgh sent Lieutenant Cherry and guide Joe Rankin downstream to investigate the crossing; they reported that the stream was not a steady flow but only lingered in stagnant pools. The two men also described warm campfire ashes near the creek, fresh horse trails from a large body of Indians, and smoldering grass, probably from fires set by the Indians to keep the cavalry back where there was more feed for the horses.[13]

This troubling news forced Thornburgh once again to reconsider his strategy. Warm ashes and fresh trail sign proved that Indians were nearby, and Ute scouts were probably watching the command's every move. Payne's plan to advance troops up to Yellowjacket Pass after dark now seemed to be an impossibility, but neither could the command make camp near the crossing at Milk Creek. Thornburgh didn't think there was enough grass for the stock or enough water in the creek to sustain more than 150 men and three hundred animals while negotiations took place at the agency.

Thornburgh asked Joe Rankin where the nearest water might be. Rankin suggested camping at Beaver Springs northeast of Yellowjacket Pass and well within the Ute Reservation. Thornburgh conferred with Captain Payne and decided to advance the entire cavalry column south of Milk Creek and then to assess a camp at Beaver Springs.

Lieutenant Samuel Cherry, guide Joe Rankin, and five Company E, Third Cavalry troopers, including Sergeant Frank P. Secrist, Private Amandes M. Startzell, and Private William Lewis, led the way across Milk Creek. These seven men had been riding ahead of the main column as a headquarters party since September 24, staying a half to three-quarters of a mile ahead of the cavalry column.[14] They crossed Milk Creek on the main wagon road about 10:30 A.M.

Cherry touched his hat as he passed the major and rode forward with his small scouting party. They pulled up just south of Milk Creek where the wagon road turned west downstream into the narrowing valley. Here a shortcut trail took off almost due south, avoiding the lower end of the valley. Rankin recalled directing the squad up the shortcut trail through Sarvisberry Draw [sic], which was separated from Little Beaver Creek by two low ridges.[15] Travel would be faster on this route since the squad was small and not hindered by the lumbering wagons.

Major Thornburgh followed at a distance with the two cavalry companies. He led this column with his ambulance, Private O'Malley, and Charles Lowry.[16] Trumpeter John McDonald of Company F, Fifth Cavalry served as the major's orderly.[17] Captain Lawson rode alongside

Thornburgh at the head of Company E, Third Cavalry while Captain Payne followed two hundred yards back with Company F, Fifth Cavalry.[18] Company F apparently took the lead after crossing the creek. Some baggage wagons and a two-wheeled forge accompanied the cavalry troops across Milk Creek.[19]

The hills south of Milk Creek, called Little River by the Utes, were filled with Ute warriors on the morning of September 29. Young men were determined not to let the soldiers cross Milk Creek and to enter the reservation. The warriors laughed and sang to ease their apprehension; they were primed for action by the dance held the evening before.[20]

Groups of Utes milled about small campfires. Johnson told stories of his past exploits, and Colorow sat alone, playing monte, until a runner came from the river to tell them that the soldiers were on the road and coming down out of the hills and into the valley. Colorow picked up his cards and joined the young men.[21]

Chief Jack had been watching the column from his vantage point in the hills south of the creek. It soon became clear that the entire expedition was crossing the creek onto the reservation. Jack, who had thought that Thornburgh would advance with only a few men, was incensed and sent a courier "galloping off twenty-five miles to tell Douglas at the agency that Thornburgh had broken his word about stopping the troops at the reservation boundary."[22]

While scorched forage and stagnant pools may have been sufficient cause for Thornburgh to cancel plans to make a camp at Milk Creek, his decision to advance onto the reservation sealed his fate.

Lieutenant Cherry and his party advanced about three-quarters of a mile beyond Milk Creek and down into a draw dotted with serviceberry bushes. He looked up to see three Indians about five hundred yards in front of him disappear behind the ridge above the trail on the southwest.[23]

Until that moment, Cherry had been a strong advocate of peaceful deliberation; but now he was suspicious because, at the Yampa and Williams Fork encounter, the Utes had ridden directly into camp to negotiate rather than hiding, as they did now. He divided his squad, sending some men to the left of the draw and taking the rest two hundred yards down to the right, where they crossed the stream at the bottom of the draw and climbed to the top of the ridge behind which the three Indians had disappeared. Events unfolded quickly from this point on. Joe Rankin, Sergeant Secrist, and possibly Private Startzell were probably with Cherry, and up the draw they saw about twenty-five mounted Indians leave other Utes on the next ridge to the west. This second ridge overlooks the main wagon road as it winds up through Little Beaver Creek ravine about one thousand yards from where Cherry's party now stood. The mounted Indians made a mad dash to head the soldiers off along the trail and gathered at a point a short distance ahead of the headquarters party.[24]

Cherry turned back toward the main column and waved his hat to Major Thornburgh to signal him to fall back with the two cavalry companies. He then retreated with his squad down the hill toward the rest of the command, which had followed him up the shortcut trail at a distance of about three-quarters of a mile. Company F, Fifth Cavalry had just begun to descend into the draw when Cherry signaled.

Cherry returned from the ridge and reined in on the trail next to Thornburgh and reported that after first seeing the Indians, he had ridden with his unit up the first ridge toward the southwest, until they were within one hundred yards of the second ridge, which overlooked the main wagon road. He saw Utes dispersed between the first and second ridges and on the second ridge above the main wagon road. The Indians on top of the second ridge were each about a yard apart and were lying down behind the ridge with guns in hand. Cherry estimated the line to contain from three hundred to four hundred Utes deployed over four hundred yards along the ridge. He also noticed that the Utes had pastured their ponies way off to the right, probably near the Danforth Hills. Cherry speculated that the Indian plan had been to wait for the column to pass within two hundred yards of their position on the agency road and then to ambush the expedition as it trailed up Little Beaver Creek. The fact that Thornburgh had followed Cherry's party up the shortcut trail behind the Indians' position probably saved the entire command from annihilation.[25]

The brief conference between Cherry and Thornburgh ended about 11:00 A.M.[26] Thornburgh still wanted to conduct a peaceful negotiation. He sent Cherry with orders to Captain Payne, who had already had his company dismount, maneuvered oblique (slanting his line away from Lawson's company), and deployed them in skirmish line along the slope on the left flank. Payne was told not to fire a shot unless the Indians fired first.

Cherry switched mounts at Payne's position and saddled up Tip, his favorite horse, which had been led all morning and was still fresh.[27] He rode back to Thornburgh's position. In the meantime, the major had ordered Captain Lawson to deploy his company in skirmish line on the right flank along the first ridge between the agency road and the shortcut trail (see Maps 4.1–4.5). The disposition of the two companies now resembled the letter V, with the point toward the southwest, facing the Indians. Payne's easternmost wing was deflected to the left to prevent the Utes from turning the soldiers' flank.

Payne's command of the left line and Lawson's of the right departed from the standard division of a cavalry battalion into company skirmishers based on seniority. Normally the senior ranking captain, Payne in this case, would have commanded the right flank. This departure from prescribed tactics indicates that they were responding to a rapidly developing situation, and that they had not planned an offensive maneuver.[28]

With his skirmishers arrayed in battle formation and spaced about ten to fifteen feet apart, Thornburgh issued another order. Cherry was to take fifteen men from Lawson's company, move out by the right flank below Lawson's skirmish line, and cross the ravine between the first and second ridges; he was to attempt to communicate with the Indians from this advance position.[29]

Cherry started down the first ridge with his squad of Company E, Third Cavalry. Simultaneously, fifteen or twenty Indians moved down from the second ridge across the ravine, but Cherry couldn't determine why the Indians were moving up; they were either coming to talk or to head off the soldiers. Both detachments proceeded cautiously.

In the meantime Thornburgh and Payne stood together far off on the left flank. They signaled with a wave of their handkerchiefs to a separate band of Utes on the slope above Company F and four hundred yards to their left. Two or three of these Indians returned the signals and cautiously approached the soldiers while keeping concealed and out of range.[30]

The Indians on the right flank near Cherry came in full view from behind the second ridge once Cherry's command moved four hundred to five hundred yards beyond Lawson's company. Cherry took off his hat and waved it in a friendly manner over his head; it was just before 11:30 A.M.

His gesture was answered with a shot. Cherry later claimed it had been fired by one of the Indians who had come forward to meet them, while Indians testified that either a soldier or an unknown participant was at fault.[31]

In the days and hours leading up to this armed confrontation, Chief Jack and the Utes had been just as tense as the expedition's troopers. The Indians also had been equally active since Jack had last met with Thornburgh at the Yampa River four days before, on September 26. Jack had left Thornburgh that evening, returned to White River, then moved his camp to the Little Beaver Creek country north of Yellowjacket Pass. Based on his meetings with Thornburgh and others, he had expected that the column would camp at Milk Creek rather than march all the way to the agency.[32]

On the morning of September 29, Jack left camp with seven or eight other Indians. They rode down toward Milk Creek to look for the soldiers whom they expected to reach the valley that day. When Jack and his group reached the top of a hill and looked across the valley, they saw the troopers coming down on the other side.

Jack and his men were unarmed; he intended to meet with Thornburgh and take the negotiating party to the agency while the rest of Thornburgh's command stayed at the stream.[33] However, Black Wilson, who was in charge of a trading post on Spring Gulch, recalled meeting five Utes at Thornburgh's Williams Fork camp on September 27 who told him to go home. They said, "Utes fight soldiers; no wanna kill you."[34] If Wilson's story is true, it too would indicate premeditation on the part of the Utes.

Colorow and a large group of armed Indians moved toward the column from behind Jack's group. Cherry may have first seen part of Jack's group on the ridges, then later they probably moved to the hill south of Payne's position as part of the band who maneuvered to stop the soldiers' advance on the trail. Jack told his people, "The soldiers will be likely to think that things look bad over here."[35]

When the troops dismounted and deployed into skirmish lines, Jack spoke, perhaps to Colorow's armed braves or possibly to the soldiers, "You now see what you have brought upon yourselves by not attending to my advice; I have always told you to live in peace, and quietly; but now no one can tell what may happen."³⁶ Jack had been a friend, scout, and traveling companion of General Crook during 1876 campaigns against the Sioux. He recognized the skirmish lines as preparation for battle, and this convinced Jack that the soldiers intended to fight rather than negotiate.³⁷

Even so, Jack tried to stop the armed Indians from moving toward the troopers. About the time an Indian named Unco saw a soldier waving his hat, Jack heard the first shots; the Indians and soldiers were about five hundred yards apart where the gunfire began.³⁸

Chief Jack urged his people not to return fire, not even after the first volley. But firing ensued on both sides, between perhaps one hundred Indians and about one hundred troopers in the skirmish lines.³⁹

To the north, the government wagons and Davis's team were just pulling over the divide and into sight of Milk Creek. Thornburgh ordered Rankin to ride back to the wagons and tell the drivers to stop and corral.⁴⁰ The scout galloped through the valley and up toward the divide. He reined in and told Lieutenants Paddock and Wolf of the Indian encounter, but the situation was obvious because the sounds of the fight echoed from the valley below.

Paddock advanced the wagon train another mile toward Milk Creek so the men and livestock could be near water; he passed Gordon's train on the way. Paddock's group corraled their wagons about two hundred yards from the creek and had a clear view of the battle raging to the south.⁴¹

Colorow watched as the wagons came into the valley and told several young braves near him: "In those wagons is food for the soldiers. If we have those wagons, our bellies will be full and we will all feel good. But those soldiers will have nothing in their bellies, and after a while they will go home."⁴² Some of the men ran down to their horses and galloped out of the hills toward Paddock's position to try to cut the wagons off from the soldiers who were fighting south of the creek.

Cherry's hands were full on the right flank. The shot by the Indians that apparently started the battle had been fired at him when he waved his hat. The bullet missed him but wounded Private Willard W. Mitchell, who was ten feet behind him, and killed Mitchell's horse.⁴³

After the shot, Cherry ordered the men to dismount, scatter, and hold their position. Their advanced position gave them a tactical advantage because they controlled the hill crest at the northern end of the first ridge just above Milk Creek. He sent a courier to report to Thornburgh that mounted Indians were riding around their right flank and trying to cut the advance companies off from the wagons. Thornburgh received this information and fell back to a position nearly opposite to, and east of, Cherry's skirmishers.

Payne, who had been the most eager to engage the Indians, wasted no time after hearing gunfire from the right flank at Cherry's advance position. He immediately ordered his command to open fire. Company F, deployed on the high ground east of the trail, was at a disadvantage because they were still below the Indian position. The nearest Utes probably were in Chief Jack's group, which was now armed and included a growing number of Indians who were moving eastward along the slope from the second ridge. The soldiers had to fire uphill toward the enemy. Payne's front was totally dominated by Indians on higher ground. The Utes poured a devastating barrage into his skirmish line. After only a few minutes the Indians killed two troopers, Privates Michael Firestone and Amos D. Miller, Private Oscar Cass was slightly wounded, and many other soldiers were hit. The soldiers killed perhaps a half dozen Indians.[44] Troopers gathered up the wounded, and Captain Payne recognized that his position was untenable.

Thornburgh was near the northeast end of the first ridge. By now he had received Cherry's message about the flanking maneuver to the northwest. Other Utes were attempting to flank Payne's company to the northeast. After about twenty minutes of fighting, Thornburgh prepared orders to withdraw.[45]

Private Startzell carried the order to Payne, telling him to fall back down the slope. The captain slowly withdrew his troop, firing all the way and keeping the led horses between his skirmish line and that of Lawson's company. Fighting became so intense that he had to leave the bodies of Firestone and Miller behind. It was all his men could do to keep themselves alive and to prevent the Indians from surrounding the two companies. The elapsed time from the first shot through this period of tactical withdrawal was probably less than forty-five minutes.[46] It was now shortly after noon.

The Indians pressed hard against the skirmish lines and intensified their flanking efforts by concentrating their force on the wagons far behind the advance cavalry companies. Some warriors congregated south of Milk Creek, beyond carbine range, to attempt to divide the command by isolating two-thirds of the cavalry from the wagons that held ammunition stores, medical supplies, and rations.[47]

Thornburgh noticed that Utes were gathering on a hill between the advance troops and the wagon train; he recognized that they were going to try to pinch the retreating troops off from the wagons. He sent a message with Private Startzell to Captain Payne telling him to take twenty men from Company F, mount up, and charge the hill to the left and rear (northeast) of the two cavalry companies. This would open the way to the wagons for the led horses and retreating skirmishers.[48] The balance of Company F would fall in with Lawson's Company E. Thornburgh ordered Captain Lawson to fall back with Company E, Third Cavalry and their horses. Cherry was ordered to try to hold his position long enough to keep the Indians from reaching the gullies and ravines along Milk Creek while Payne's and Lawson's companies fell back. Once the withdrawal was well under way, Cherry could fall back as well.[49] Timing was critical. Cherry had to be careful not to separate too far from Lawson's larger detachment and thereby expose the rear of his squad to additional flanking maneuvers by the Utes.

Joseph Lawson's company had been in the thick of the fight from the first shot. His troopers returned fire from a skirmish line on the first ridge while every fourth man held the horses.[50] While Lawson's men fired volleys, the Indians rapidly appeared on all sides, in the ravines, and on almost every rise. The fighting order on the right flank became less linear and more general by the minute.[51]

Thornburgh told Lawson to fall back while Payne withdrew in a "charge" to the northeast knoll. Lawson passed the word to Cherry to fall back on Lawson's company while Company E covered Cherry's retreat. Thornburgh left Lawson while the skirmishers, fighting all the way, continued to withdraw.

Payne, aboard his horse, Charger, prepared to carry out Thornburgh's order, but the horse was shot just as the charge began. The saddle girth broke, and Payne took a bruising fall to the ground. When he stood up, he found himself alone; his detachment already had swept over the knoll and was disappearing into clouds of dust and powder smoke.

A Ute noticed the captain's plight and approached to within fifty yards of the now unarmed soldier. Fortunately, First Sergeant John Dolan of Company F had circled back when he noticed the captain missing. The fifty-five-year-old veteran dismounted and offered his horse to the captain. Payne refused, and Dolan stayed with his commander.

Apparently, the Ute retired once the odds became two to one. Soon Carpenter, a young recruit, brought up a led horse, and the three men made it to the corral without further incident.[52]

After giving the withdrawal orders to his company commanders, Major Thornburgh started back alone toward the road crossing on Milk Creek. Payne's small force had just charged over the area five minutes before, and Paddock was beginning to circle the wagons north of the creek. Only one company guarded the supplies, and Thornburgh wanted to concentrate his entire force there against the Indians, who now were rapidly gaining control of the high ground. Thornburgh didn't make it to the wagons. The major was shot and killed right after crossing the creek. He fell from his saddle a half mile behind Lawson's company and within five hundred yards of the corralled wagons. Thornburgh was thirty-five years old and had served in the army since he was a teenager. He was almost a full year younger than Custer was when he was killed with all of his men on the Little Bighorn.

Payne later speculated that the major had been riding back on the road toward the wagons at a leisurely pace, looking over the battle and deciding what to do next. He must have been picked off by a sharpshooter at long range. Payne recalled that his detachment had charged through the area just before or slightly after Thornburgh's movements.[53] However, Payne was not in the charge due to his fall; he was not familiar with the details as the charge moved toward the knoll.

The major probably was killed by a single sniper concealed in the ravine. Likely a lone Ute, hidden by cottonwoods, crept up or down Milk Creek and moved close to the crossing and remained behind the retreating troops of Company E, Third Cavalry.

The circumstances surrounding Major Thomas Tipton Thornburgh's death at Milk Creek are among the most discussed and controversial topics related to the battle. Sources vary. For example, M. Wilson Rankin claimed,

> Shots from the same band of Indians that fired on Payne's men, apparently wounded Thornburg [*sic*] and his horse, which slackened speed. The Indians, seeing he had no firearms, swooped down from the hill and surrounded him. Private Tom Nolan, one of Lawson's men, who was holding horses while the troops were fighting, at a considerable distance, saw the Indians drag Thornburgh from his horse and beat him. His horse was fatally wounded and died a few hours after.[54]

Another source, published within months of the battle, describes Thornburgh as having recognized the situation at the wagons and then leading a squad of twenty mounted cavalry in a gallant charge against the Indians; the charge caused his death and the deaths of thirteen bold followers.[55] Eyewitness testimony debunks these facts. Sergeant Dolan was the ranking soldier who took part in the charge; Captain Payne was not a participant because his horse had been shot and he had been left behind.

Thornburgh may have been unarmed when he was killed, according to some authors, because he had been planning to negotiate with the Indians and possibly follow them to the agency when the fight started. Some eyewitnesses mention having seen him with the revolver given to him on his thirty-first birthday. Thornburgh probably did not have that revolver in his possession; it may have been with other personal belongings in the ambulance. Descendants of J. M. Thornburgh, the major's brother, have what appears to be this weapon; if it had been with the major when he was killed, the Utes probably would have taken it.[56]

Chief Jack witnessed Major Thornburgh's death from his vantage point in the hills south of the creek but did not provide detailed testimony of the incident.[57] The Ute leader sat alone pondering the implications of the engagement. He lit his pipe, the smoke spiraling up and mixing with the powder smoke from the discharge of hundreds of revolvers, carbines, and rifles. The air reeked of burned sulphur. Jack rose, cradling his rifle beneath his arm, and slowly walked away.[58]

Lieutenants Paddock and Wolf, John C. Davis, and others who had been with the wagons, pulled them together with the help of scout Rankin and wagon master William McKinstry. McKinstry was killed before they finished.

About twenty minutes later, the twenty members of Company F, Fifth Cavalry galloped in from the bluff five hundred yards to the south, where they had just broken up the Indians' flanking effort. Payne, Nolan, and Carpenter were with the company by now, having caught up with them after the charge. The Indians followed Payne's detachment closely, and only the fusillade from the wagon train kept Utes from surrounding the small cavalry detachment. Two of Payne's men were wounded and a horse was killed just as they entered the circle.[59]

The wagons were parked in an oval with the wagon tongues pointed to the inside, so the men had some protection while they unhitched the teams. The wagons formed about three-quarters of the defense perimeter while the twelve-foot-high bank down to the Milk Creek streamed completed the circumference. Running water, such as it was, was about two hundred yards away.[60] Payne remembered that "the wagons [were] very badly parked, a great many horses killed, and a large number of them wounded. They were all concentrated in a little space, perhaps not over seventy-five yards long by twenty-five wide, and the Indians upon the high bluffs upon the north and the south side of the position were pouring a plunging fire into this corral."[61]

Dr. Grimes had moved his ambulance to the train and assisted in directing the defensive efforts. He tried to make a double circle of wagons, but the Indians created such a barrage of lead that only a partial single circle could be finished.[62]

Captain Payne ordered thirty to forty wounded horses destroyed and their carcasses used by sharpshooters for cover. Marksmen took up their positions and quickly returned fire against the Utes. Their efforts slowed the deluge of bullets whizzing into the wagons, and the men within the circle began to feel a bit more confident.

Some soldiers unloaded the wagons and formed a breastworks along the perimeter of trunks, bundles of bedding, grain, sacks of flour, and mess boxes. The greenhorn Lieutenant Paddock, who was in his first fight, was painfully wounded in the hip. Captain Payne received a bullet wound through his left shoulder and arm. In spite of increasing casualties, the defenses took shape and began to offer some security to the fragmented command. But the situation had far from stabilized.[63]

The Indians continued to press Lawson's and Cherry's retreating skirmishers south of Milk Creek. Both units were running short of ammunition. According to Rankin, Lawson sent Private John Donovan back to the wagon train to bring up more cartridges; it was Donovan who noticed Thornburgh's body on his way back to Lawson's company with ammunition and informed Lawson of the major's fate.[64]

The Utes tried desperately to break the skirmish line by maneuvering toward the crest of a hill that would exploit a break in the line and give them advantage over the retreating soldiers. Payne apparently saw the tactic from his vantage point at the wagons and ordered Sergeant Edward Grimes to rush the hill with two soldiers. Grimes and two men left hurriedly and beat the enemy to the position. They held their ground until ordered to leave, then presumably mixed in with Cherry's retreating troops.[65]

Cherry's advance detachment was dangerously low on cartridges, and he was a thousand yards from the wagons when he needed to send someone through the gauntlet for more ammunition. By this time, Sergeant Grimes had joined Cherry's skirmishers, and he volunteered to return to the wagons.

Cherry hollered, "Go, Grimes, and I will never forget you."[66] Grimes mounted his twice-wounded horse, galloped for the corral, emptying his revolver as he went, and made it to the wagons unscratched.

Whether Grimes ran the gauntlet again isn't known, and an 1879 source suggests that Cherry received his ammunition from Lawson, who was cool and courageous throughout the retreat.[67] This account may have been describing a different incident or perhaps was confused about the circumstances of Grimes's trip. Nonetheless, it illustrates that the cavalry companies maintained discipline within their ranks during the retreat and were able to execute controlled tactical maneuvers. Their discipline contrasts starkly with the chaos that characterized the five companies with Custer at Little Bighorn three years earlier.[68]

Captain Lawson and Sergeant Neurohr of Company E, Third Cavalry were still mounted when ammunition was brought up from the wagon train, and then they learned about Thornburgh. Lawson tried to reach the major's body but his horse was shot out from under him for the second time that day. Sergeant Neurohr's horse also was killed. They each had to take remounts from the led horses, but neither man reached Thornburgh.

It is not clear whether Private Donovan or Sergeant Grimes reported the news about Major Thornburgh. Private Donovan's name isn't in official records. Sergeant Grimes's activites, on the other hand, are described and his bravery earned him the Medal of Honor; the citation reads, in part, for having "voluntarily brought up a supply of ammunition while under heavy fire at nearly point blank range."[69]

Lawson and Cherry still had a difficult retreat even after they received more ammunition. Payne sent Sergeant John A. Poppe of Company F, Fifth Cavalry with ten men out to help cover their withdrawal. Poppe's detachment dislodged some Utes hidden in ravines and behind the creek banks, where they had taken position between the wagons and the two companies of cavalry. The ravines were about five hundred yards from the wagons, near where Thornburgh was killed, and in direct line of the retreating cavalry.[70]

Payne could only speculate how things were going with the retreating troops. Most of their led horses and the men leading them had returned to the wagon circle, but the skirmishers were still out. The captain hoped Poppe's squad would make a difference.

Lawson's men fought their way back, bringing all of their wounded with them. The Indians pulled up a bit in their fight on the right flank when they concentrated on the wagons, allowing the soldiers to reach Poppe's relief squad which was on the banks of Milk Creek and protected by cottonwoods. Once the troopers made the final five hundred yards to the wagons, they counted about twenty wounded among them.[71]

Payne's company also had several wounded, but the only fatalities outside the wagon circle were troopers Firestone and Miller, and Thornburgh himself. Private Donovan told Payne about Thornburgh's death, and Payne, as senior ranking officer, took command of the expedition.[72] It was not quite 1:00 P.M.

The Utes observed the retreating skirmishers from high ground. Colorow squinted at the encircled wagons from his hilltop position; he recognized that the soldiers had gained a defensive advantage once all of the men reached the wagons. Acari sat beside him and stretched as Johnson approached the pair carrying his Sharps rifle and a new one belonging to his son, Tatit'z. Robert Emmitt included in *Last War Trail*, published in 1954, that Johnson informed Colorow and Acari that a son had been killed during the skirmish—although Johnson later testified that his sons were not in the fight. Johnson left the new rifle with Acari, then moved downhill to shoot into the barricade.[73] If his son had been killed, the price Johnson paid for fighting with Agent Meeker had just become a very personal one.

Captains Lawson and Payne assessed the situation once both were in relative safety behind the barricade. Payne asked Lawson to take overall command since he was not wounded, but Lawson refused because Payne's shoulder wound and bruises were of too little consequence to affect his command ability.[74]

Captain Payne said that he would move the camp back toward Rawlins but offered no plan. Lawson asked, "How will you do that with our horses and mules killed?" and added, "I will stay right here with my wounded men."[75]

While the besieged troopers were fighting for their lives on the morning of September 29, the Interior and War Departments processed standard correspondence related to the expedition. John E. Summers, surgeon at Omaha Barracks, sent a telegraph to Fort Fred Steele:

> Headquarters Dept. of the Platte
> Medical Director's Office
> Fort Omaha, Neb. Sept. 29, 1879
>
> To: Post Surgeon
> Fort Fred Steele, W. T.
>
> Sir,
>   A communication has been received at this Office requesting that additional Medical Supplies be sent to the Ute expedition under command of Major Thornburgh, which you will please put up in such quantities as may be

required by a command of its proportions for a period of two months, including a good supply of bandages and plaster of Paris, and have them forwarded by the first opportunity.

I am, Sir,
Very respectfully,
Your obedient servant,
Jno. E. Summers
Surgeon, U.S.A.
Med. Dir. Dept.[76]

When Thornburgh sent his request to Omaha for more medical supplies is not known. He may have sensed the possibility of a fight as early as his first meeting with the Indians at the Yampa River on September 26 or at the conference with Colorow at Williams Fork on September 27. As negotiations soured, the major probably realized that his expedition might take twice as long as expected, and, if so, there could be a greater need for medical care.

Meeker was concerned about the growing tension and aware of increased Indian movements around the agency and completed a telegraph message to the Interior Department's commissioner of Indian Affairs:

September 29, 1879

Sir:

Major Thornburgh, Fourth Infantry, leaves his command 50 miles distant, and comes to-day with five men. Indians propose to fight if troops advance. A talk will be had to-morrow. Captain Dodge, Ninth Cavalry, is at Steamboat Springs, with orders to break up Indian stores and keep Indians on reservation. Sales of ammunition and guns brisk for ten days past. Store nearest sent back 16,000 rounds and 13 guns. When Captain Dodge commences to enforce law, no living here without troops. Have sent for him to confer.[77]

Agent Meeker was still under the impression that Thornburgh would leave his cavalry somewhere around Williams Fork or probably no closer than Deer Creek. He hadn't yet received Thornburgh's message sent from Deer Creek Sunday evening, September 28, explaining that his troops would be close to the agency, that he would not arrive at a stopping point until September 29, and that they had left Williams Fork that morning.

It's interesting that Meeker knew the Indians would fight if the soldiers entered the reservation, and this coincides with what John Gordon and his men told Thornburgh at the bench north of Milk Creek. Unfortunately, nobody but the Utes knew how far the soldiers could advance without precipitating hostilities.

Within a few hours of sending his message to the Interior Department, Meeker received Major Thornburgh's correspondence from Deer Creek. He prepared a quick reply:

United States Indian Service
White River Agency, September 29, 1879 – 1 p.m.

Major T. T. Thornburgh
White River Expedition, in the Field, Col.:

Dear Sir:
    I expect to leave in the morning, with Douglas and Servick, to meet you. Things are peaceable, and Douglas flies the U.S. flag. If you have trouble in getting through the canyon to day let me know in (what) force.

We have been on guard three nights, and shall be tonight, not because we know there is danger, but because there may be.

I like your last programme, it is based on true military principles.

Most truly, yours,
N. C. Meeker
Indian Agent[78]

Meeker was content with the change in plan and finally agreed to meet Thornburgh on the road. He handed his response to Wilmer Eskridge, who was ordered to deliver it to Thornburgh.

No employee at the agency yet knew that the Milk Creek battle had been raging for an hour and a half. The Utes, however, had runners moving back and forth between the agency, Milk Creek, and their camp near Beaver Springs. The Utes were in control: they could communicate freely with warriors at Milk Creek. Meeker's belated approval of Thornburgh's plan was too late; Thornburgh was dead, and Eskridge was killed before he could deliver Meeker's message.

Back at Milk Creek, the Indians controlled the entire valley. They moved in to surround the wagons, taking positions on each of the nearby bluffs, in the streambed, and behind any cover they could find.

John Gordon and three of his men, Bullwhacker Jack, Hamilton, and Hornbeck, were still laboring with their wagon train northeast of the wagon circle. They quickly realized the deteriorating situation and abandoned their freight wagons about fifty yards up the road from the expedition's defenses. Gordon unhitched the oxen from his ten wagons. The Indians then either killed or drove off the animals and wounded one of Gordon's men. After freeing the teams, each man scurried for cover behind the army wagons and dug in with the soldiers.[79]

While the Indians controlled the battlefield, the cavalry had secured a single fighting position, and now the battle commenced in earnest. Bullets rained into the circle that was crowded with more than 150 soldiers and civilians, 153 mules, and 186 horses.[80]

The Indians were armed with Winchester repeating rifles and the latest models of Sharps, Henrys, and Remingtons; even though no reference mentions bows and arrows, it does not mean they weren't used.[81] Their weapons fired more quickly or had greater range than the cavalry's .45-70 Springfield carbines. Range wasn't always a factor, however, because the Indians sometimes crept to within thirty yards of the barricade. The soldiers hunkered down and tried not to present themselves as easy targets, likewise the Indians were well-concealed and poor targets, too.

Indians hidden behind the benches along the north bank of Milk Creek kept up such lethal fire that soldiers could not get to the wagons to get picks and shovels needed for digging trenches. Most of the men could only hide beneath the wagons while others sought refuge behind the layered bodies of horses and mules.

Sergeant John Dolan, who had saved Payne a couple hours earlier, saw how frightened the men were and shouted at them to help gather bedrolls and corn sacks from the wagons to reinforce the barricade. Too many soldiers were slow to respond. Dolan threatened the timid men, "If you don't get out and help, I will kill you myself."[82] He was shot dead by the Indians as he finished his sentence.

Payne, according to Theo F. Rodenbough in *Uncle Sam's Medal of Honor*, published in 1886, agonized over the loss of his first sergeant and good friend, "He (Dolan) was the bravest and most loyal soldier to his officers I have ever known . . . In his long service of thirty-seven years he had met with many adventures; had been wounded twice, had innumerable horses killed under him, and had been a prisoner at Andersonville." The year before he was killed, a bill was favorably reported in Congress that placed Dolan on the retired list as a lieutenant, but he was killed before it was enacted.[83]

Troopers continued to return fire and to reinforce the defensive position. Several prepared sixteen to seventeen dugouts or pits, each sixty to seventy feet long, about three feet wide and four feet deep as measured from the height of the dirt breastworks that were piled alongside. Many pits were in the open area of the wagon perimeter and faced the creek. Breastworks lined each side of the dugouts, and a sentry was posted behind the completed breastworks at the end of each pit. The fighting was so intense in one area that dead soldiers eventually were wrapped in blankets or canvas, piled up, and then covered with dirt to provide more protection.[84]

Dr. Grimes tended the growing number of wounded as best he could, moving amid the whizzing lead and passing from soldier to soldier. His responsibilities were just as dangerous as those of the troopers who were firing at concealed Utes. When Grimes reached over to open a medicine chest to get a bandage for Private Emil Kussman, he was hit by a bullet in the left shoulder.[85]

Indians made repeated attempts throughout the afternoon to dislodge the soldiers from behind the barricade. A steady wind had arisen and was blowing up the creek from the Danforth Hills, clearing the powder smoke from the battlefield. It was a cold wind that smelled of coming snow and "stirred the brush and chilled the bare, damp bodies of the men in the hills."[86]

The Indians took advantage of this breeze at about 3:00 P.M. by setting fire to dry grass and low sagebrush at the foot of the benches three hundred yards upwind (southwest) from the soldiers' wagon circle. Flames whipped skyward, fanned by the gusting afternoon wind. Fire spread back into the Danforth Hills and crept forward up the valley dangerously close to the soldiers' position. According to one participant, about 150 Indians followed behind the wall of flames as it neared the barricade, shooting as they went.

Also spiraling above the Danforth Hills was smoke rising from fires set by the Utes at the White River Agency.[87] Violence had erupted with a vengence at White River Agency only hours after the Milk Creek battle began. Utes attacked the agency staff, killing Meeker and his male coworkers and setting fire to buildings.

At Milk Creek Captain Lawson called up some men to fight the blaze at the barricade. They set small counter-fires around the outside perimeter of the wagons to prevent the main blaze from encompassing their barricade. Thanks to this countermeasure, there was very little of the corral exposed to flames when the main blaze reached the wagons.[88]

The soldiers fought the flames with blouses and burlap sacks. Some spread dirt on the fire by digging into the terrace with their scabbard knives. Corporal Charles F. Eichwurzel, Company E, Third Cavalry, was wounded about this time.[89] Rankin recalled that Private James Hickman, who was on the outside of the barricade fighting the fire and being shot at, managed to pull off a wagon sheet from its frame after the canvas caught fire, saving the wagon from incineration. Unfortunately, there is no Private James Hickman on the muster rolls.[90]

Meanwhile, Captain Payne noticed that the Indians would gain an advantage if they could position themselves behind John Gordon's abandoned wagons fifty yards up the road to the northeast of the barricade. He ordered Sergeant Poppe to take three or four men and, under cover of the smoke from the Indians' fire, to set fire to the grass just beyond the corral toward Gordon's wagons. Poppe said he would do it alone and jumped over the breastworks. The sergeant put a match to the sagebrush in several places before he returned. Payne later testified that the counter-flames set to protect the soldiers position blew into the Gordon train and burned the wagons before Gordon or anyone else could extinguish the fire.[91] One of Gordon's men was wounded while trying to save these wagons, but because they were not part of the barricade they would have had to be destroyed anyway to prevent the Indians from taking shelter behind them. It was a necessary loss.

All this time the Indians were having a good laugh. It looked to them as though the breeze changed a bit in direction and that the soldiers' counter-fires were now threatening the barricade. The Utes chuckled at the soldiers dancing about trying to put out the flames. They could have picked the troopers off but too many sharpshooters were rolling on the ground, doubled up with laughter.[92]

The period of midafternoon fire fighting was the most dangerous time in the battle. Payne concentrated on the northeast perimeter and Lawson on the southwest as the encircled command sustained several casualties. Five men were killed and about twelve were wounded, one mortally, in the span of a few minutes. Among the dead were teamster Thomas McGuire, Private Samuel McKee of Company F, Fifth Cavalry, Private Thomas Mooney with Company D, Fifth Cavalry, and Private Dominick Cuff, Company E, Third Cavalry.[93]

Payne was slightly wounded by a glancing shot across his abdomen while working the fires near Gordon's wagons—his second wound. Corporal Charles F. Eichwurzel, Company E, Third Cavalry, was wounded by two shots, and a third shot pierced his uniform beneath the armpit. Charles Grafton Lowry, Thornburgh's guide and courier, was mortally wounded. When offered medical assistance he muttered, "Never mind me; I am done for." He then became silent, and the troopers thought he had died. The wounded who couldn't man the barricade were kept in three large trenches dug in the center of the circle.[94]

At dusk, about ten mounted Utes loped toward the barricades from the northern ridge, came within forty yards, and stampeded thirty head of horses and mules. They herded them down Milk Creek and turned them south toward White River. The soldiers fired on the band in vain.[95]

Too much cover had burned away for the Indians to get close enough to attempt running off the rest of the soldiers' livestock. The Utes felt that the animals would have to be shot to prevent anyone from using them to ride for reinforcements. This task was handled with great solemnity, as no warrior was happy about shooting horses.[96]

The Utes had maintained continuous fire into the entrenchment until dusk, about 5:30 P.M. Snipers aimed at the flour and grain sacks on top of the breastworks so their bullets would penetrate the sacks and drain their contents. Repeated hits eventually depleted all of the flour and grain and reduced the effective height of the barricade. Soldiers soon mitigated this problem by piling dirt over all of the sacks.[97]

By nightfall, the Indians had reinforced their positions in the hills overlooking the wagons and in the ravines along the creek.[98] Many were concealed within thirty to forty yards of the soldiers, but return fire forced them to keep down, so they could not take very accurate aim. Each shooter had to rise from cover and fire quickly at the corral rather than aim carefully at a specific target.

Even with quick firing and poor aim, the soldiers' casualty list had grown considerably by nightfall. Nine men were killed at the barricade and one was fatally wounded. Privates Michael Lynch and Charles Wright of Company D, Fifth Cavalry had been added to the list of fatalities, as was Private John Burns of Company F, Fifth Cavalry.[99] Three men already had been killed before reaching the wagons. An additional forty-three were wounded, including those wounded outside the corral.[100]

All of the fatalities sustained by the White River Expedition had occurred by about 5:30 P.M. on the first day of battle, September 29 (Appendix B). Most of the wounds also were received on this day. Lowry, already mortally wounded and presumed dead, did not expire until the morning of October 5.

The Indians had killed 127 mules and 183 horses, leaving very few head of livestock alive.[101] Often the Indians intentionally wounded the animals inside the corral rather than kill them outright so that they would kick and roll within the defensive positions.

Payne set about to strengthen their position to withstand a prolonged engagement.[102] He ordered Corporal Hampton Roach to set up a water detail between the corral and Milk Creek, two hundred yards to the south. Troop mobility was severely reduced now that there were fewer than one hundred uninjured men and fewer than fifty live horses and mules.

The Indians were better supplied, more strategically positioned, and could move more easily at any point along the perimeter. The White River Expedition had left Fort Fred Steele nine days earlier with a thirty-day supply of rations and fifteen days of forage. The bulk of Payne's resources was either lost, damaged, or dwindling, and the Utes could wait the troopers out and likely win the battle by attrition if the expedition was not reinforced in the next several days. Two Denver correspondents who wrote about the engagement before the end of 1879 claimed that the soldiers were down to only six days of rations.[103] The troopers were probably better stocked than that, unless a disproportionate amount of supplies had been left at Fortification Creek or destroyed during the initial attack at Milk Creek.

Payne prepared a dispatch to inform the army of their situation. He needed couriers to carry correspondence to Lieutenant Price at Fortification Creek, to Captain Francis S. Dodge, on detached service with Company D, Ninth Cavalry and known to be scouting for possible Indian troubles somewhere in the mountains, and to General Crook via the telegraph at Rawlins. His message read:

> Milk River, Colo., September 29, 1879
> 8:30 P.M.
>
> This command, composed of three companies of cavalry, was met a mile south of Milk River by several hundred Ute Indians who attacked and drove us to wagon train which had parked with great loss. It becomes my painful duty to announce the death of Major Thornburg [*sic*], who fell in harness; the painful but not serious wounding of Lieut. Paddock and Dr. Grimes, and [killing of] ten (10) enlisted men and a wagon master, with the wounding of about 25 men and teamsters. I am now corralled near water, with three quarters of our animals killed after a desperate fight since 12 o'clock N. We hold our

position at this hour. I shall strengthen it during the night and believe that we can hold out until reinforcements reach us if they are hurried through. Officers and men behaved with greatest gallantry. I am also slightly wounded in two places.

Payne, Comdg[104]

Four men volunteered to carry copies of the message out of the valley. Guide Joseph Rankin and teamster boss John Gordon knew the country well enough to run the risk, so they would go. Two Fifth Cavalry corporals also volunteered, George Moquin of Company F and Edward F. Murphy of Company D.[105]

The moon would be full on September 30.[106] While the couriers waited for dusk, they selected the best remaining horses for the trip. Rankin had lost his own mount during the first siege at the wagons earlier that afternoon. Two of the horses selected may have been Fort Fred Steele stock and, if so, may have been the only cavalry horses ridden to Milk Creek to survive the battle.[107]

Hours passed. Hardly a breeze blew, and the flames from the Indians fires pointed straight up to the heavens. Some of the young braves crept through the battlefield and brought back soldiers' clothing, caps, guns, and money. They played games around the campfire most of the night and took turns watching the wagon corral. Others leaned over the fires, cupping the heat beneath blankets spread on their backs. The older men started back to the big camp, carrying the dead and severely wounded.[108] The Indians eventually admitted that about twenty-three of their number had been killed during the first day of battle at Milk Creek (Appendix B).

The cavalry officers met briefly with the couriers about 10:30 P.M.; the four men would move out before midnight. One authority argues that the moon wouldn't have reached its meridian until about 11:30 P.M.[109] By then the Indians probably would have settled down and the couriers would still have had about six hours of dark in which to cover as many miles as possible.

Payne repeated the dangers involved in carrying messages through enemy lines. Chances were slim that all four men would get through safely. All volunteers still expressed a desire to go, so he gave each of them a copy of his dispatch.[110] Just before midnight, four tired and sore men climbed into McClellan saddles cinched tightly on battle-weary mounts. Without hesitating, they began the risky journey to seek relief for the expedition. The rest of the command settled in behind the barricade, making themselves as comfortable as possible. It had been a long day for everyone.

Legend for Maps 4.1-4.5:

- ～～～ = Milk Creek.
- ～～ = Agency Road.
- ·-~-~-- = Cut Off Trail.
- ⊠ 5D = Company D, Fifth Cavalry Position.
- ⊠ 5F = Company F, Fifth Cavalry Position.
- ⊠ 3E = Company E, Third Cavalry Position.
- ⊠ C = Lieutenant Cherry's Position.
- ☐ G = John Gordon's Wagons.
- ▱ / △ = Ute Positions.
- ⇨ = Ute Movements.
- o T = Position Where Thornburgh is Killed (see Map 4.3).
- ⋯ = Wagon Circle (see Map 4.5).
- ▪▪▪▪ = Gordon's Burned Wagons (see Map 4.5).
- ※ = Dead Horses and Mules (see Map 4.5).

(Maps based on USGS Thornburgh Quad.)

80 Hollow Victory

Map 4.1

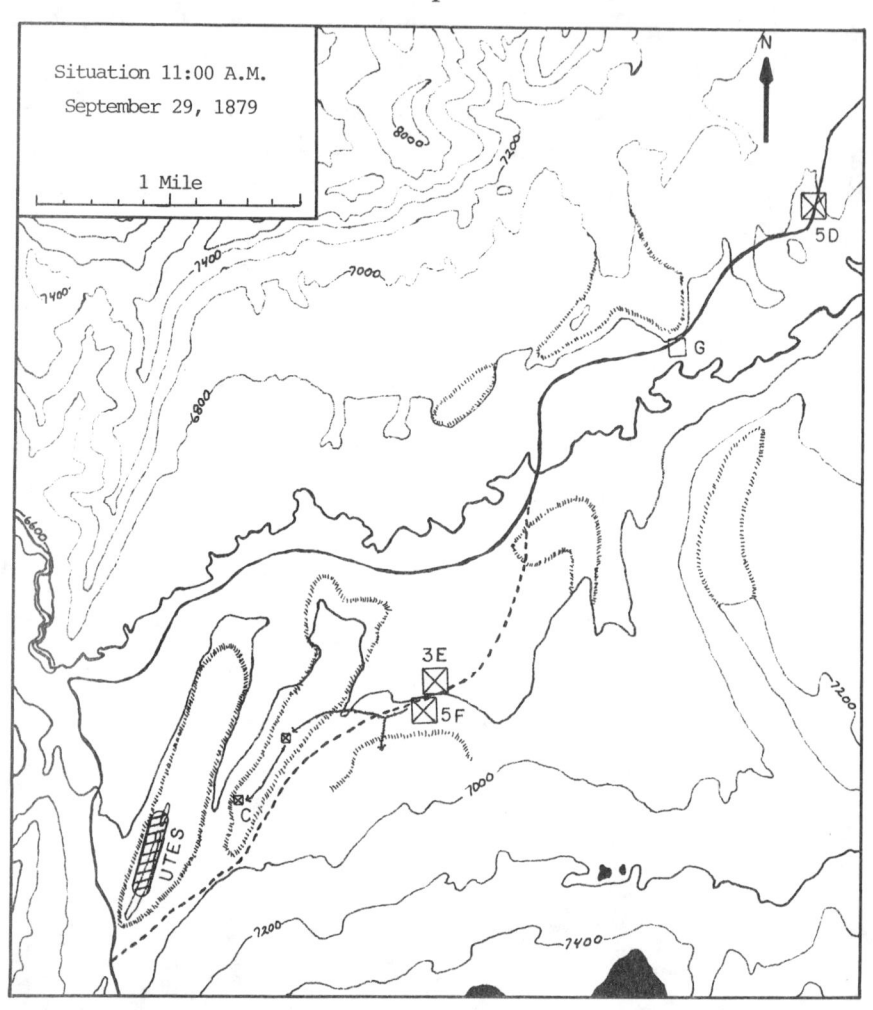

Situation 11:00 A.M.
September 29, 1879

1 Mile

Map 4.1: Situation 11:00 A.M.
Lieutenant Cherry crosses Milk Creek at 10:45 A.M. with the advance guard, taking the shortcut trail east of two long narrow ridges. He moves out three-quarters of a mile ahead of Thornburgh, Company F, Fifth Cavalry, Company E, Third Cavalry, and over two miles ahead of Company D, Fifth Cavalry, which was guarding the wagon train. John Gordon's wagons are on the north bench above the creek. At 11:00 A.M. Cherry is three-quarters of a mile south of Milk Creek when he notices three Indians disappear behind the easternmost of the two ridges, five hundred yards ahead of and above his party. He divides his advance guard, sending some to the left and taking the rest to the right. Cherry travels two hundred yards, crosses a stream, then rides to the top of the easternmost ridge. He advances up this ridge and discovers the ambush line of Utes on the westernmost ridge about one hundred yards away.

Map 4.2

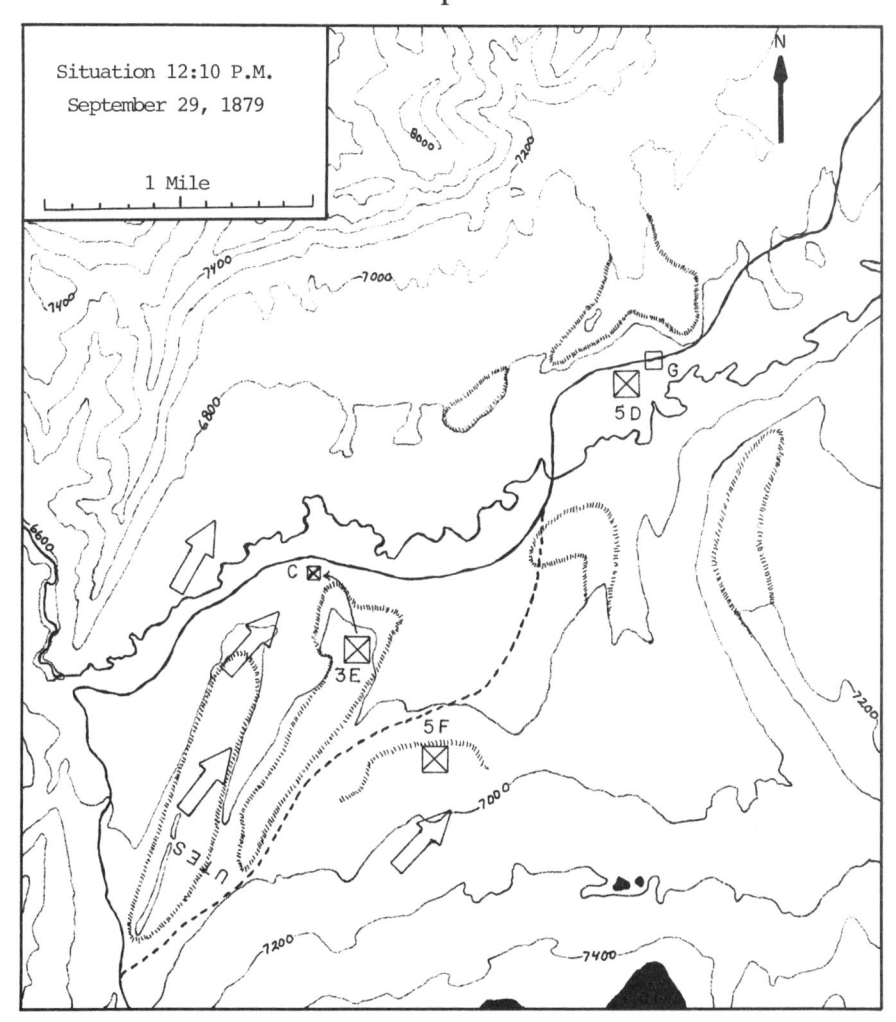

Map 4.2: Situation 12:10 P.M.
Cherry rides back to Thornburgh. The major deploys Payne's company to the left flank and Lawson's to the right. Skirmish lines form a V pointing toward the Indian position. Chief Jack and others move in front of Payne's position as Cherry takes a small detachment toward Indians below Lawson's position. Colorow moves with fifteen to twenty Utes to face Cherry. A shot is fired at 11:30 A.M. and the fight begins in earnest. The wagons are ordered corralled. About 11:50 Payne begins a slow withdrawal down the slope keeping led horses between him and Lawson. Indians attempt to turn the flank of Payne's skirmish line and ride across the creek to get between Lawson's company and the wagons. Payne's line is deflected on the left to prevent the tactic. Withdrawal of Payne's line continues until shortly after noon. Lawson and Cherry continue to hold the ridge on the right flank. Government wagons pass Gordon's position, reach a point two hundred yards from the creek, and begin to circle.

Map 4.3

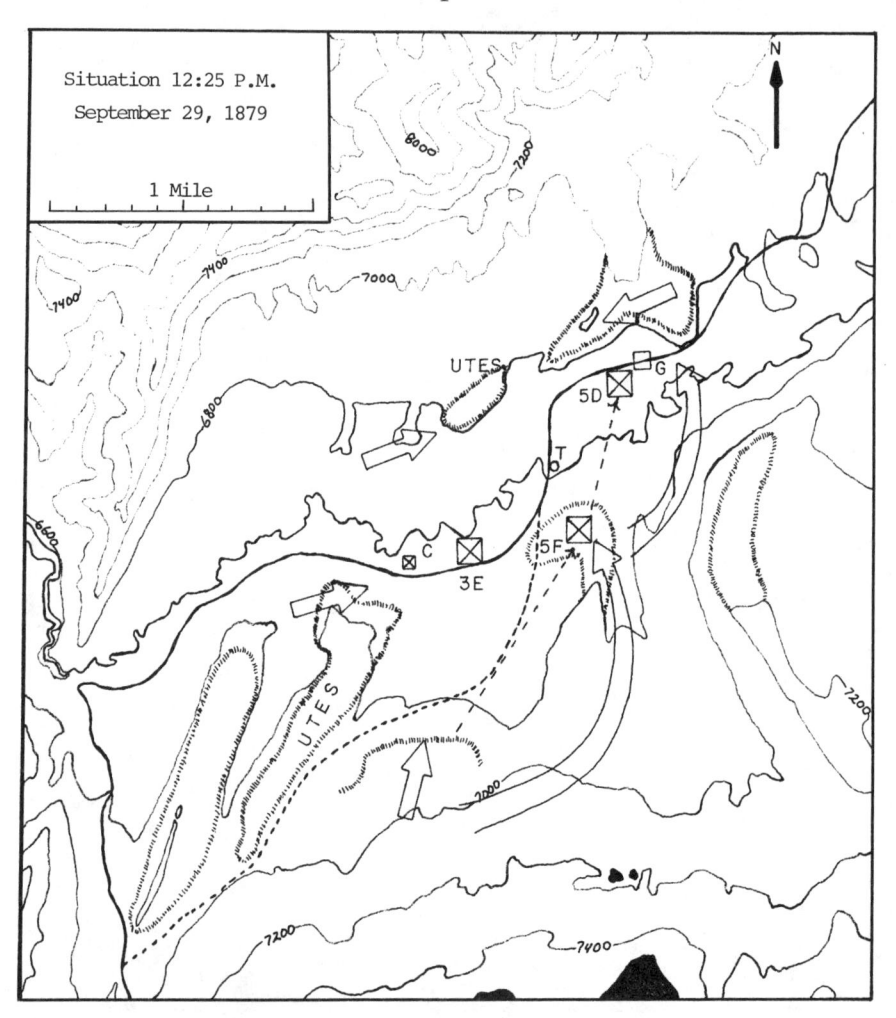

Map 4.3: Situation 12:25 P.M.
Indian flanking efforts are concentrated toward the circling wagons. Utes occupy a knoll between the retreating cavalry companies and the wagons. Thornburgh orders Payne to charge the knoll with twenty men of Company F, Fifth Cavalry. The balance of the company continues to withdraw and blends in with Lawson. Payne's detachment charges the knoll, drives the Indians off, then charges into the corral. Thornburgh is killed after he crosses the creek. Indians begin to occupy all hills around the wagon circle and continue attempts to cut off the retreating skirmishers. Gordon abandons his wagons.

Map 4.4

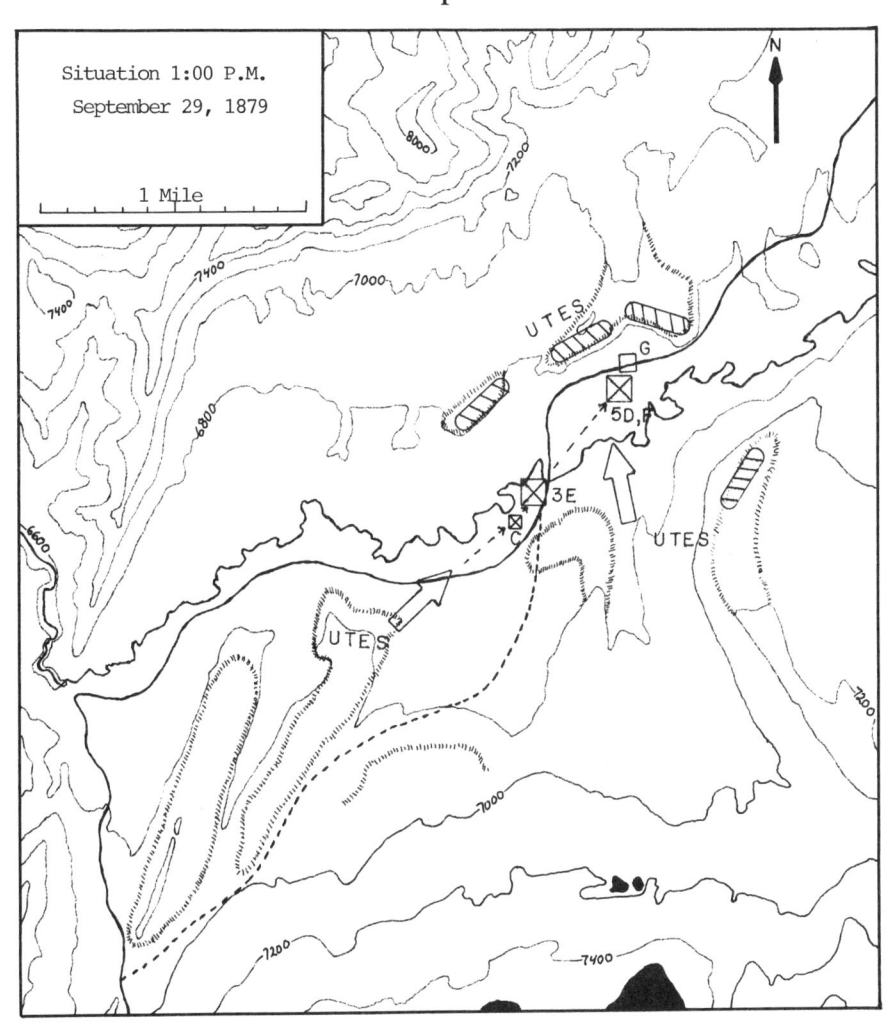

Map 4.4: Situation 1:00 P.M.
Payne, Paddock, John Gordon, and their men are pinned down in the wagon circle by Utes occupying hills and other cover to the northwest, northeast, and southeast. Indians maneuver toward ravines in Milk Creek to cut off Lawson's and Cherry's retreat from the southwest. Utes are pushed back from the line of retreat. Shortly before 1:00 P.M. all of the troops are behind the wagon circle. The Indians take up positions along the creek, surrounding the command.

84 Hollow Victory

Map 4.5

Map 4.5: Situation 3:00 P.M.
Indians command all strategic positions around the barricade except for Gordon's abandoned train. Utes begin a brushfire southwest of the circle and follow in behind the flames, firing as they go. Payne orders a counter-fire and destroys Gordon's wagons. Indians settle into their sharpshooter positions and begin killing stock. Troopers strengthen defenses and pull dead animals out later that evening. From 3:00 P.M. on September 29 until 5:30 A.M. on October 5, the battle is waged against the wagons. Indian and soldier positions remain more or less the same throughout this period.

5
Entrenchment at Milk Creek

This bad smell will bring many flies—big, fat, blue flies.
—Colorow, September 30 to October 1, 1879[1]

Meeker's zeal, the Utes' strong will, and Thornburgh's indecision combined to produce the bloody incident at Milk Creek, Colorado, on September 29, 1879. Two Denver-based correspondents, Thomas F. Dawson and F. J. V. Skiff, compiled and published a lengthy manuscript about the tragic affair less than two months after the battle. Their account is clearly biased and smattered with the colorful lexicon of the day. They describe the morning of September 30 at the barricade, "As the dark mantle of night was lifted and the first day of the siege came on, the orb of light was greeted by the groans of the dying, the moans of the wounded and the wild cry of the disabled horses. The hours of the first night had seen the soldiers laboring hard to complete their defense as far as possible and secure to themselves all the protection which the desperation of a forlorn hope could call upon men to devise."[2]

These correspondents wrote that the soldiers had completed about seventeen pits, each nearly seventy feet long by two and a half feet wide and two feet deep.[3] Pits were reinforced with breastworks of dirt piled two to four feet high. With these dimensions, the combined surface area of the pits would have covered about 32 percent of the nearly 9,400-square-foot area within the wagon enclosure. Lookouts were stationed on each end of every hole; thirty-four men were on constant guard while the others rested and nursed their wounds.

The bodies of dead horses and men began to smell as the sun warmed the valley on September 30. Each time the firing from the surrounding hills stopped, soldiers moved animal carcasses from the enclosure and piled more bodies of dead comrades beneath canvas and dirt in the barricade. Soldiers used horse carcasses for three of the breastworks and the bodies of fellow soldiers for one.[4]

The tattered remnant of the White River Expedition began their vigil. Each huddled group of soldiers was issued rations and ammunition, and now they crouched in the trenches trying to keep from becoming a sharpshooter's target. They were a mix of seasoned veterans from the Sioux war of 1876 and raw recruits with no experience in fighting Indians. In spite of their plight, officer and private, veteran and novice, mingled "together as pleasantly as boys playing truant from school in a haystack."[5]

Even with cheerful camaraderie, there was work to be done, wounds to tend, and bullets to dodge. The Indians kept up a constant barrage most of Tuesday, September 30, beginning at reveille and ending only at nightfall; they killed most of the remaining animals.[6] Just before sundown, after the Indians ceased fire, a party of Utes rushed the barricade and attempted to drive off the surviving stock that had broken loose from pickets during the day. Marksmen fired directly into the horde, turning them back and thwarting the effort.

A few Indians stayed awake, and those who did sleep were "distressingly prompt about arising at daylight. They always brought their guns into play just about the time the boys were stirring about and preparing for breakfast."[7] Cold rations were the order of the day since troopers couldn't risk cooking because too many fires would provide an easy target for the Indians. Even so, the weary soldiers risked detection by starting a few small fires to boil hot coffee; probably a greater necessity than food in the growing chill of fall.

Running errands within the enclosure was like being a pigeon at a skeet shoot. A soldier would rise, run, and scamper back to cover as quickly as possible. The Indians would fire a score of shots at him. This pattern of run and shoot was repeated when soldiers made trips to the creek for water.[8] Occasionally a shot would strike a soldier and the wounded man would have to crawl back to the central pit, which was used as a field hospital, and be treated by Dr. Grimes.

Sometime during September 30, Utes reached McCargar's two freight wagons that had been abandoned the night before about eleven or twelve miles away, on Deer Creek near where the expedition had camped the night of September 28; they ransacked the wagons, scattering flour, soap, and sugar. They also broke up several cases containing small hatchets that Meeker had ordered for Ute children to use as play tools. The

Indians tried but failed to burn the wagons because there was nothing flammable in them.[9]

By dawn on October 1, the soldiers had reinforced the barricades well enough to defend the position for a month. That evening, a small water detail was fired on at close range and Private William Esser of Company F, Fifth Cavalry was shot in the face. The bullet ripped through his mouth, cheek, and the back of his neck, producing a particularly painful, though not fatal, wound. Eventually the guards returned fire and killed one Indian.[10]

The Indians at Milk Creek knew that Chief Douglas and others had killed Meeker and his staff at the White River Agency on the same day that the Milk Creek battle began. Douglas's Utes had taken the agency women and children as hostages and moved them out of Powell Valley. Still, the Indians at Milk Creek kept up their fight. Once the soldiers were behind the barricade, it took relatively few well-placed shooters to keep them pinned down.

Little was seen of Chief Jack after the initial engagement. He would come to the battle, watch for a time, and then leave in silence. He returned to a new camp south of White River where Johnson had gone after the death of his son and where the white captives were held. He was clearly bothered by the events of the past few days.[11] Jack knew the military resources of the United States, and, because the Utes had not been able to overwhelm the soldiers in two days of fighting, he could see that the Utes' situation was futile. The Indians could not dislodge the troopers, and sooner or later other soldiers would come to find them. The Utes' certainly would lose any negotiations now that blood had been spilled. Neither could they be punished by being sent back to the reservation; they had never left it as hostiles in the first place. He could see that the true price of resistance might be the Ute reservation land itself, the homeland of their ancestors.

As Jack withdrew, Colorow emerged as the leader of those who were fighting the soldiers. He had successfully directed the fight that had trapped the soldiers. Now he wanted to force the soldiers to abandon the field of battle. He spoke with Yaminatz and Acari as they looked down at the barricade, "This will not be so bad," he said. "This bad smell will bring many flies—big, fat, blue flies. Those flies will get even fatter on those dead horses, and when the soldiers run out of food, they can roast them."[12]

A shot from behind the barricade interrupted Colorow. Lieutenant Cherry had just put his wounded greyhound, Frank, out of his misery; the Indians who had heard the dog squeal thought that the soldiers were shooting dogs for food.[13] Several soldiers had brought dogs along on the campaign, and Lieutenant Cherry had often let his greyhound loose to run to the creek for a drink of water. On this evening, Frank had hobbled back; a soldier had mistaken the dog for an advancing Ute and had shot off one of its paws.[14]

About this time, Payne recalled an interesting incident that occurred when he was dozing in a trench alongside Captain Lawson. Payne awoke to Lawson's exclamation, and he pointed to the sky: reflected in the heavens was a perfect mirage of the creek bed and barricade, giving the temporary illusion that troopers were exposed to Ute snipers if only the Indians fired at the suspended images.[15]

Even with continually strengthening defenses interspersed with regular intervals of sniper fire, some monotony set in. Payne ordered a time call every half hour so occupants in each trench would sound off. He would sit beside Cherry and announce, "number-one, ten o'clock, and all's well." The call would be repeated in each trench, but by the time the turn reached halfway around the corral, troopers had embellished it with humorous anecdotes, comments on world events, and epithets directed at the Utes. Payne ignored protocol and let the command enjoy whatever relief the opportunity allowed.[16]

The third night, Wednesday, October 1, was almost as quiet as the previous night.[17] Even so, the soldiers couldn't let their guard down. They could expect the Utes to begin firing as soon as the moon rose to cast light over the trenches. Muzzle flashes marked where Indians fired their rifles; the bright flashes added to the glow from campfires and pale moonlight.[18]

While the soldiers at Milk Creek adapted to what was to become a siege, news of the battle reached the outside world. Slightly before midnight on September 29, Joe Rankin and the other three volunteers, John Gordon, Corporal Edward F. Murphy, and Corporal George Moquin, had begun their ride for reinforcements. Rankin, whose own horse had been killed earlier in the day, had taken the best remaining mount, a horse that was still bleeding from a wound in its neck.

Rankin and the other couriers left the entrenchment, picking their way through the brush, moving beyond the sleeping Utes, and avoiding the guarded passes. Their route probably followed the cover of Milk Creek upstream for about two miles to where the creek bends south. To avoid noise, the couriers may have led their horses to this bend, mounted, and ridden north toward the divide between Milk Creek and Stinking Gulch, where they would be in rugged country well beyond the main Indian lines. The four men rode quietly to the north for about four or five miles under cover of aspen groves, evergreens, and tall brush.[19]

The couriers' route took them over the divide into the valley of upper Morapos Creek, where they would have trailed down Morapos Creek to the agency road crossing, and from there the group may have split up.[20] Joe Rankin followed the Morapos Trail and had ridden his wounded horse about twenty-seven miles by the time he approached the Yampa River at dawn, about 6:00 A.M. on September 30. The courier's horse was played out, so he took a remount from saddle stock at Hulett's (Hewitt's) cattle ranch and told the residents about the engagement.

Rankin rode his fresh mount north along Fortification Creek to the agency road about twenty-two miles until he reached Lieutenant Butler Price's Company E, Fourth Infantry camp, most likely at Fortification Rocks. Rankin told the lieutenant about the attack and handed him orders from Captain Payne. Joe may have switched horses once again if Lieutenant Price still had a fresh mount. Price wrote an additional dispatch for Rankin to take to the telegraph office at Rawlins:

Fortification Creek, Sept. 30, via Rawlins, Oct. 1.

I am left at this point with thirty men; 25 miles behind Capt. Payne's intrenchments. I have just received orders to intrench and fortify well.

Price,
Lieut. Commanding[21]

The mileage was wrong, but the message was clear.

The next leg of the journey took Rankin another twenty-four miles or so to Snake River crossing, where he ate a light lunch and saddled another remount from the Harrah ranch. The horse was named Joe Busch, and Rankin knew it to have good staying power.[22] Joe Busch carried the tired courier another thirty-six miles, to Sulphur Springs ranch. A team of Rankin's own horses from his livery business in Rawlins had just been driven to the ranch on the old Overland Trail. Rankin selected one of the team that was in good condition but not broken to ride. He saddled up after a quick meal and set out for the last twenty-eight miles of his ride to Rawlins. The horse bucked for the first mile or so, then held a steady gait the rest of the way.[23]

Rankin reached the telegraph office in Rawlins between midnight on September 30 and 1:15 A.M. on October 1. Robert M. Galbraith, a one-time master mechanic for the Union Pacific Railroad, witnessed Rankin's arrival at the telegraph office, and soon thereafter the telegraph operator sent Captain Payne's dispatch to military authorities. The telegram, addressed to the Adjutant General at Omaha Barracks, Nebraska, was received in Omaha at 2:25 A.M. their time.[24]

Allowing for the one hour time difference between Rawlins and Omaha, a few minutes for Rankin to put the dispatch into the telegrapher's hands, and time to transmit it, the telegram itself is convincing evidence that Rankin arrived in Rawlins no later than 1:15 A.M. He had covered around 140 miles in not more than 25.5 hours, for an average speed of 5.5 miles an hour.[25]

Joe Rankin's ride to Rawlins is the second most famous gallop in Wyoming history. Only John "Portugee" Phillips's ride from Fort Phil Kearny to Fort Laramie in December 1866 to announce the Fetterman disaster ranks higher in prestige. Subsequent events, however, show that the threat to Payne's command in 1879 was more real and immediate than was the perceived threat to Colonel Carrington's outpost in 1866. Utes at Milk Creek kept up a continuous fight after the initial attack, while Sioux at Fort Phil Kearny moved away for the winter. Reinforcements at Milk Creek were a lifesaving necessity.[26]

Price had sent another message from his Fortification Creek camp by courier on October 1 to Captain Bisbee at Fort Fred Steele. The text refers to the Fortification Creek supply camp and reads, "The existence of the command depends solely on the haste with which reinforcements are gotten here. Am entrenched here as Payne has directed me, simply to hold my camp and not advance. Signed, Price."[27]

While Rankin had gotten the message out, the other three couriers were still on the road. After the four riders had split up, John Gordon and Corporal Edward F. Murphy may have doubled back to the south on the agency road looking for Gordon's brother. Corporal Moquin may have followed them for a way and then turned back toward Rawlins. If Gordon and Murphy reached Stinking Gulch, a little over five miles northeast of the Milk Creek battle site, they would have found burning wagons and scattered agency supplies, and the bodies of John's brother, George, and two teamsters lying near the wreckage.[28] One hundred Winchester cartridge cases were scattered around Gordon's body, testifying to a hot fight.[29]

The two couriers couldn't linger; they probably turned back north on the road. They, too, may have followed the Morapos Trail so they could warn settlers and gather reinforcements in case Rankin didn't get through. They may have found McCargar and his son somewhere along Deer Creek and enlisted them to ride for help. If these two contractors knew something was wrong at Milk Creek, they may have hidden near their wagons and hoped that hostiles wouldn't find them. At any rate, the McCargars rode on to Snake River while Gordon and Murphy stopped at Iles's ranch on the Yampa River. Jimmy Dunn, likely a local resident, was there, and he was told to locate and notify Captain Francis Dodge and his troops of Company D, Ninth Cavalry. Dodge's company had left Fort Lewis in southern Colorado on July 21, and he was now believed to be in or near Twenty-Mile Park south of the Yampa River and east of the Williams Fork Mountain.[30]

On his way to Steamboat, Dunn met Ed Clark, a surveyor from Greeley, Colorado, who had been at Crawford's in Steamboat. Clark was on his way to the White River Agency to conduct some surveying for Agent Meeker. Dunn asked Clark to help him find Dodge; although apprehensive, Clark agreed to help. He went a short distance on the Twenty-Mile Park Road but turned around, apparently afraid to venture too far. Clark wrote a note, tied it to a tall sagebrush along the road, and hoped Dodge would find it. Clark headed to Iles's place to join other settlers who had gathered for safety. Settlers throughout the Hayden Valley between the agency road crossing on the Yampa River and Steamboat and adjacent areas had received word of the battle, joined into larger groups, and prepared to defend themselves either in communities or at individual ranches.[31] Everyone feared the worst.

Captain Dodge already had received mail from Sandy Mellen, a mail carrier from Middle Park, with orders from headquarters in the District of New Mexico telling him that his company was needed by Agent Meeker at the White River Agency.[32] This message, of course, had preceded the outbreak of violence. On September 29, the captain and his company started for the agency, crossed the Gore Range, and headed down through Twenty-Mile Park toward Hayden. On October 1 Sandy Mellen, whom Dodge had hired as a guide, discovered a slip of paper tied to a sagebrush at the side of the Twenty-Mile Park Road. Addressed to Captain Dodge, the message read: "Thornburgh killed. His men in peril. Rush to their assistance." It was signed E.E.C.[33]

The company quickened pace to Tom Iles's ranch at the Yampa River crossing, where they ate and visited with John Gordon. Gordon had been drinking heavily but volunteered to ride with Dodge to Milk Creek. Dodge sent seven wagons, the teamsters, and an eight-man guard detail to Lieutenant Price's camp on Fortification Creek. Sending the wagons to Price enabled his column to move much faster toward Thornburgh's expedition.[34]

Dodge's relief column rode up Morapos Trail toward Milk Creek on the evening of October 1. His force included two officers, thirty-five soldiers, and four citizens, including John Gordon, Sandy Mellen, and a Mr. Lithgow. Each trooper carried 225 rounds of ammunition and three days' rations.[35]

It snowed that night in Milk Creek Valley. The smell of decaying flesh was still strong in the chill dawn beneath the gray clouds of October 2. The soldiers were most apprehensive about bad weather because they had inadequate clothing, flimsy shelter tents, and no firewood. Soaking autumn rains would chill them to the bone, but they could brush a light snow from their uniforms.[36]

A few Indians noticed the approach of Dodge and Company D, Ninth Cavalry as they entered Milk Creek Valley and recognized them as Buffalo Soldiers, black cavalry troopers. No one fired a shot; the Indians, curious about the color of the troopers' skin, merely watched.[37] More Indians drifted down to vantage points overlooking the barricade.

Some among the Utes wanted to renew the battle. But Ute strategy began to divide between age groups: young braves wanted to fight again as intensely as they had on the first day while older men did not. The killing on both sides was about even now, and the elder Utes thought that the best thing to do was to wait until the soldiers got so tired they simply went home.[38] The battle had been much easier to start than it would be to finish.

6

The Whitest Black Men in the Cavalry

They . . . have proven themselves good soldiers and reliable men.
—Captain Francis S. Dodge, October 19, 1879[1]

The Indians made their own breastworks seventy-five yards from the corral on Wednesday night, the third evening of battle. Soldiers could hear the Utes passing orders in English, and one Indian spoke directly to them, "We will kill you all."[2] Other Utes taunted the soldiers, describing how they would scalp and mutilate them and leave them naked on the battlefield. These graphic threats did little to ease tensions behind the barricade.

Gunfire continued during daylight hours. Every so often a bullet would strike its target. John C. Davis was shot in the heel as he made an incautious approach toward his sutler wagon for provisions; he had a limited supply of regulation hardtack and raw bacon in his wagon and a little liquor, a godsend to the wounded.[3]

Although Private Esser was shot in the face while on water detail during the night of October 1, the rest of the evening was relatively quiet.[4] Most of the Utes spent the night at their advance camp about a mile south of the battlefield, near Beaver Springs and present-day Aldrich Lakes.

The besieged expedition had now been fighting sporadically for three days, and the troopers were beginning to tire. Rations dwindled, and the stench from putrefying horses, mules, and oxen lingered in the cool morning air. Acrid, eye-stinging powder smoke hung in the valley. About the only thing to be thankful for was that it had not snowed heavily or rained. One common thought in the mind of every trooper was, Had any of the couriers gotten through?

While Utes were aware of Dodge's approach from the north on October 1, they chose, for some reason, not to attack. Shortly before dawn on October 2, Captain Dodge's command reached a point five hundred yards from the barricade. He halted his troop and sent John Gordon and Sandy Mellen toward Payne's command to announce their arrival. When they were challenged as they approached the barricade, they answered that they were part of a cavalry company. Someone in a trench replied, "That's a damned lie; it's an Indian ruse—look out."[5] John Gordon identified himself, and the besieged men recognized his voice.

Dodge's command was told to come in, and a crescendo of cheers arose from the wagon circle. Grateful men shouted, leapt from the pits, and greeted the new arrivals with hearty handshakes and cheers.[6] At least one courier had made it through enemy lines. Everyone hoped that the others had made it, too, so that more reinforcements would be on the way.

One of Thornburgh's soldiers interviewed by Dawson and Skiff recalled how he felt when Dodge's troops arrived:

> We were getting pretty d—d tired about that time. It was the third morning after we were corralled, and of course we didn't know whether any of our messengers sent out from camp had struck help or not. Suddenly that morning in the dusk we heard a noise. Even by that time some of us had begun to fear that the Indians would charge us, and we all then supposed it might be Indians. If it hadn't been for the voice of John Gordon, the scout, who was riding in the advance, we might have poured in a volley at them; but you bet your life there wasn't no volley except cheers when Gordon rode in with five or six darkies alongside of him. Pretty soon he told us what was up and what to expect, and when Captain Dodge came up at a canter, leading the rest of his men, we didn't take much account, except to wonder a little at the color of their faces. We forgot all about the danger of exposing ourselves, and leaped up out of the pits to shake hands all around. Why, we took those darkies in right along with us in the pits. We let 'em sleep with us, and they took their knives and cut off slips of bacon from the same sides as we did.[7]

Dodge speculated that the Utes had not attacked them and had held their fire because they were anticipating a much stronger force and were reluctant to expose themselves. The new arrivals tied their horses inside the enclosure, quickly unsaddled them, and took shelter in the pits, where room was readily made for them.[8]

Captain Lawson, a Kentuckian, abandoned his normally quiet demeanor and offered a heartfelt, if not obtuse compliment: "You men of the Ninth Cavalry are the whitest black men I have ever seen."[9] No sooner had Lawson finished speaking than the Indians finally opened fire.

The loud greetings had aroused the Indian scouts and the Utes quickly took positions on the hills. Daylight brought a rain of bullets from the surrounding ridges and creek bank.

Dodge suggested that a charge would dislodge the Indians. Veterans persuaded him that his tactic would only cause more casualties because a charge would have to be up some hills that were almost perpendicular. In addition, there were only enough horses for Dodge's own company, which was too small a force to undertake a frontal charge at fortified positions. The Utes were too well entrenched in rifle pits and behind rock piles with loopholes. Soldiers would have to content themselves with firing only at fleetingly exposed targets because both terrain and cover favored the Utes.[10]

Dodge, senior in rank to Payne, relaxed and pondered their predicament. They had only the makeshift barricades to protect them until a larger relief force arrived. Rather than saving the trapped command, Dodge had become trapped himself. He took comfort knowing that his reinforcements strengthened the perimeter and gave everyone hope.

The horses once again became the primary target for Indian sharpshooters, and one battle veteran told correspondents,

> Every few minutes, you heard the dying gurgle of a horse or a mule, and although we fastened them as securely as possible at night, their pangs were such that they would often break away after being hit, threatening the men's lives in the trenches. Once a wounded horse leaped in his agony right into the pit we had dug for the wounded,

where Lieutenant Paddock and seven men were lying at the time. It was a miracle, almost, that he did not trample them to death. As it was, we all opened a terrific fire on the bluffs, so as to make the Utes stop firing, and under cover of this fusilade a lot of our boys jumped up and hauled the horse out of the trench.[11]

Soldiers believed that much of the stock slaughter was being done by a red-shirted Ute stationed below the creek bank. The Indian was often seen at close range, but none of the Wyoming soldiers knew his name. They nonetheless admired old Red Shirt's marksmanship.

Periodically, a soldier raised his hat on a stick and waved it above the trenches. There would be shots from Red Shirt's position, and when the trooper would lower the stick, his hat would be riddled with bullet holes. After the battle, the sniper's nest was found to contain over two hundred .45 caliber cartridge cases from a Sharps, and Red Shirt's sharpshooting would be attributed to Johnson.[12]

The Indians continued to shoot to wound the animals within the wagon circle rather than to kill them, because the wounded animals would lunge, break their tie ropes, and stagger among the trenches, causing more hardships for the soldiers. Some stock tried to crawl to the trenches. Dr. Grimes watched for these wounded animals and shot them in the head before they reached pits that were crowded with men.

One wounded horse fell into the hospital trench that held forty-two wounded men. The animal landed on its hindquarters and knocked down the board covering the pit. Dust billowed up from the hole, and only quick reactions by nearby Ninth Cavalry troopers, who dragged the horse from the trench, saved already injured men from more injuries.[13]

The soldiers didn't like killing wounded animals any more than the Indians enjoyed wounding them. Love and respect for horses were nearly universal feelings among those who relied on these animals. Horses were more than transportation, they were companions and pets. This sentiment was as true for F Company's bays that lay dead at Milk Creek as it was for the Utes' mountain-bred pintos grazing below the camp near the springs and lakes at the head of Beaver Creek.[14] Troopers staked their lives on the government-owned cavalry horses. Private Henry Perkins recalled that Private Joseph Patterson got three flesh wounds in trying to save his horse's life. Finally, the horse was shot through one of his forelegs. Instead of writhing around like the others, he came hobbling up to the edge of the pit where Joe and I were and looked down at Joe, as if to say, "Help me, for God's sake!" Joe turned to me and said, "You'll have to finish him, Hank; I can't do it; by God, I can't!" I watched my chance as the horse turned and put a ball in right behind his left ear, and dropped him. That night we hauled him outside with the rest.[15]

All but seven of Dodge's cavalry horses were dead by noon; 148 horses and mules had already been killed. Many carcasses still littered the wagon circle and trenches, while others had been dragged out to the creek bank and dumped over the edge. Not even the oxen survived. Several oxen that John Gordon and his teamsters had cut loose on September 29 were slaughtered by the Utes for food.[16] Only five horses and two mules would survive the rain of Ute lead. Each head of livestock exhibited constant fear throughout the siege: "Every crack of a rifle caused them to shudder and tremble violently."[17]

Later in the day, Captain Dodge became concerned that his troopers were intruding on the soldiers who were cramped into existing trenches. During a lull, he had his men start to dig their own trenches. Utes immediately fired into the work party. A trooper from Company E, Third Cavalry observed the scene and remembered how the soldiers "made ten feet every jump and leaped head first into the trenches like frogs."[18]

During another lull, a trooper from Company D witnessed a burly Buffalo Soldier climb to the top of a trench wall, wave his rifle at the surrounding ridges, and yell, "Show me a Ute!" No Ute reacted, so the soldier sat down on a wagon tongue. Just as he relaxed, a bullet struck the corner of the wagon bed, only a foot away from his head. He dived back into the trench and sat silently amid the muffled laughter of his comrades.[19]

Chief Jack rode to the Indian battle positions later that evening along with Sowawic, Douglas, and Pauvit'z. Douglas and Pauvit'z had been at White River and were visiting the battlefield for the first time;

Sowawic had been at Milk Creek on the opening day of battle. Everyone but Colorow looked up and greeted the riders. Colorow's aggressiveness since the first shot had distanced him somewhat from the more conciliatory philosophy of Jack. Piah, a Ute who had been at Milk Creek all day, told Jack about the Buffalo Soldiers. Colorow listened to the conversation, then suggested that he might go down to the soldiers tomorrow and shake hands. Deliberations continued into the night. Winds blew down from the snowy high country, and cold sleet rattled onto sagebrush and among cottonwood and aspen leaves.[20]

Between the night of October 2 and the morning of October 5, monotony became the routine, interspersed with occasional sniper fire and Payne's continued regimen of calling the hour. Once most of the animals had been killed, it became a question of waiting for a full-scale rescue.

Cavalrymen created diversions for themselves to pass the long hours. Troopers in one trench formed a debating society and argued about many subjects, including the properties of electricity. (Thomas Edison had been through Fort Fred Steele the year before while on a trip to see the solar eclipse; some say this is when he conceived the idea of the incandescent light bulb.) Some soldiers organized a minstrel show and sang ballads, and others cracked jokes and recited puns. Private Michael Hogan, Company D, Fifth Cavalry, attempted to tell a few stories.[21] The men simply were too tired to remain in constant fear.

Peace within the barricade, however, was often disrupted by violence when soldiers ventured outside. On the evening of October 2, several men left the trenches to gather sagebrush for a fire. Their desire for hot coffee surpassed their fear of snipers, and their activities attracted more gunfire that night than any other night of the siege.

Sergeant Henry Johnson of Dodge's company left his rifle pit under heavy fire to make the rounds of the trenches to see that all was well. He later went with a water detail toward Milk Creek, attracting more heavy fire from the ridge tops and creek banks.[22] His heroism earned him the Medal of Honor (Appendix C). Similar acts of bravery were almost common, because water sorties were a nightly detail.

Carnage was everywhere in the valley. More than three hundred dead animals lay between the creek and the soldiers, within one hundred yards of the barricade. During the day a gentle breeze blew the odor away, but at night, when the winds were calm, cold, heavy air would bring with it the stench of putrefying carcasses.[23]

Crows and magpies settled onto the bones and rotting flesh of horses and mules in the predawn of October 3. Calm prevailed as these carnivorous birds and even packs of coyotes feasted on the carrion. Shortly after dawn the birds rustled, bobbed their heads up from feeding on decomposing meat, and cawed. As one, they stopped feeding, rose into the sky, and flew away. The soldiers knew the Indians were moving into position once again.[24]

The sun shone. By now most Indians had lost interest in escalating the confrontation. Most of the Utes engaged in lazy activities, played a simple game, or had a quiet talk. Several warriors continued to shoot into the entrenchment; some were protected in seven pits on the heights surrounding the wagon circle.[25]

Daily jeers were shouted back and forth between the cavalrymen and English-speaking Indians. Among the Utes at Milk Creek who knew English were Piah, Cojo, Chief Jack, Johnson, Charlie, who was one of the few Uncompahgre at the battle, and Henry Jim, the interpreter who had accompanied Colorow to see Thornburgh on Saturday, September 27. Some of these men situated themselves along the creek banks near the soldiers to exchange derogatory remarks.

Milk Creek may be unique among battles of the Indian wars because it was one of the few encounters that was so long that there were periods of relative quiet when daily conversations were possible between opponents. Little Bighorn, the Fetterman disaster, and the Wagon Box fight, which took place near Fort Phil Kearny in 1867, certainly were not as lengthy. Milk Creek also seems to have been one of the few battles at which several Indians were bilingual and eager to talk to the soldiers. Utes had scouted for the bluecoats and some, like Chief Jack, had made lasting acquaintances.

Soldiers couldn't always hear the gibes shouted from the distant ridges, but the taunts from the creek banks were clear enough. One Indian, or a renegade with the Utes, yelled, "Come out, you sons-of-bitches and fight like men."[26] Another chided, "Utes kill your horse and mule, and kill you too." When a horse or mule dropped from a bullet, an Indian would yell, "Better go out and harness him again for your funeral." When good targets were scarce, one Indian said, "Lift up you hats and give us a mark."[27]

Private Eugene Schickedonz from Captain Payne's company had been wounded in the right arm and was so sick that he lost his appetite for two days. One morning he turned to a black soldier and said, "Here, pard, stop shooting at them bluffs, and for the Lord's sake make me a little coffee."[28] Without a moment's hesitation the trooper silently went about the task. A comrade in an adjacent pit tossed over some coffee, but they were out of wood to build a fire. The Buffalo Soldier broke for the sutler's wagon, stripped off the side of a provisions box, and returned. There was a brand new hole in the board made by a bullet just fired at the man. Without complaint, he sat down, built a fire, then served his comrade a cup of coffee.[29]

At one point, Captain Lawson recognized Colorow among the enemy because he knew the Comanche from past experiences in New Mexico and had also seen him at the Williams Fork camp a couple of nights before. Lawson pointed Colorow out to Captain Payne. This is one of the few instances that a cavalryman identified an individual Indian during the battle. Robert Emmitt's 1954 study relied in part on the recollections of Saponise, a fifteen-year-old Ute participant at Milk Creek who identified many of the Indians and related incidents during the battle.[30]

Elsewhere the plight of Thornburgh's command was on the mind of every citizen who had heard news of the battle. Could the engagement evolve into another catastrophe like the Little Bighorn three years earlier? Townspeople and settlers alike prepared for the worst.

Bisbee and his meager garrison at Fort Fred Steele also dealt with the situation. On the morning of October 1, Captain Bisbee notified Mrs. Thornburgh about her husband. He waited until the family finished breakfast, then went with two others and Dr. Semig to the commanding officer's quarters. He could only tell Lida that the major had been wounded; nothing else would come out. Bisbee was concerned that Lida might be too fragile emotionally to hear that the major had been killed, because their three-year-old son had died earlier that year. She became suspicious of his abbreviated report and begged permission to go to the front to be at her husband's side. Later in the day she heard the whole truth and accepted the facts as any army wife would.[31]

Concern about the engagement reached a fever pitch by October 2, and Bisbee had to handle the growing fear that spread throughout the settlements. A Snake River rancher named Morgan reported in Rawlins that he had heard heavy firing in Milk Creek Valley on the morning of September 30, and this news aroused the citizens even further.[32] Bisbee sent a message to the headquarters at Omaha Barracks of the Department of the Platte and received a telegram reply the same day. He was authorized to issue arms and ammunition to settlers between Fort Fred Steele and the scene of the battle.[33] All of south-central Wyoming and northwestern Colorado prepared for a possible escalation of hostilities.

At Fortification Creek supply camp on October 3, Lieutenant Butler Price wrote a letter to his wife with news of the expedition. "I have seen no Indians in this vicinity," he wrote, "with my twenty-nine men I can stand off three hundred Indians. A company of the Ninth cavalry, 50 strong, reached Payne yesterday morning, the 2d inst."[34]

FIGURE 1 Milk Creek Valley looking north from Rio Blanco County Road 15, which is County Road 45 in Moffat County. The barricade was on the terrace at the foot of the mountain beyond Milk Creek

FIGURE 2 Milk Creek Valley looking north from Rio Blanco County Road 15. The farthest south advance of the cavalry was to the ridge in the right center and foreground, which was briefly occupied by Company E, Third Cavalry.

FIGURE 3 White River Utes, Chief Douglas, *left*, and Johnson, *right*. Johnson's brief fight with White River Indian Agent Nathan C. Meeker, September 8, 1879, led to Meeker's successful plea for military assistance at the agency. Courtesy, Colorado Historical Society, (F1209).

FIGURE 4 Nathan C. Meeker social reformer and neophyte Indian agent, whose policies helped precipitate the tragedy of September 29, 1879. Courtesy, The Denver Public Library, Western History Department, (F23161).

FIGURE 5 Chief Jack, or Nicaagat, the White River Ute who had scouted for General George Crook in 1876. He and his band blocked the advance of the White River Expedition toward the White River Agency once the troops entered the reservation at Milk Creek, shortly before noon September 29, 1879. Courtesy, Colorado Historical Society, (F40475).

FIGURE 6 Colorow, *seated far right,* with his band in Colorado Springs, 1875. Colorow made the tactical decision to cut the cavalrymen off from their wagons and nearly succeeded. Courtesy, Colorado Historical Society, (F7051).

FIGURE 7 Major Thomas T. Thornburgh, Fourth Infantry, commanded the White River Expedition of 1879 and was killed in action at Milk Creek, Colorado. Courtesy, National Anthropological Archives, Smithsonian Institution, Photo No. 77-13323.

FIGURE 8 Chief Ouray sent dispatches from Los Piños Agency in the southern part of the Ute Reservation, which helped end hostilities October 5, 1879. Courtesy, Colorado Historical Society, (F13030).

FIGURE 9 Captain J. Scott Payne, Company F, Fifth Cavalry, took command of the expedition when he learned of Thornburgh's death. Here he is with Charger, the horse that was shot out from under him at the battle of Milk Creek. From Theo. F. Rodenbough, *Uncle Sam's Medal of Honor* (G. P. Putnam's Sons, New York, 1886, page 358).

FIGURE 10 Stanley J. Morrow photographed five officers, a private, and a scout, all of the Third Cavalry, who had prominent roles in the battle of Slim Buttes in 1876. His photo is entitled "Colonel Mills and Officers of his Battalion." Joseph Lawson, then a first lieutenant, is seated at the far right. Captain Lawson led Company E, Third Cavalry at the battle of Milk Creek. Morrow Photograph No. 28, Courtesy United States Military Academy.

FIGURE 11 Sergeant Edward Grimes, Company F, Fifth Cavalry, Medal of Honor recipient for valor at the battle of Milk Creek. From Theo. F. Rodenbough, *Uncle Sam's Medal of Honor* (G. P. Putnam's Sons, New York, 1886, page 359).

FIGURE 12 Sergeant John S. Lawton, Company D, Fifth Cavalry, Medal of Honor recipient for valor at the battle of Milk Creek. From Theo. F. Rodenbough, *Uncle Sam's Medal of Honor* (G. P. Putnam's Sons, New York, 1886, page 363).

Figure 13 Sergeant Henry Johnson, Company D, Ninth Cavalry, Medal of Honor recipient for valor at the battle of Milk Creek. Courtesy, Library of Congress, LC-USZ6912.

Figure 14 Private A. M. Startzell, Company E, Third Cavalry, who was with Lieutenant Cherry's advance squad when they first saw the Utes on September 29, 1879. Courtesy, Wyoming State Museum, Department of Commerce, Cheyenne.

Figure 15 Private John Mahoney, Company E, Third Cavalry, was one of the Certificate of Merit winners for conspicuous gallantry at the battle of Milk Creek. Courtesy, Catherine Joan Mahoney Page, Rawlins, WY.

Figure 16 Guide Joseph P. Rankin. Courtesy, Carbon County Museum, Rawlins, WY.

Figure 17 John Charles (J. C.) Davis post sutler employee at Fort Fred Steele. Courtesy, J. C. Davis Collection #801, Photo 25976, American Heritage Center, University of Wyoming, Laramie.

Figure 18 Jim Baker, trapper, scout, and guide, who accompanied Colonel Wesley Merritt's relief force to Milk Creek. Courtesy, Carbon County Museum, Rawlins, WY.

Figure 19 "The Ute War—Major Thornburgh's Last Charge," sketched by J. Viele in *Harper's Weekly*, November 1, 1879. Twenty men from Company F, Fifth Cavalry took part in the charge; Thornburgh was not present. Courtesy, The Denver Public Library, Western History Department, (F10882).

Figure 20 A sketch from *Frank Leslie's Illustrated Newspaper*, November 8, 1879 entitled "Death of Major Thornburgh While Leading a Charge to Secure the Wagon Train." Thornburgh did not lead a charge; in fact, he was alone when he was shot. Otherwise this sketch seems fairly accurate. However, the cavalry sabres may have been left at Fort Fred Steele. Courtesy, The Denver Public Library, Western History Department, (F10364).

Figure 21 "The Thornburgh Battle With the Utes on Milk Creek." Painting by Robert Lindneux from a sketch made at the site in September 1935. Courtesy, Colorado Historical Society, (WPA 299).

Figure 22 *Frank Leslie's Illustrated Newspaper,* November 8, 1879, sketch entitled "The Barricade Constructed Between the Two Bluffs Occupied by the Indians." The officer with his arm in a sling is probably Captain Payne, who had been shot in the left shoulder and arm. Courtesy, The Denver Public Library, Western History Department, (F10354).

Figure 23 "Behind the Breastworks," by Frederic Remington. The officer striding by the wounded men strongly resembles Captain Joseph Lawson. At least some of the weapons appear to be long rifles used by infantry rather than the shorter carbines that were issued to cavalry troopers. Courtesy, Frederic Remington Art Museum, Ogdensburg, NY.

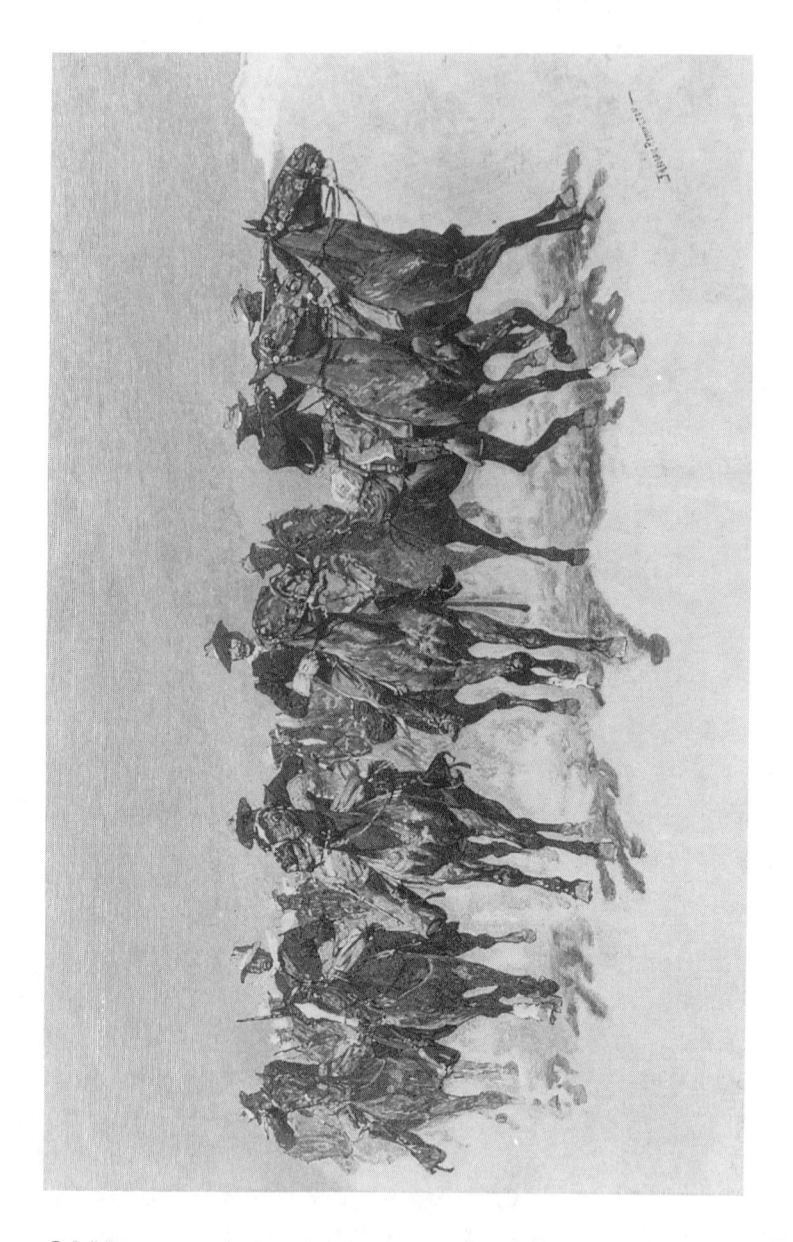

Figure 24 "Captain Dodge's Colored Troops to the Rescue," by Frederic Remington. The White River Expedition of 1879 inspired several artists, but Remington's work probably has been the most enduring. Courtesy, Frederic Remington Art Museum, Ogdensburg, NY.

Figure 25 "Fighting for Water," by R. F. Zogbaum. Water detail during the siege at Milk Creek. This illustration suggests a healthy stream flow; had this much water been present in the streambed, the expedition may have camped here rather than cross into the Ute Reservation. Nawrocki Stock Photo, Inc. NSP-HF-HM-495-737.

Figure 26 "The Relief of Payne's Command—The Trumpet Signal," by R. F. Zogbaum. The two individuals behind the trumpeter may represent guide Jim Baker, *left*, and Colonel Wesley Merritt, *right*. Nawrocki Stock Photo, Inc. NSP-HF-HM-4890-479.

7

Merritt's Lightning March

One of the most successful forced marches of modern times . . .
—Colonel Wesley Merritt, March 1888[1]

It was 5:00 A.M. on October 5, 1879, and the White River Expedition had been under siege for 138 hours: six long nights and six weary days. The men were bone-tired, the water they drank was stagnant, and the air they breathed was tainted by gun smoke and the odor of decaying flesh. Food rations were dwindling, but troopers hadn't yet resorted to eating horse and mule meat, as some of these same men had done three years earlier on Crook's Big Horn and Yellowstone Expedition. Captain Lawson was a veteran of Crook's starvation march and had openly disdained eating horseflesh at the time, a few days before the battle of Slim Buttes, saying, "I'd as soon think of eating my brother!"[2] Yet even old Joe was forced to survive on pony meat before that campaign ended.

For the past four days, Colonel Wesley Merritt had been directing the movements of the final relief force to Milk Creek. Merritt was a successful Civil War general who became a very competent regimental commander on the western frontier during the Indian wars. He was in command of Fort D. A. Russell near Cheyenne when he was ordered to move reinforcements to the front. Merritt's rescue of the White River Expedition would become one of the best-executed military maneuvers of the Indian wars. In his own words,

> One of the most successful forced marches of modern times was that made to the relief of the Thornburg [*sic*] command by a battalion of the 5th Cavalry in the autumn of 1879. . . . The distance accomplished was 170 measured miles. The time from 11 A.M. October 2d, to 5:30 A.M. October 5th. This was at the rate of sixty miles per day for

two and three-quarter days. This march is mentioned as being peculiarly successful for, in brief, the following reasons:

First.—The distance accomplished in the time.

Second.—No horses were lost or disabled on the march, and there were noticeably no sore-back horses after its completion.

Third.—The command—men and horses—were in good condition for service at once after the march.[3]

The colonel's philosophy of how to conduct a cavalry march provides a glimpse into what his 1879 relief command accomplished. Merritt spoke about the marching cavalry to his comrades at a meeting of the U.S. Cavalry Association in 1888, nearly a decade after the march to Milk Creek.[4] His perspective had been formed through years of service and based on a rigid adherence to sound military principles. He advocated, for example, that every camp duty should be initiated by a trumpet call: "Reveille," then "Stables," "The General," "Boots and Saddles," "Mount," and "Forward." Each call was to be sounded at a specific time that was stated in advance and maintained for the duration of a march. A large troop aggregate, such as a battalion, he decided, must march in a column of fours, keep closed up, and try to minimize dust.

In the fall, a march generally would start by 6:30 A.M. or 7:00 A.M. This would leave ample time after reveille to care for animals, eat breakfast, and pack the wagons or mules, in that order. Merritt believed that livestock always came first and that the speed and success of a march always depended on the endurance and ability of the weakest animals. If not properly kept, the stock would slow the entire column and put the expedition at risk. To minimize the gamble, most of the saddle stock probably was between five and eight years old, in their prime. Merritt advocated strict obedience to ensure organization and maintain discipline. No man was allowed to leave the ranks mounted, and no horse was to be watered unless all of them could be watered. He recommended the arrest of any officer or confinement of any trooper "who wilfully neglects attention to the smallest details of the march, so necessary to the preservation of the endurance of the men and horses."[5]

As for forced marches, Merritt believed that daily marches should not exceed fifty miles if a total distance to be covered was to be more than 150 miles. However, he was able to meet and exceed this daily distance in 1879 with remarkable success.

Merritt's overall philosophy was outlined when he chose to cite in 1888 General Philip St. George Cooke, renowned authority on cavalry tactics: "any unusual success I may have had in cavalry marches, I suspect may be attributed to my constant thoughtfulness and attention—my great interest felt in the welfare and comfort of horses and men—I fear in that order."[6] This philosophy and Merritt's rigid discipline combined to bring the necessary factors together that were required to save Thornburgh's command.

Two historical accounts provide some personal detail of Merritt's forced march to Milk Creek in early October 1879. One account is by Merritt himself; the other is by Dr. James P. Kimball, medical officer from Fort Sanders, near Laramie, Wyoming, who accompanied the relief force.[7]

The Fort D. A. Russell garrison near Cheyenne, Wyoming received telegraphic news of the Milk Creek disaster on the morning of October 1, possibly at 8:00 A.M.[8] The message had been wired to Cheyenne, then carried by a courier who galloped the two miles to the military post. Orders from Omaha read, in part, "You will proceed with all available troops in your command to the rescue of Payne and his sorely pressed command."[9] Colonel Merritt was sick in quarters but pulled himself out of bed and began the necessary preparations to rescue his comrades.

In October 1879, the regular garrison at D. A. Russell consisted of Companies A, B, D, F, I, and M of the Fifth Cavalry, and Company I of the Fourth Infantry, in addition to the field staff and band.[10] Companies D and F were already at Milk Creek and probably included most of the four commissioned officers (counting Volkmar) and 114 enlisted men who were listed in Post Returns as being on detached service since September. Merritt mustered every one of his remaining Fifth Cavalry companies—A, B, I, and M—for the relief force. This assignment placed on detached service for October a total of fourteen commissioned officers and 304 enlisted men from his regiment.

Subtracting Companies D and F, the relief force of the Fifth Cavalry then included about ten commissioned officers and 190 enlisted men. Each company consisted of about forty-five troopers.[11] Added to these were Merritt, six commissioned officers, and two enlisted men of the Fifth Cavalry Field Staff and Band. Three commissioned officers and forty-two enlisted men also were taken along from Company I, Fourth Infantry, Thornburgh's regiment.

The total relief force from Fort D. A. Russell may have included up to twenty commissioned officers and 234 enlisted men (Appendix A).[12] Solomon Brock, veterinary surgeon, also accompanied the Fifth Cavalry to the front. First Lieutenant William B. Weir, an ordnance officer in charge of government rifle repair works at nearby Camp Carlin, volunteered to go. So did Paul Humme, a rifle tester at the repair works whom Merritt appointed as chief scout, perhaps because of his familiarity with the region.[13] More soldiers from other outposts would follow Merritt's column in the days following.

Merritt summoned the officers and set them to preparing their companies for the journey. They gathered the necessary ingredients for the command from Camp Carlin, a mile from the post. Tom Moore, chief packer, took charge of loading two special Union Pacific trains for the expedition.[14]

Preparations were completed in only four hours from the time the first message of the disaster was received. The troops, horses, and equipment were on railroad cars speeding west toward Rawlins shortly after noon.[15] Each train had double engines to pull and double engines to push them over the summit of Sherman hill.[16] After a brief stop in Laramie to feed and water the stock, the force continued across the Laramie Plains toward Rawlins. There were no shenanigans with the citizenry this time.

The D. A. Russell troops arrived in Rawlins at 5:30 A.M., October 2, at the same moment Captain Dodge and the Buffalo Soldiers were reinforcing Payne's wounded command on Milk Creek.

Three companies of Fourth Infantry from Fort Sanders near Laramie, Wyoming had arrived in Rawlins on the evening of October 1 and were waiting for the cavalry.[17] The Fort Sanders contingent consisted of Company B under Captain Thomas F. Quinn, with First Lieutenant Edward L. Bailey, Second Lieutenant Carver Howband, and thirty enlisted men; Company C under First Lieutenant George O. Webster, with Second Lieutenant Leonard A. Lovering, and thirty-nine enlisted men;

and Company F under First Lieutenant Henry E. Robinson, with Second Lieutenant Edward H. Browne, and twenty-nine enlisted men. Browne had just arrived at Fort Sanders from leave on the day they received orders to move out. The Fort Sanders command was accompanied by Captain James P. Kimball of the Medical Department and Hospital Steward S. W. Richardson.[18] These companies brought the total infantry battalion to around 150 men.[19]

Rumors flew around Rawlins Monday morning, October 2. While troopers unloaded the Union Pacific cars and organized the column for the march, unconfirmed reports persisted that the southern Utes were moving to reinforce the White River Indians at Milk Creek. Concern deepened for Payne and his men. Merritt may have been aware of Thornburgh's earlier request for additional medical supplies and perhaps wondered now if their supplies were holding up. The colonel also worried about Payne's rations: some thought that he had only five days of rations at the beginning of the siege, which meant Merritt had just three days left to reach the beleaguered remnant of Thornburgh's White River Expedition.

The relief force, however, could not sacrifice strength for speed. They had to arrive quickly and in force. While cavalry was faster than infantry, there were not enough troopers in the relief force. Merritt needed the entire command. He secured light wagons and harnessed the best teams available around Rawlins to haul the infantry. Without transportation, there wasn't a prayer that foot soldiers could keep up with the cavalry on the forced march.[20]

Other wagons and pack animals were loaded with supplies for the entire command. In addition, chief packer Tom Moore supervised the light packing of provisions on fifty mules so they could be led during a speedy march if the cavalry had to separate from the main supply wagons.

As Moore worked, a nineteen-year-old lad with a revolver hanging from his belt came up to him. Apparently the teenager had stowed away on the train at Laramie and smuggled in with the troops to Rawlins. He asked Tom if he could accompany the soldiers. Tom acquiesced and assigned him a mule to ride and duties to help the cooks and packers.[21]

Merritt spoke with Joe Rankin about the Milk Creek situation. Rankin advised Merritt to hire Jim Baker to help out when they got to

Snake River. Merritt agreed. An old-time guide and trapper, Baker's knowledge of the country and the Indians was second to none. At 10:00 A.M., Rankin and Lieutenant Colonel Charles E. Compton left Rawlins for Snake River. Once there, they were to go upriver twelve miles from the road crossing to Baker's cabin and hire him to help scout for the expedition. Joe Rankin would accompany the expedition to Milk Creek, but then he would return to attend his livery business.[22]

Another civilian joined Merritt before he left Rawlins. Colorado officials sent John C. Dyer from Denver to serve as a correspondent for the *New York World* and the *Chicago Tribune*.[23] He would be the first newsman on the scene. Thornburgh, unlike his friend General George Crook during the Big Horn and Yellowstone Expedition in 1876, hadn't taken any correspondents on the White River Expedition, most likely because he hadn't had time to organize a press corps.

The relief force began the march at 11:00 A.M. Merritt mapped their course almost due south toward Bridger's Pass, taking the steeper but shorter of the two routes to White River. The rugged road, however, may have been too much for the wagons. It also is conceivable that the entire command took the longer basin route that Thornburgh had used, or that the cavalry took the mountain route and the wagons took the basin route, meeting up again at Snake River. Val McClellan, in *This is Our Land,* indicates that the relief force made it to Cow Creek late the first night, which suggests that at least some of the command did take the basin route.[24]

Each cavalryman carried a blanket, carbine, small knapsack containing hardtack, and a canteen of either water or coffee. A train of fifteen wagons led by wagon master John McAndrews followed several hours behind with supplies.[25]

Correspondent Dyer rented a spirited horse from Rankin's livery stable. He couldn't handle the animal; the horse took the bit in its teeth and lurched forward. Out of control, the correspondent broke ranks and passed the column. Dyer was commanded to halt more than once, and his vain efforts to close up must have given the soldiers quite a chuckle until they got farther south, near hostile territory.

Now Merritt's tactical knowledge of cavalry marches came into play. Years of study and firsthand experience served him well. He measured the distance, weighed the odds, and assessed the condition of his command. He had to reach the barricade in three days yet not diminish his troop or animal strength in the process. Impulsive actions had nearly destroyed the cavalry at the Little Bighorn, now purposeful calculations must save it at Milk Creek.

The relief command likely paid close attention to taking halts that were so critical in maintaining the condition of horses and men, although each halt was not chronicled by eyewitnesses. Normally, a mounted battalion would halt after the first hour for about fifteen minutes so troopers could adjust their saddles and "go to the rear" if needed. Each hour thereafter would either end with a five-minute halt or be divided into a two-minute halt, a twenty-minute dismounted walk leading the horses, another two-minute halt, a fifteen-minute mounted trot, then a standard mounted walk for the balance of the hour. Horses and men received needed exercise with the repetition of this variety, which generated a lighter work load, prevented saddle sores and chafing, and produced a timely march. Variations probably included ten-minute trots twice during each of the last three hours of the daily march, and an occasional seven- to ten-minute gallup with appropriate rests. Commanders in charge of forced marches normally exercised these standard maneuvers for the first four to five hours or so. At the completion of the first third and second third of the march, a two-hour grand halt was ordered near water to feed and refresh the horses and men. Horses were unsaddled so they could lie down, roll, eat, and drink.[26]

Variations of this marching pattern were used for Merritt's relief force in October 1879. He ordered his column to stop briefly for coffee at 3:00 P.M., four hours into the march, then it continued until roughly 9:00 P.M. and covered forty-five miles in ten hours. Colonel Merritt reviewed the command and determined it to be in good condition. He then called a halt for the night.[27]

Dr. Kimball's account of the first day's march differs slightly from Merritt's. The doctor states that the relief force marched until 10:30 P.M. and covered forty-two miles before halting for the night.[28]

Kimball and Merritt noticed different things during the march. The full responsiblity for the safety of his command and the salvation of Payne's rested on Merritt's shoulders: he recalled the tactical elements of his march most vividly. Kimball, a more passive participant, chronicled daily experiences as seen by one who obeys rather than commands: he noted the weather and geography.

Kimball recalled that the days were reasonably warm. With each order to move out, stifling dust billowed up from a thousand hooves and wagon wheels. The first hours of evening, however, were cooler and brightened by the moon. Temperatures dropped considerably after sunset and nights became downright cold, with ice forming on standing water along the route.[29]

The relief column marched out at 7:00 A.M. on October 3. Cavalrymen alternated walking, trotting, and leading their horses. Merritt sent out an advance guard and periodically ordered flankers to prevent any ambush by Indians, but the second day was quiet.[30]

At Baggs's crossing, Merritt picked up Jim Baker and Tom Duffy, a cowboy volunteer. Baker was dressed in buckskin and toted his Sharps across the pommel of his saddle, and was riding his horse, Brownie.[31] Presumably Rankin and Colonel Compton also rejoined the command here.

An hour's halt was called shortly after noon. The men unsaddled their horses and rested. Except through occasional patches of sand, the infantry wagons had been able to keep up with the cavalry throughout the day.

The command made camp on Fortification Creek by 9:30 P.M., some fifty-eight miles beyond their morning bivouac. Merritt's column had covered 100 to 103 miles since leaving Rawlins a day and a half before and spent about twenty-three hours of actual marching.[32] Over four miles per hour was very good time for a cavalry and infantry battalion with loaded wagons, but this was still less than two-thirds of the anticipated distance to the beleaguered command. Time was becoming critical.

The march recommenced at dawn, October 4. M. Wilson Rankin described the next leg of the journey:

> When Merritt arrived at the Thornburg [*sic*] reserve camp on Fortification Creek, Lieutenant Price with Troop I [probably means E], of the 4th Infantry, and Captain Dodge's mule teams with supply wagons, were taken along. At Bear River, Merritt's command was joined by

Bill Lisco and a small party from the Iles's ranch. Arriving at Williams Fork the evening of October 4th, they made camp until two a.m., when they moved to the trenches.[33]

Merritt probably did enlist the services of Price's company at Fortification Creek, but there is some question as to how long the command stopped at Williams Fork. The remainder of the distance between Fortification Creek camp and Payne's command had to be covered in twenty-four hours if relief was to arrive at Milk Creek before Payne's rations might run out. Merritt calculated that they were still seventy miles from Milk Creek and Kimball figured sixty-five, but both estimates were high by about ten to fifteen miles. They still would have to travel day and night to get there in time; it meant maintaining a constant three-miles-per-hour pace.

The colonel had ordered this dawn start on Saturday morning, October 4, and the troopers were mounted and moving out by 6:00 A.M. They reached the Yampa River at noon and the cavalry rested while the wagons kept on. Troopers met several settlers at the river who were fleeing the country because of the uprising. There were wounded among the settlers: some men had encountered roving bands of Utes, and Dr. Kimball stayed behind to treat them. One severely wounded citizen was resting on a makeshift bed in a wagon; he had been found lying beside the corpse of his partner and had been left for dead by the Indians. Soldiers treating him noticed that the wagon bed was half full of loose cartridges, the remains of ammunition the citizen had been trading to the Indians. Sympathy for the injured man quickly diminished.[34]

The Fifth Cavalry battalion was exhausted, and when Dr. Kimball looked up from tending the wounded settlers, the scene remained etched in his mind for decades. In front of him was "a field covered with men and horses stretched upon the ground as profoundly still as though the sleep of Sennacherib's host had fallen upon them."[35] The cavalry column moved on at 3:00 P.M.

Troopers left the open river valley and entered canyons in the Williams Fork Mountains about sunset; moonlight didn't brighten their way until almost midnight. These canyons angled down both sides of the mountains toward Williams Fork. They soon overtook the infantry wagons and leapfrogged ahead.[36]

Night traveling was dangerous with such a large force in unknown, rugged country. Merritt called a couple brief halts of a few minutes each to rest the column and keep it together. He also sent staff officers

> to the rear to direct the column in the darkness and see that all kept well closed. After a seemingly interminable season of marching by the uncertain light of a waning moon, in which objects were dimly defined and always distorted, the hour indicated to the weary though watchful horsemen that they were approaching the scene of the conflict. Not a sound broke the stillness of the chilly night save the steady tramp of the horses and the rattle and jingle of the equipments of the men.[37]

They were getting close. The night march, however, did little to ease their growing apprehension. Shadows cast by moonlight distorted images on the nearby canyon slopes and played games in the minds of every trooper. Each hill offered an uncertain fate awaiting them on the far side.

At Stinking Gulch, Merritt's column passed the ashes and blackened debris of George Gordon's wagon train that had been bound for the White River Agency. The Indians had killed the teamsters and burned the wagons and their stores. Iron fragments, pieces of chain and harness, and rubbish were strewn about, and the bodies of the teamsters lay beside the ashes. Their features were distorted; their "staring eyes, told all too plainly of their short run for life—of the mercy they had pled for, and how their prayers had been answered by the merciless foe."[38]

Merritt pushed on, well ahead of the trailing infantry wagons. An advance guard of eight men kept about a half mile ahead of the main column. A man named Chris Madsen was in charge of this group.[39]

A guide, probably Joe Rankin, said for the third time, "It can't be far from here."[40] He raised his hand and pointed to a hill dimly outlined a quarter of a mile away. The rest of the column halted. Everyone strained their eyes to see and listened for any sound from the battlefield. "There is the hill," the guide said, "and to the left of it was the corral."[41] It was 5:30 on the morning of October 5, about an hour before daylight.

On command, a bugler blew "Officers' Call," a call used by the cavalry to prevent accidental engagements between friendly forces. The clear notes floated through the valley to the weakened command at Milk Creek and "awakened the echoes of the night."[42] The music testified to their imminent rescue, and for Thornburgh's White River Expedition, the beginning of the end was at hand.

Payne's command had spent the night of October 4 huddled in the trenches behind the barricades, and the captain had pondered their chances for rescue all night. He had profound faith that the United States Cavalry would come, and he was sure that Colonel Merritt would accompany any relief force.

Captain Payne had served with Merritt during the Sioux campaign of 1876. Payne had made a forced night march to overtake Merritt, and when he reached the rendezvous at 3:00 A.M., Merritt was not to be found. Tired from extended travel, Payne sounded "Officers' Call" to alert any troopers who might be nearby. Merritt heard the call, and response became a regimental tradition. Payne was sure Merritt would remember the call and save his command.[43]

By the time Merritt's bugler broke the silence of the gray dawn, Payne's bugler had been ready to respond for several hours. The captain anticipated that help should arrive soon, and he wanted a trumpeter to listen for and respond to the familiar notes. He answered "Officers' Call," and Merritt's men rode forward at a gallop. Men at the barricade cheered, rushed from the trenches, and shouted as they ran through the dark to greet their saviors. Kimball recalled that, "men tumbled out of the pits and ran around in the chill morning, throwing their arms wildly and falling on one another's necks, showing by every gesture the sudden revulsion of feeling."[44]

Payne observed, "brave men wept, and it was touching to see the gallant fellows hovering around to get a look at the general whose name had been on their lips for days, and who, as they heard from their comrades just arrived, had risen from a bed of sickness to make a march unparalleled in military annals."[45] The two comrades, Payne and Merritt, threw their arms around each other, overcome with gratitude and relief. Some brave men's tears apparently were the captain's.[46]

One of the besieged soldiers went up to Merritt and offered him a can of peaches that he had been saving for the last meal. The colonel refused the generous offer and said that the soldier could end his waiting and eat the peaches now.[47]

Kimball wrote that the march had been made in just "two and three quarters days, at an average speed of sixty miles per twenty-four hours."[48] M. Wilson Rankin calculated the statistics of Merritt's lightning march: the total time from Rawlins to Milk Creek, including stops to feed, a two-hour stop at Price's camp on Fortification Creek, and eight hours at Williams Fork, was 66.5 hours. According to Rankin, this feat broke all records filed by the War Department for distance and time in a forced march of cavalry, and both the Colorado and Wyoming legislatures would pass resolutions complimenting the success of the relief force.[49]

Merritt met with Captains Payne, Lawson, and Dodge. The soldiers quickly took control of the terrain adjacent to the barricade. Some were sent to hold a nearby hill that had been used daily by the Indians to shoot into the trenches. As the sun crept up over the eastern horizon, the Utes awakened at their camp a half mile away and saw new soldiers commanding their position. A large group moved quickly toward the troops, giving some soldiers the impression that the Utes were going to attack.[50] The troopers advanced, and after only a few shots the Utes scattered into the hills. Only one man and a horse were slightly wounded.[51]

The infantry wagons finally caught up with the cavalry at the barricades at 9:00 A.M. or sooner, at which time Kimball indicates hostilities ceased. Rankin, however, states that infantry soldiers were involved in the morning's combat.[52]

Then a large troop, including the Fourth Infantry and the men who had defended the barricade for six days, were ordered to advance along the ridge formerly held by Indians and along the bluffs on the north side of Milk Creek. Merritt kept the main relief force in ready reserve near the trenches.[53]

Robert Emmitt, in *The Last War Trail*, published in 1954, implies that the infantry were involved in the final fighting at Milk Creek. He describes the soldiers moving toward the Indian positions by crawling along through the brush. At clear daylight, probably well before 9:00 A.M,. the Indians had congregated on the two hills where the battle had begun on September 29 to watch these new maneuvers. After getting into position, the soldiers north of the creek fired long-distance volleys into the Indians. Long-distance firing would have required rifles rather than carbines, and the rifles were infantry issue. A Springfield rifle in the hands of a sharpshooter could be a lethal weapon at ranges of one thousand yards or more, whereas the Springfield carbine with its twenty-two-inch barrel and fifty-five-grain powder charge was practically limited to half that distance. While the Springfield Trap-Door rifles had been criticized for their awkward breech-loading system, they were beyond reproach for long-distance accuracy.[54]

Some Utes fired back, but no one was in any real danger. In fact, most of the Indians probably were in council. Rankin estimated their strength at the time of Merritt's arrival at 175 to 200 men.[55] If the battle had begun with four hundred Utes, the rest must have left during the ensuing period for the Indian camp or destinations to the south.

The Indians began to pull back from the skirmish when some heard horses coming from the direction of Yellowjacket Pass. Two riders came in: one was Sapavanero, Ouray's brother-in-law, and the other was Joe Brady, a white employee from Los Piños Agency. Brady handed a message to Chief Jack:

> Los Piños Indian Agency
> October 2, 1879
>
> To the chief captains, headmen, and Utes at the White River Agency:
>
> You are hereby requested and commanded to cease hostilities against the whites, injuring no innocent persons or any others farther than to protect your own lives and property from unlawful and unauthorized combinations of horse-thieves and desperadoes, as anything farther will ultimately end in disaster to all parties.
>
> Signed, Ouray[56]

Ouray was respected and generally recognized as an influential leader in the Ute Nation. His opinions could not be ignored. The huddled

Indians discussed this missive as the distant sounds of gunfire continued between the young men and soldiers. Perhaps if they stopped, the white men in Washington would send the soldiers home. Then the courier handed Jack a second letter:

> Los Piños Indian Agency
> October 2, 1879
>
> To the officers in command and the soldiers at the White River Agency:
>
> GENTLEMEN: At the request of the chiefs of the Utes at this agency, I send by Jos. W. Brady, an employe, the inclosed order from Chief Ouray to the Utes at the White River Agency.
>   The head chiefs deplore the trouble existing at White River, and are anxious that no further fighting or bloodshed should take place, and have commanded the Utes there to stop.
>   I hope that you will second their efforts, so far as you can consistently with your duties under existing commands.
>   Thus much for humanity.
>
> Very respectfully, your obedient servant,
> W. M. Stanley
> United States Indian Agent[57]

Chief Jack became more deliberate in his actions than at any other time since the initial engagement on the morning of September 29. He had pondered the battle for many hours these past days. Now he made a flag of white tent cloth. Shortly after 9:00 A.M., soldiers saw the Indians raise the white flag from a distant hill. The shooting stopped and a sense of relief and resolve pervaded the scene. The battle of Milk Creek ended 142 hours after it had begun.

Several Indians rode with Joe Brady toward the troops. Brady left the group and rode ahead at a gallop toward the soldiers, carrying the white flag with him. He reined in next to Merritt and handed him the two notes. Brady said that the Indians wanted to quit fighting and wanted a new agent. They wanted to live in peace on the reservation. Merritt had Lieutenant Cherry tell Brady that he would not withdraw all of the troops but would look after the Utes. Brady returned to the Indians; the Utes decided to quit the fight even though the soldiers were to remain on the reservation. They left the battlefield and headed south through Yellowjacket Pass.[58]

Kimball helped Grimes treat the wounded while a burial detail removed the soldiers' bodies from beneath the tent canvas and dirt that had been piled upon them as part of the barricade wall. Scout Charles Lowry, who was thought mortally wounded while fighting the fire the afternoon of September 29, was among the corpses. After five and a half days, Lowry was still alive. Apparently the canvas held back dirt from his face and enabled him to breath while in a semiconscious state throughout the ordeal. His surprised friends helped him up. He was unable to move well or speak coherently because of his wound, but he "rose shakily to his feet from his grave of loose dirt in the animal breastworks. He murmured, 'What's the matter boys?' took a sip of coffee and died for good as Merritt's surgeon, Dr. A. J. Kimmell [*sic*] probed for a bullet in his head."[59]

Merritt sent Lieutenant Price, Sandy Mellen, and a small party of troopers toward the trail crossing of Milk Creek to retrieve Major Thornburgh's body, which had lain there since September 29. The two correspondents from Denver state that a Lieutenant Hughes was one of the first to see Thornburgh's body on October 5. The body lay where it fell. Hughes recognized five or six wounds and noticed that the scalp had been taken. The major was naked, lying on his back, and a photo of an Indian lay on his breast.[60] So many different names for the Indian in the picture appear in the literature that his true identity cannot be established. If this picture was intended as a signature of authorship for the bloody deed of killing the commander, the perpetrator's identity has been lost.

Lieutenant Cherry wrote Mrs. Thornburgh that the major "must have been killed instantly by a shot thru the heart, as he had only one or two other slight wounds—one in the face after his death."[61] Cherry added that he and ten men had gone out to gather the body, and that Cherry himself, who had tried three times during the battle to retrieve it, was the first to see Thornburgh's corpse after the battle. No one could have brought the major back before the end of the battle because the Utes were watching the spot and sniped at any movement. According to Cherry, the major was found lying on his back, feet together, arms folded across his breast, and unmutilated. Cherry could have omitted the reference to scalping to save the major's widow from further distress, but it also is remotely possible that Thornburgh was not scalped.

Thornburgh's body was remarkably well preserved after five days of exposure. His face had been blackened somewhat by gunpowder but otherwise was natural, showing no evidence of prolonged suffering at the time of death. The powder burns suggest that the facial wound(s) occurred at close range and, consequently, had been inflicted after death. Cherry had the body wrapped in canvas and temporarily interred until it could be taken back to Fort Fred Steele.

Dr. Kimball identified what probably was the fatal chest wound on the major's body. Dr. Grimes also stated that the immediate cause of death was "a gunshot wound of chest, the ball passing from left to right, through both lungs."[62] Marshall Sprague presented a less likely scenario: that Thornburgh "was riding alone in the tall grass short of the Milk Creek crossing when a big slug from some Ute's Sharps rifle struck him above the ear."[63]

The *Cheyenne Daily Leader* interviewed Dr. Grimes, who had been present throughout the battle, in the latter part of October, after the troops returned to Fort D. A. Russell. One newspaper article states that Thornburgh's body "was afterwards found with the scalp taken—the only one of the dead. The body was stripped of clothing. In the right hand, which lay across the breast, was a photograph of the young chief, Wammaniche. Maj. Thornburgh's body contained five or six wounds. After death some miserable Indian emptied his revolver into the body, hitting the left eye and cheek, the latter place twice."[64] It is likely that Thornburgh's wounds were described accurately if the newspaper used the information from Dr. Grimes. However, the account also could have used other, less reliable informants.

While troops scouted the surrounding hills, Captain Jacob Augur, Company A, Fifth Cavalry, was placed in charge of the burial detail and its escort. The bodies of Firestone and Miller, the two Company F, Fifth Cavalry men who died during the early moments of fighting south of the creek on September 29, were brought in and buried.[65] There are no details of the condition of their bodies. All of the dead, except for Thornburgh, were buried near the trenches.[66]

Kimball, in *A Soldier-Doctor of Our Army*, published in 1917, mentioned that all bodies were accounted for but one.[67] He recalled that once the troops moved on to White River a few days after the relief, a body was found two or three miles beyond the barricade, probably to the south. Apparently, the man's horse had bolted and carried him into enemy lines, where he and his horse were killed. No records indicate who this soldier was, if indeed he was a soldier. If it was not Firestone or Miller, none of the official accounts mention this body. It may be a confused incident in Kimball's recollections, because the troopers had dismounted into skirmish lines before gunfire broke out on September 29.

Malachi W. Dillon, Company E, Third Cavalry, was in charge of a small infantry detail that accompanied Chris Madsen, leader of an escort troop of Fifth Cavalry, that went to Stinking Gulch. Indians had attacked George Gordon's wagon train, and the detail was sent to bury Gordon and his two teamsters, J. H. Brigham, and Brigham's son.[68]

Meanwhile, Merritt moved the soldier camp a mile east and up Milk Creek from the barricade because of the stench of dead livestock. Apparently, the water and grass there could have supported a much larger force than the original White River Expedition. Had scout Rankin considered this spot on September 29, the ensuing battle may have been avoided. Kimball recounted the first hours after their arrival and the reasons for the move:

> It was necessary to move to a new camping-ground, as the old one was far from water, and the decaying bodies of over three hundred animals tainted the air. Another site was chosen, and the wounded were cared for. I had a busy time, having no assistant, except the wounded surgeon, who was able, however, to administer chloroform. In the

evening, cheerful camp-fires dotted the valley, the soldiers talked, laughed, and smoked, as usual; even the stock jokes between horse and foot were overheard — Cavalryman: "Why do they call you dough-boys?" Infantryman: "Because we are so much *needed* when you get into trouble." "Got a brush and comb?" "No; when we get over and have a brush with the Indians, they will fix your hair for you." The horror of the past week remained a memory only. Give a rouse for the Cavalry![69]

Another account comes from Edward A. Matthews, who was assigned to Company I, Third Cavalry in the fall of 1879. Apparently Company I followed behind Merritt's initial relief force. Years later, his memory perhaps clouded by the passage of time, Matthews said that the dead had been taken back to Fort Steele and buried. "Yes," he said, "it was pretty hard; many of the boys were our friends."[70] Several primary sources and secondary sources, however, mention that the dead, except for Thornburgh, were buried at the battlefield.[71]

Merritt's survey of the battlefield involved considerably more than the burial detail. Troopers found officers' trunks that had been captured by the Indians on the first day of battle emptied of their contents. Lieutenant Cherry's fine broadcloth dress suit was missing and undoubtedly now the property of a fashion-conscious Indian. Some troopers also found a photograph of Cherry lying on the ground. The Utes had cut his scalp out of the picture.[72]

The Denver correspondents, Dawson and Skiff, recounted that, "during the stampede of the wagon train by the Indians the trunk of Lieutenant Cherry, who covered the retreat and brought off the wounded, was secured by the Indians and broken open. They took everything of the contents but a bible, and left Lieutenant Cherry's picture in the trunk with the scalp of the likeness carefully cut out."[73]

Most of the trunks that had been used as breastworks were damaged beyond repair. Dr. Grimes's trunk was so was riddled with bullet holes that the folded contents were shredded. A newspaper noted that leaden Winchester balls were found in the trunk, souvenirs for the doctor.[74]

Payne had lost a field table that was found set up; the Indians had used it as a gun rest to shoot at the barricade.

The Utes had captured at least one tent, probably the forage type used by most of the men, and pitched it on the battlefield. Several empty bottles found in the tent indicated that some Utes, like some soldiers, had drunk heavily during the engagement. This tent may have been the source for canvas used in the truce flag.

Dawson and Skiff speculated that the ambulance taken on the expedition by Major Thornburgh would doubtless be preserved at Fort Steele as a relic of the siege. It had been parked with other wagons near the center of the entrenchment, and they described it as having been ventilated by thirty or more bullet holes. During the siege's first day, Joe Rankin got under it "for a nap and was awakened by a ball which struck one of the spokes within two inches of the top of his head."[75] This probably occurred during the late afternoon or early evening of September 29, while the couriers rested up for the night ride.

Survivors of Thornburgh's White River Expedition prepared wagons and themselves for the long march back to Fort Fred Steele. Their duty was done, their mission a failure.

The survivors of the White River Expedition and the settlers who had volunteered to go with Merritt on his forced march left the battlefield on the morning of October 10 under the command of Captain Dodge.[76] Thornburgh's body had been treated by Dr. Kimball, then sewed in canvas for transport with the column. Colonel Merritt rested his stock at Milk Creek and awaited the arrival of his supply train before leading his full force farther onto the reservation.[77]

Merritt finally advanced toward the agency and established a fort at the White River cantonment on October 11. The location was about three to four miles upriver from the agency where, on September 29, Nathan C. Meeker had been killed. In addition to Meeker, the fatalities at the agency and along the road included Frank Dresser, Harry Dresser, George Eaton, Wilmer Eskridge, Carl Goldstein, Julius Moore, William H. Post, Shadrack A. Price, Fred Shepard, and Arthur L. Thompson.[78]

8
Aftermath

No doubt you have heard of our engagement with the treacherous Utes.
—Captain Joseph J. Lawson, October 9, 1879[1]

Historians, anthropologists, and dedicated students of Western history have debated the causes of the 1879 Ute outbreak for decades. Still, no simple explanation emerges from the range of possibilities. Students of the tragedy conclude that several factors were at work, including Meeker's obsession with reform and the Utes' resistance to change. Like the rest of the Indian wars, myriad cultural differences ensured that the Ute outbreak was virtually unavoidable. The eminent military historian S.L.A. Marshall explained: "violence beset the western frontier and lasted and lasted because the fundamental interests of the two sides were so wholly irreconcilable as to leave little or no room for compromise. Due to the absence of any middle ground, there occurred intolerable grievances to white man and red. When these basic conditions are present, war or revolution becomes inevitable."[2]

But for all of the complex problems facing human settlement in northwestern Colorado in 1879, no scholar can ignore the fact that Meeker clearly misunderstood the Utes and their cultural values. His fanatical, utopian ideals clashed with a social system that was thousands of years old. His attempt to alter Ute subsistence economy from hunting to agriculture ignored how hunting permeated so many aspects of Native American culture.[3] Forcing acculturation threatened enduring Ute customs and compelled the Utes to defend their traditional way of life.

When tempers at the agency reached the boiling point in early September 1879, Meeker either misinterpreted or exaggerated the magnitude of the physical threat directed at him and at his family. Meeker's actions prove that he blew Johnson's aggression out of proportion. He had not been seriously injured, because he wrote cogent, articulate letters and moved freely about the agency shortly after the incident. His concern over the Indians' response to military actions several days later implies that he regretted his hasty decision to ask for such forceful military intervention. The whole history of the expedition would have been different had Meeker requested a commission to arbitrate differences rather than the cavalry to prosecute offenses, most of which were imagined.

When the army was called to respond, its agent, Thornburgh, who had been largely sympathetic to the Utes in light of Meeker's constant complaints, made strategic errors that sent the wrong message to the Indians. First, his expeditionary force was too large to convince the Utes that he came in peace. The battalion, however, was too small to succeed in an all-out war. Thornburgh had indicated to Meeker only a few weeks earlier that he could easily advance to the agency with fifty men if ordered to do so. But even fifty men may have been too many to convey peaceful intentions.

Thornburgh's fatal error was not to camp at Milk Creek, the commonly accepted northern boundary of the Ute Reservation. Instead, when he found Milk Creek too dry and with insufficient firewood and too little grass for stock, he ordered his command to advance toward Beaver Springs. Why did Joe Rankin, or others who may have been familiar with the terrain, ignore an alternative campsite a mile up the creek and instead recommend another place four miles into the reservation? Contrary to Thornburgh's decision not to camp on Upper Milk Creek, whatever it may have been based on, Merritt's relief force found the site adequate and camped there for several days after the battle ended. Thornburgh's smaller command only needed it for one night, and the location was still at the traditional reservation boundary rather than on Ute soil. Had the expedition camped up the creek, Thornburgh still could have taken a five-member squad to the agency and Payne could have advanced the entire command later, under cover of darkness. There is no evidence or testimony to indicate that the Utes would have attacked the soldiers if they had camped anywhere along the east-west course of Milk Creek rather than entering the reservation.

The tactical maneuvers of the Utes and the cavalry once troopers crossed the creek are fairly clear from eyewitness testimony. Specific details and unit positions, however, could be clarified with systematic archaeological investigations.

Most of the Indian combatants on the morning of September 29 were from White River Ute bands. A few members of other bands were probably there, but they did not constitute a significant number. At best, the warriors outnumbered the expedition by only a few men. Census figures suggest that there were not even as many White River Ute warriors as there were troopers. The Ute advantage lay not in overwhelming numbers but in their knowledge of the terrain and their occupation of the high ground when the shooting began.

Had the Indians significantly outnumbered the cavalry, they could easily have overrun Payne's skirmish line during the early phase of fighting. Yet Payne's company maintained volley fire for over twenty minutes without retreat, so the Indians must have been held in check at a reasonable distance, perhaps three hundred to four hundred yards, where their repeating rifles were less effective. The soldiers could fire at least four rounds a minute with their Trap-Door carbines, but they may have had only forty rounds of carbine ammunition apiece since offensive maneuvers were not anticipated when ammunition was issued at the Deer Creek camp. Consequently, troopers would have had to conserve their ammunition before they returned to the wagons. An overwhelming force of Utes would have made this nearly impossible.

The Indians maintained an element of surprise and the benefit of high ground in spite of the soldiers' detecting the planned ambush along Little Beaver Creek. The Utes' first reaction after their discovery was to block the column's advance by repositioning warriors and firing into the V-shaped skirmish lines in an attempt to collapse the defense and scatter the led horses. This frontal attack failed, so they initiated simultaneous flanking maneuvers to bypass the two skirmish lines. The eastern flankers occupied a small knoll between the advance companies and the wagons. The western maneuver enabled Utes to cross Milk Creek and attack the wagon train while the two skirmish lines south of the creek were still engaged with Utes on the hillside. These three coordinated maneuvers would have required more than the fifty warriors mentioned in Chief Jack's testimony but would not have required the three hundred to four hundred estimated by Lieutenant Cherry.

Cavalry units repulsed both the knoll occupation and the initial pressure on the wagon train. The Indians then resorted to increased pressure on the wagons from additional flanks, combined with an attempt to cut off the retreating skirmishers. This too failed because of the timely arrival of a small squad from the wagons.

Once the skirmishers reached the wagon circle, the Indians infiltrated the surrounding terrain and took up numerous firing positions within thirty yards of the wagons. The expedition, however, had time to set their initial defenses, and troopers held off deeper infiltration. The Utes were forced to attack from behind a wall of flames in an effort to dislodge the soldiers, but this too collapsed due to the timely advance of counter-fires ordered by Payne. Even an evening mounted attack to run off livestock failed to breach the entrenchment. Further infiltration was impossible, so the Utes killed horses and mules to prevent their use in any attempt to go for reinforcements. After this series of movements, the entire battle settled into a monotonous defensive stand at the barricade. Offensive tactical maneuvers by either side essentially ceased until the arrival of Colonel Merritt on October 5. Merritt's large command prevented any further offensive moves by the Utes, who withdrew after a brief exchange.

As the beleaguered White River Expedition began the march back toward Rawlins on the morning of October 10, 1879, survivors could reflect on their recent ordeal. Their horses were dead and a third of the men were wounded. Many wounded troopers had to ride in wagons. They mourned the loss of their commander and hoped that the relief force would avenge his death.

The army established a camp on the Snake River and used Rawlins as the supply depot. For a time in the early 1880s, this part of Wyoming was transferred from the Department of the Platte under Brigadier General George Crook to the Department of the Missouri under Brigadier General John Pope.[4] This administrative change placed the military supply line in the same department as the White River Agency to facilitate command and control. There had been no need for this reorganization before the 1879 outbreak, because the Utes had been at peace until Meeker's tenure at White River.

Several officers who participated in the Milk Creek battle prepared official reports or statements following the hostilities (Appendix D). These men returned from the battlefield with the wounded and reached Rawlins on October 18, after nine days of travel. The return trip was made in chilling rain after they crossed Fortification Creek.[5]

Native-born Americans and immigrants with diverse ethnic backgrounds made up the White River Expedition. For example, data collected at Fort Fred Steele in June 1880 lists forty-two troopers in dwelling 189, apparently the enlisted men's barracks for Company E, Third Cavalry. Most of the men were veterans of Milk Creek; 55 percent of them were native-born Americans, whereas eighty percent of their parents were foreign-born. Only two of the soldiers had been born west of the Mississippi River.[6]

It is safe to say that few, if any, of the enlisted men knew many details about the problems at White River.

As the White River Expedition of 1879 closed and the column returned to civilization, the careers of each captain took different directions. Captain J. Scott Payne had been ill before the battle, and his condition worsened afterward. He retired from active service in 1886, and then served in Washington on the Pension Board until his death in 1895.[7]

Captain Dodge, who had ridden to the relief of the expedition and was senior in command at Milk Creek from October 2 to 5, left the wounded at Rawlins and departed for Fort Union, New Mexico. Eventually he quit field service to work paymaster duty and became paymaster general in 1904.[8]

Perhaps the most colorful career was that of the unheralded captain of Company E, Third Cavalry. Prior to Milk Creek, Joseph J. Lawson had participated in some of the most notable engagements of the Indian wars, campaigning in New Mexico, Arizona, upper Nebraska, Dakota, Montana, Wyoming, and Colorado.[9] He had been with General Crook at the battle of the Rosebud in 1876 and, three months later, with the Big Horn and Yellowstone Expedition at Slim Buttes.[10] Quite possibly, Lawson became acquainted with Chief Jack during this period.

One of Stanley Morrow's photographs of some Slim Buttes veterans taken in September 1876 shows Lawson and other expedition members sitting in front of a captured tepee with a recaptured Seventh Cavalry guidon that had been lost at the Little Bighorn in June (see Figure 10). Lawson appears as a lean and lanky individual with a straggly beard. He was about six feet tall and his features in late 1876 reflect several arduous weeks of campaigning under extremely stressful field conditions. Lawson was a lieutenant in Company A of the Third Cavalry at the time.[11]

John F. Finerty, a correspondent for the *Chicago Times*, traveled with General Crook and the expedition, and he had ample opportunity to become acquainted with Lawson. Finerty described him as

> an Irish Kentuckian and as gallant an old gentleman as ever drew a sword. He was an original in every way, and joined the Union army on principle at a time when nearly all of his neighbors of fighting age were donning the rebel gray. Lawson was absolutely without fear, but his many peculiarities induced his brother officers to quiz him when they had nothing else to do. He bore it all with supreme good nature, and on the day of battle showed the whole brigade that an officer need not always hail from West Point in order to gain that place in the affections of his soldiers which dauntless courage alone can win.[12]

Author J. W. Vaughn considered Lawson as one of the most interesting men who ever served in the cavalry, due to his personal character.[13] Younger men would often badger Lawson during a campaign, but the captain would shrug it off good-naturedly. When the opportunity arose, however, he would get even during evening chats around the campfire. Lawson would spit a chaw, let it dribble down his beard, and yawn loudly once or twice when these same soldiers recited their own brave deeds of heroism.

Lawson was born in Ireland in February 1821 and immigrated to Kentucky, where he operated a grocery store near the Ohio border. He was forty years old when the Civil War broke out, and, in spite of having a wife and children, he organized a company of the Eleventh Kentucky Cavalry to fight for the Union. By the end of the war he had reached the breveted rank of major.[14]

Joseph Lawson died of paralysis January 30, 1881, a month short of his sixtieth birthday, while he was still stationed at Fort Fred Steele. He was buried at the post cemetery following a grand funeral march and brief ceremony involving the entire garrison. Fort Fred Steele was abandoned by the army in November 1886, and Lawson's body was removed and reinterred on August 25, 1887 in San Francisco National Cemetery.[15] He was the only officer to be buried at the outpost on the North Platte River in Wyoming.

Lawson was a loyal and thoroughly qualified officer. Next to Lieutenant Colonel William B. Royall, also of the Third Cavalry, he was considered to be the best judge of horses in the cavalry and capable of putting most men to shame with his riding skill and endurance. J. W. Vaughn wrote that he simply wore himself out serving in the frontier army.[16]

The veteran lieutenants of the Milk Creek battle went on to diverse careers. Second Lieutenant Silas Wolf returned to Fort Fred Steele, and in December 1879 the White River Ute Commission returned Wolf's gold watch, which he had lost during the battle.[17] One of Wolf's duties was to record the identity and layout of Fort Fred Steele buildings, a task certainly less stressful than the defense at Milk Creek. On January 8, 1880, scarcely three months after the battle, he sent his report and map to the Department of the Platte. This correspondence has proven to be one of the most informative accounts ever prepared of the military buildings at Fort Fred Steele. Wolf eventually rose to the rank of lieutenant colonel before retiring in 1910.[18]

Second Lieutenant Paddock suffered considerably from wounds sustained at Milk Creek and carried two bullets in his body for the rest of his life. Paddock eventually had to retire from the army due to disability caused by the wounds. He died at home in Chicago on August 7, 1907.[19]

Second Lieutenant Samuel A. Cherry, the battalion adjutant during the White River Expedition, returned to Rawlins and spent considerable time refitting his company because it lost so much equipment in the battle. Of his personal gear, the Indians captured and burned all but two valises. Cherry was killed only nineteen months after Milk Creek, on May 11, 1881, at Rock Creek, Dakota Territory, while in command of a detachment in pursuit of desperadoes. Four men had robbed a saloon and bawdy house called the Hog Ranch near Fort Niobrara, Nebraska, where Cherry was stationed at the time. The desperadoes, however, did not kill the lieutenant—one of Cherry's own men did. Private Thomas Locke was in the detachment and was coming off of a two-week drunk. He developed delirium tremens and while in this altered state began shooting at all of the soldiers in sight. The only fatality in the unfortunate incident was Cherry.[20]

A few colorful personalities emerged among the enlisted men. Amandes M. Startzell, a private in Company E, Third Cavalry, had been in the small headquarters group with Lieutenant Cherry that advanced to the position nearest the Indians on the morning of September 29, when the Utes were first sighted. Startzell, whose parents were Swedish, was born January 6, 1848 in Jefferson County, Pennsylvania, one of thirteen children. He worked as a carpenter until August 28, 1876, when he enlisted in the United States Cavalry. Startzell mustered out in 1881 and remained in Rawlins. He and another veteran of the battle, Private John Mahoney, Company E, Third Cavalry, engaged in wool growing, and Amandes maintained interests in the local livestock business, banking, and other ventures.[21]

Startzell, a Republican, was elected to the Wyoming House of Representatives, serving in the 1890–1891 term, the first after statehood. He married Alta Evelyn Kirk Holt, the widowed second daughter of Civil War veteran and educator Henry Kirk, in 1890. Sometime prior to July 27, 1931, Startzell wrote a brief account of the Milk Creek battle. He died in Rawlins on May 26, 1938, at the age of ninety, after a long and successful life spent mostly in south-central Wyoming.[22]

Startzell's good friend, John Mahoney, carried a bullet in his thigh that had been acquired in the battle; he won the Certificate of Merit for his actions at Milk Creek and lived until 1931.[23]

Through the ensuing years, battle veterans occasionally revisited the Milk Creek site or reminisced about the ordeal to the *Meeker Herald,* which chronicled at least two visits. One brief account mentions John Costigan, a member of Company D, Fifth Cavalry, while Eugene A. Patterson, who fought with Company F, Fifth Cavalry, provided a longer story.[24]

Seventy-one-year-old Costigan wrote a letter to the newspaper in 1929 inquiring as to whether or not anyone was planning a memorial of the battle on its fiftieth anniversary. He was working as a night watchman at a place called the Mississippi Warrior docks at the time, but the hardships faced in 1879 were still keenly etched in his memory. Costigan mentions in his letter that Thornburgh's command had gone into action with about 170 men, counting soldiers and civilians. He also recalled that the state of Colorado had promised a bonus of ten acres to each soldier who fought there, and added caustically, "like a great many other things in regard to Indian war veterans, we were forgotten."[25]

Eugene A. Patterson was born on March 23, 1855 in New Lisbon, Ohio. He was eighty-one years old when he revisited the battlefield in the summer of 1936, fifty-seven years after he had left it in October of 1879. Patterson was one of the twenty men of Company F, Fifth Cavalry who stayed with Cherry and Lawson to cover the retreat after the other half of Payne's company charged the knoll and returned to the wagon train.[26]

Patterson remembered the deaths of Privates Firestone, Burns (who had been a remarkable violinist), and Miller (Patterson's "bunky," or bunkmate). The elderly veteran also recalled that he had tried to rescue the mortally wounded Amos Miller while mounted on Captain Payne's horse, probably a replacement for the dead Charger, and to move Miller to safer ground. Patterson had seen Miller fall near the high point where the Utes later raised the white flag. He said that he rode past Thornburgh's body and found Miller's body nearby. The newspaper account states that "the body was placed on the horse by Patterson and taken to cover. About the high point the ground looked as if plowed, with bullets striking the earth everywhere."[27] This account is the only mention of such a rescue attempt, but other records also suggest that if Miller died outside of the barricade he must have fallen about a mile south of where Thornburgh died. Patterson's recollection makes a good story, whether true or not.

Patterson also remembered a central pit inside the wagon circle that was used as a field hospital, and observed that nearly every wounded man had been shot in the legs. However, he didn't speculate why this was the case. He also recalled the guide, Lowry, who, with a shot in the forehead, was believed dead and whose body was brought into the hospital enclosure and dirt thrown over it. According to Patterson, Lowry survived six days only to die while in transport in an ambulance.[28]

The *Meeker Herald* account documented one amusing and somewhat racist but dangerous incident after Dodge's company of Buffalo Soldiers arrived:

> Out came the cooking equipment and the negroes started making coffee. "Come on up and get some coffee," the negroes called. "There ain't no Indians around heah." Almost immediately, however, the vicious crossfire rang from the rocky ridges. The negro troopers rose and ran pell-mell for the earthworks and dived helter-skelter into the enclosure. Mr. Patterson recalls that the face of one white soldier was cut open by the impact of a terror-stricken negro who came from above.[29]

The soldiers made a survey of the battlefield once Merritt arrived, and Patterson remembered that only one Indian body was found. The body had been shallowly buried; other bodies had been carried away by the Utes.

The *Herald*'s 1937 story describes the first encounter with Indians on the morning of September 29 and includes unlikely details not recorded elsewhere:

> Company F had cantered across the valley near what is now known as Thornburg, Color. and entered a canon. Part way down the decline the soldiers saw Indians. They dashed back to the head of the canon and on a high point a white flag was run up, asking for a parley. The invitation of the Indians had too long been scorned, however. The bearer of the white flag was shot down and instantly rifles barked from behind rocks and trees. Indians were everywhere on the slopes of the ridges on either side.[30]

The article further states that Patterson held a distinguished service certificate "doubtless for his heroism in attempting rescue of his friend Miller."[31] Patterson did receive a Certificate of Merit, but it was not issued for rescuing Miller's body (Appendix C).

Patterson found what he thought to be several .45 caliber shells of the rimfire variety during his 1936 visit to the battlefield. He concluded that they were used by the negro troopers, because Thornburgh's men used centerfire. He may have been confusing some of the Utes' .44 caliber Henry cartridges, unless he only collected within the barricade. Patterson also noted great ridges of bones where the dead horses, mules, and oxen had been stacked.

Patterson also saw the monument that had been erected on October 20, 1881 by order of the War Department; an obelisk of gray Indiana granite weighing nine tons. It had been carved in Chicago and engraved with a list of the military men killed and wounded. The monument was shipped in two sections to Rawlins and freighted to Milk Creek by Sam Fairfield, using two bull teams.[32] Patterson observed during his 1936 visit that the position of the monument was about a quarter mile from the actual scene of the engagement. The monument has since been relocated: in 1995 the monument was closer to Rio Blanco County Road 15 and next to two monuments commemorating the Utes.

A complete list of civilian veterans has not yet been found, although several names are known (see Appendix A). William "Dad" Sherrod claimed to have been there, even though he would have been about sixty-six at the time of the battle. Joe Rankin went back to Rawlins after the incident, operated his livery business, and eventually became a United States marshal for Wyoming.[33]

One interesting anecdote is how J. W. Hugus, post sutler at Fort Fred Steele, interpreted word of his employee J. C. Davis's wound. Davis had reached the Snake River with the other battle casualties when he encountered a man headed to Milk Creek with a long wooden box on the bed of his wagon. Davis recognized the driver and asked where he was going. The driver didn't know Davis, and answered that Hugus had sent him with a casket to bring back the remains of J. C. Davis, who had been killed in the recent battle. Davis looked up and said, "You go back to Fort Steele, and tell Judge Hugus that Jack Davis ain't ready to go in his coffin yet, and tell him I'll bring in my remains myself, as soon as my foot gets a little better!"[34]

Back in Colorado, Colonel Merritt was ready and eager to press his military advantage over the Utes. However, almost as soon as the Utes abandoned the battlefield, civilian authorities began exerting their influence through governmental action. By late October 1879, Merritt received word that Secretary of the Interior Carl Schurz was attempting to establish and convene a special commission to investigate the incidents at Milk Creek and White River.

Brevet Major General Edward Hatch of the United States Army was elected president of the commission, and members included General Charles Adams of Colorado and Chief Ouray of the Ute Nation. First Lieutenant Gustavos Valois, of the Ninth Cavalry, was the recorder and legal advisor.[35] The commission met at Los Piños Agency in southern Colorado from November 12, 1879 through January 7, 1880. Members took direct testimony from White River Utes Douglas, Johnson, Sowawick, Colorow, and Captain Jack; Uncompahgre Utes Yanco, Wash, and Charley; as well as Joseph W. Brady, who was a miller at Los Piños, and Henry Jim, the White River Ute interpreter. Written statements were read from former captives Mrs. S. F. Price and Agent Meeker's wife, Mrs. A. D. Meeker, and daughter, Josephine Meeker.

One purpose of the commission was to identify those who had destroyed the Indian agency and killed eleven agency employees and freighters at White River. Utes involved only in the battle of Milk Creek escaped being charged with anything because the battle had been a military action between two armies, not an attack on civilians.

The commission chose to hold Douglas, an acknowledged head chief among the White River Utes, as well as any other Utes who could be identified as having taken part in the Meeker incident, as responsible. On December 6, 1879, twelve Utes were identified through testimony and were required to turn themselves in to stand trial. These were Chief Douglas, Chief Johnson, Wausitz (Antelope), Ebenezer, Pasone (Big Belly), Ahu-u-tu-pu-wit, Johnny (son-in-law of Douglas), Serio, Cre-pah, Tim Johnson, Thomas (a Uintah), and Paruitz.[36] Johnny surrendered, but his father-in-law, Douglas, would pay the heaviest price in answer to the charges.

The U.S. House of Representatives' Committee on Indian Affairs convened a hearing in relation to the Ute Indian outbreak scarcely a week after the Ute commission at Los Piños ended its deliberations.[37] Ouray, Chipeta (Ouray's wife), Jack, Sowawick, and other Utes left Colorado on

January 16, 1880 to testify in Washington before this House committee. Douglas accompanied them as far as Fort Leavenworth in Kansas, where he was jailed for his role in the affair. He was released 348 days later, after he had been diagnosed as insane.[38]

The Committee on Indian Affairs examined seventeen witnesses between January 15 and March 22, 1880 in an effort to determine the circumstances of the Ute outbreak. They heard from Commissioner of Indian Affairs Hayt, U.S. Cavalry officers Payne and Cherry, Governor Pitkin of Colorado, and several Utes, among others. There were more than two hundred pages of testimony.[39] But it seemed as if the fate of the Ute Nation had already been decided.

Chief Jack, who testified in Washington, was one of the most colorful participants in the Milk Creek battle. He was a well-known figure in the late nineteenth century and known by many different names in the literature on the Indian wars, including Captain Jack (not to be confused with the Modoc Indian of the same name) and Chief Jack. He was identified as Ute John when he was a scout for General Crook in 1876 during the battles of Rosebud and Slim Buttes.[40]

Jack may have rescued Captain Guy V. Henry of the Third Cavalry, who was seriously wounded during the Rosebud battle. While it is not known for sure the identity of the person or persons who saved Henry's life, one eyewitness stated that the hero was an Indian named Yute John.[41] This spelling most likely is a variation of Ute John.

Captain Henry recovered somewhat by 1879 and was part of the relief force that followed a few days behind Merritt's battalion.[42] It would be a bitter irony indeed if the Indian who saved the life of Captain Henry at Rosebud also led the force that took the life of Major Thornburgh at Milk Creek, and that Henry himself should be part of the military relief force.

Ute Jack and several other Indians who testified in Washington regarding the Meeker incident feared retribution for their role in the outbreak and were worried about losing the reservation. Jack returned to Colorado from Washington in April 1880 and eventually went north with three companions to the Wind River Reservation in Wyoming, where they used to trade.

The commander of Fort Washakie learned of Jack's presence among the Shoshone and Arapaho and wired Washington, fearing Jack's violent reputation. He received orders to arrest the Ute and sent a cavalry detachment to do the job. When Jack was ordered to surrender his rifle, he shot and killed a sergeant, then dodged into his tepee. The cavalry withdrew beyond rifle range and fired a mountain howitzer into the tepee. The shot riddled the dwelling and ended the life of Chief Jack.[43]

Ouray also was quite concerned over the United States government's plans for the Ute Nation. On March 6, 1880, before the House Committee on Indian Affairs even ended its hearing, the Treaty of 1880, dictated more than negotiated while Ouray and the others were in Washington was signed: it provided for the removal of Utes from Colorado.[44] However, it still needed to be ratified by three-fourths of the Ute males. Ouray, who was ill, urged his fellow Utes to sign the document, believing it offered the best peaceful option for the Indians.

Treaty ratification still had not been accomplished in August, when Ouray's physical condition worsened. He had neglected treatment for a hernia because he was so preoccupied with getting the necessary signatures to ratify the treaty. Everyone was worried that if Ouray died, the White River Utes would not sign the treaty. The noble diplomat passed away on August 24, 1880, before ratification.[45]

The treaty was finally ratified on September 11, 1880 amid claims of bribery and in spite of problems associated with determining valid signatures to demonstrate agreement by three-fourths of the Utes. The Utes lost their reservation, and between September 1–8, 1881, Utes were removed from Colorado to Utah across the Grand River, guarded by Colonel Ranald MacKenzie and a military escort. Chief Colorow was the last to leave the Utes' ancestral land. The *Ouray Times* described Colorow's final departure as "a dull, prosaic dash of copper at the end of a long Indian sentence."[46]

But Colorow was a popular and persistent leader who would return to Colorado time and again through the years. He was a talkative sort and would often visit tourist spots to tell tales to the visitors.[47] Once, in August 1887, he entered Colorado with a small band of Utes to hunt for game. The group was attacked by a game warden's posse, then forced by militia to return to the reservation in Utah.[48]

That was the last engagement for the Ute whose tactics forced the White River Expedition into a defensive posture on September 29, 1879. He remained a proud and defiant man to the end. Truly the spirit of Colorow, and of the nation he represents, belongs in the annals of the state that grew up in Ute country. Ironically, Chief Colorow was also known as "Colorado."

More than a century has passed since the bloodshed at Milk Creek and the abject failure of the White River Expedition. The intervening years have dimmed our perspective of the most significant military engagement between the United States and the Ute Nation. Dimmed, perhaps, but not erased. Those men who fought and died in this mountain valley were victims of confusion and poor judgment, but the sacrifices rendered on both sides of the battle line are not forgotten. Today Milk Creek cuts across the land like an old scar on the face of a warrior. The wound's pain is gone, but the memory of its sting remains.

Appendix A

Roster of Expeditionary Troops and Civilians

I have compiled a list of 191 officers and enlisted men and sixteen civilians who I believe served in the White River Expedition. Dodge's first relief force also is listed, as are the officers and companies who participated in Merritt's forced march. Soldiers' names were taken from company muster rolls for the two-month period from August 31 through October 31, 1879 and from McClellan (1979). The muster rolls are on file at the National Archives in Washington, D.C. I gathered the civilian names from a variety of sources listed in the bibliography, for example Rankin (1944, p. 99) and Owens (1937, p. 6). Those officers and enlisted men who probably did not serve in the campaign due to duty assignments, arrest, or other reasons have been omitted.

COMMAND STAFF (TOTAL 7)

- Major Thomas Tipton Thornburgh, Fourth Infantry, Commander
- Second Lieutenant Samuel A. Cherry, Company F, Fifth Cavalry, Battalion Adjutant
- Second Lieutenant Silas A. Wolf, Fourth Infantry, Acting Assistant Quartermaster and Acting Commissary of Subsistence
- Doctor Robert B. Grimes, Medical Officer
- Private Samuel W. Hagerman, Company H, Fourth Infantry, Ambulance Driver
- Private William LaParle, Company E, Third Cavalry, Hospital Steward Second Class
- Private O'Malley? (Mentioned only by Rodenbough, 1886, p. 347 and Sprague, 1957, p. 193 as orderly/ambulance driver.) It is possible that there was no such individual, because he is not listed on company muster rolls for any of the expeditionary companies. Another possibility, if O'Malley existed at all, is that he was detached from Bisbee's company and just was not mentioned on Fort Fred Steele Post Returns.

Third Cavalry, E Company (Total 50)

Captain
Joseph Lawson

Sergeant
Allen Lupton
James Montgomery
Joseph Neurohr
Thomas Nolan

Corporal
Charles F. Eichwurzel
Frank Hunter
Frank P. Secrist

Trumpeter
Andrew Downs

Farrier
William M. Schubert

Blacksmith
Seves Glande

Saddler
Peter Hollen

Private
Christopher Ayers
Daniel Ackley
Michael Brannon
John Breeman (Brennan)
Joseph Budka
Henry Burton
William H. Clark
James Conway
John Crowley
Dominick Cuff
Samuel L. Dance
Malachi W. Dillon
John Donovan
Orlando H. Duran
Thomas Ferguson
Michael Glennon
Lewis S. Grigsby
Marcus Hansen
Frederick Heinrick
Thomas Hogan
Edward Lavelle
Thomas Leahey
Thomas Lewis
William F. Lewis
John Mahoney
Robert McAdams
Thomas McNamara
Marcus Magerlein
William Miller
Willard W. Mitchell
Frank W. Morton
Joseph Patterson
William Pease
Henry Perkins
William Rice
Daniel C. Ross
Amandes M. Startzell
Charles Williams

Fifth Cavalry, D Company (Total 48)

Captain
William Jefferson Volkmar

Second Lieutenant
James Valentine Seaman Paddock

First Sergeant
Jacob Widmer

Sergeant
Charles Constantino
William Craig
John Hamilton
John S. Lawton
John Morgan

Corporal
Jacob Amberg
Francis Duggan
Edward F. Murphy

Trumpeter
Alanson H. Inman

Farrier
George Clantier

Blacksmith
Wilhelm O. Philipsen

Saddler
French Sharp

Private
Christian Ahrens
Frederick Bernhardt
Joseph Booth
James S. Burrows
Thomas Conway
John Costigan
James H. Cunningham
James W. Davis
Frank A. Douglass
Alphonse Durangean
Charles M. Gilbert
Jesse B. Hart
Nicholas W. Heeney
Michael Hogan
Francis Levalley
Michael Lynch
Thomas Lynch
William J. Marshall
James McGee
Ananias McMillan
Thomas Meguire
Thomas Mooney
Ernest Muller
Frederick Mundlien
George W.A. Peck
George Peters
Clarence E. Rand
Thomas Rogers
Charles E. Swarts
George Watson
Lut Whitbeck
Charles Wright
Enos F. Yeoman

Fifth Cavalry, F Company (Total 56)

Captain
John Scott Payne

First Sergeant
John Dolan

Sergeant
Edward P. Grimes
John Harrington
John Merrill
John A. Poppe

Corporal
John Fitzgerald
George Moquin
Hampton M. Roach

Trumpeter
John McDonald
Frederick Sutcliffe

Farrier
Samuel P. Eakle

Blacksmith
Richard C. Murn

Saddler
David Link

Wagoner
Clarence E. Carpenter
Amos D. Miller

Private
Mahlon Basford
William T. Bassett
John C. Broderick

John Burns
John W. Caldwell
Burton W. Camp
Charles J. Clark
James M. Coatney
Charles H. Cobb
Kenrick B. Combs
William Edwards
William Esser
Michael Firestone
Daniel Ford
Henry Fulk
James T. Gibbs
Richard Grinney
John M. Hatton
John Hoaxey
Spencer H. Hodges
John Hurd
Lewis Kesouth
Samuel Klingensmith
Mathew Krieger
Emil Kussman
William Marcey
Samuel McKee
Frederick C. Mimipoting
Eugene A. Patterson
Walter Peterson
Franklin H. Ritner
William Roberts
William H. Rockwell
Eugene Schickedonz
Frank E. Simmons
James W. Smith
Gottlieb Steiger
David Stephens
William Sullivan
Robert H. Walker

Fourth Infantry, E Company (Total 30)

First Lieutenant
Butler Dalaplaine Price

First Sergeant
Charles A. Dugan

Sergeant
Mitchell E. Hayes
Richard O'Sullivan

Corporal
William T. Bell
William G. Hurithberg
Michael McKenzie
William H. Nichols

Musician
John Gallen
Harvey E. Hill

Private
Lucien F. Babcock
George Carpenter
William J. Carroll
Hannibal B. Crocker
Louis Eiskamp
Jason Garrison
Charles L. Gruble
John W. Hales
Charles H. Luce
Frank Mason
George W. Masters
Theron Maynard

John Murphy
Daniel O'Brien
Robert Sanford
Joshua Scott
Martin Shea
Thomas Troxell
Charles Vailimger
John Walsh

Civilians (Total 16)

- F. E. Blake, accompanied J. C. Davis with sutler's wagon
- J. C. Davis, sutler's wagon
- John Gordon, Wagon master
- Hamilton (one of Gordon's Teamsters)
- Hornbeck (one of Gordon's Teamsters)
- Bullwhacker Jack, Teamster
- Thomas Kane, Teamster
- Charles Grafton Lowry, Guide
- Thomas McGuire, Teamster
- William McKinstry, Wagon master
- Fred Nelson, Teamster
- Joseph P. Rankin, Scout
- Rodney, Blacksmith
- Robin Saunder, Blacksmith
- William Sherrod (?)
- Emil Weber (Kid Weber)

Ninth Cavalry, D Company (Total 45)

Captain
Francis S. Dodge

First Lieutenant
Martin Briggs Hughes

First Sergeant
Albert Fowler

Sergeant
Henry Johnson
John Onley
John H. Washington

Corporal
John R. Hatchet
Gabriel Joiner
David F. Reddick

Trumpeter
Lusk Guddy

Blacksmith
William James

Saddler
Innocent Jacobs

Private
John D. Adams
George Ball
Caleb Benson
Robert Bohn
Jeremiah Bowman
Joseph Bratchet
Alexander Cook
John Crawford
Henry Dent
George H. Emanuel
Peter Ewen
Lewis Fort
George W. Goodman
Henry C. Grant
James Haskins
William F. Holliday
Madison Ingoman
Joseph Johns
John W. Johnson
Perry Johnston
Thomas Jones (1st)
Thomas Jones (2nd)
Richard Kelley
Edward Kelsey
William Langwood
Emanuel Morris
Soney Picket
David Prewit
William Reed
Edward Scott
John Shipley
Clarence Thompson
Reese Turnbull

Four Civilians
Mr. Lithgow
Sandy Mellen
John Gordon,(also on Civilians list)
unidentified person

Merritt's Relief Force: Officers and Companies

Fort D. A. Russell

Colonel
    Wesley Merritt, Fifth Cavalry

Lieutenant Colonel
    Charles E. Compton, Fifth Cavalry

Major
    Edwin V. Sumner, Fifth Cavalry

Captain
    Samuel P. Ferris, Company I, Fourth Infantry
    Robert H. Montgomery, Company B, Fifth Cavalry
    Sanford C. Kellogg, Company I, Fifth Cavalry
    John B. Babcock, Company M, Fifth Cavalry
    Jacob A. Augur, Company A, Fifth Cavalry

First Lieutenant
    William P. Hall, Fifth Cavalry Quartermaster (an ordnance officer according to Rankin[1])
    Hoel S. Bishop, Company A, Fifth Cavalry

Second Lieutenant
    Eben Swift, Fifth Cavalry, Adjutant
    Charles W. Mason, Company I, Fourth Infantry
    Henry A. Goldman, Company M, Fifth Cavalry
    Augustus C. Macomb, Company B, Fifth Cavalry
    L. C. Welborne, Company I, Fifth Cavalry

Fort Sanders

Captain
    Thomas F. Quinn, Company B, Fourth Infantry
    James P. Kimball, Medical Department

First Lieutenant
>Edward L. Bailey, Company B, Fourth Infantry
>George O. Webster, Company C, Fourth Infantry
>Henry E. Robinson, Company F, Fourth Infantry

Second Lieutenant
>Carver Howband, Company B, Fourth Infantry
>Leonard A. Lovering, Company C, Fourth Infantry
>Edward H. Browne, Company F, Fourth Infantry

Appendix B

Casualties at Milk Creek September 29–October 5, 1879

SOLDIERS AND CONTRACTORS

Military and civilian casualties were great cause for concern once the outside world learned about the Milk Creek battle. Newspapers quickly circulated unconfirmed accounts long before all of the facts were in from the front and before any correspondents were on the scene. As a result, several discrepancies emerge between primary and secondary sources. The most accurate records are assumed to be those written by actual participants once the smoke cleared at the battlefield.

The casualty list provided here (Table B.1) is largely based on two primary sources. One is a letter sent by Lieutenant Samuel A. Cherry to Lieutenant John G. Bourke, Third Cavalry aide-de-camp.[1] Cherry compiled this list on October 8, 1879 from his station at the White River Expedition's camp on Milk Creek. This was before the wounded returned to Rawlins, so he would have had direct access to each soldier and civilian who participated in the fight. His account should be particularly accurate and complete for all major battle-related injuries.

The second source is Captain J. Scott Payne's list. It was sent with a cover letter to the Assistant Adjutant General at the Department of the Platte in Omaha on October 25, 1879, after Payne returned to Fort D. A. Russell as one of the casualties.[2] Only the cover letter is dated, so it cannot be determined whether he wrote the attached list while at Milk Creek or after returning to his post. Yet one entry, discussed below, suggests Payne's letter was written shortly after the battle.

The list presented here contains the thirteen individuals from Cherry's account who were killed in action. In contrast, Payne lists guide Lowry as wounded, followed by a parenthetical note—"since died."

Payne's record of Lowry's condition suggests one of two scenarios. Either his list was compiled before the guide died sometime after 9:00 A.M. on October 5, or he was unaware of Lowry's death until after recording the casualties. The former situation is the most likely, considering Payne's responsibilities as senior officer. In either case, however, his list probably was made near the time Lowry died and before his death was common knowledge among the members of the command. Payne's official report (Appendix D), which also lists Lowry as dead, indicates that his losses had been totalled by October 5, 1879.

Major Thornburgh was the highest-ranking soldier to die in the battle. He was buried on October 22, 1879 beneath a large monument at Prospect Hill Cemetery in Omaha, Nebraska. The body of his son, George W. Thornburgh, had been exhumed from Fort Fred Steele and was placed on top of the major's coffin in the single grave. The funeral services were conducted at Trinity Cathedral.[3]

For the other troopers, the Cherry and Payne accounts of wounded-in-action differ in several respects. Cherry lists forty wounded (thirty-six soldiers and four civilians), including an unnamed freighter, who may be John Charles Davis. Payne lists thirty-nine wounded (thirty-six soldiers and three civilians), including Lowry. Cherry's account contains Private Marcus Hansen, Company E, Third Cavalry and Train Blacksmith Rodney, while Payne's does not. Payne also omits the unnamed freighter. On the other hand, Payne lists Private James Conway, Company E, Third Cavalry, but Cherry doesn't.

Each casualty is included in the following list whether he was mentioned by only one officer or by both. This comprehensive list accounts for forty-one wounded men (thirty-seven soldiers and four civilians). Additional names also are included from other sources, and discussion of these follows. Interestingly, guns are the only weapons mentioned to have inflicted wounds; it is likely that bows and arrows may not have been used in the battle.

Two Denver correspondents published a casualty list on November 25, 1879, based in part on newspaper accounts from the *Denver Tribune*, *New York Herald*, and *Chicago Tribune*.[4] They mention twelve killed (which excludes Lowry) and forty-two wounded. This reference seems to confuse the spelling of two given names. These correspondents list a James Patterson, Company E, Third Cavalry and a James Donovan, Company E, Third Cavalry, whom I believe to be Joseph Patterson, Company E, Third Cavalry and John Donovan, Company E, Third Cavalry, respectively, as mentioned in the primary sources.

Not all differences can be explained by spelling variations. The sequence in which these authors list the wounded illustrates how they came up with more casualties than either Cherry or Payne. In their account, a Private Just is listed directly above a Private Gibbs, both from Company F, Fifth Cavalry. This is probably an error either on the list they used or in their transcription. The names Just and Gibbs likely refer to the given name and surname of Private James Gibbs, also spelled James T. Gibbs, J. T. Gibbs, or Jas. T. Gibbs.

Similar discrepancies occur in their listing Private Gattlied directly above Private Steiger, probably for Gottleib Steiger, Company F, Fifth Cavalry; Private Nicholas directly above Private Heeney, for Nicholas W. Heeney, Company D, Fifth Cavalry; Private Thomas above Private Lynch, for Thomas Lynch, Company D, Fifth Cavalry; and Private Eugene Shiek above Private Edouz, for Eugene Schickedonz, Company F, Fifth Cavalry. Combining all of these given names and surnames reduces the wounded-in-action total to thirty-seven, which corresponds to the comprehensive total of soldiers from the two primary lists. The two correspondents did not list wounded freighters, teamsters, or other civilians.

The above sources account for every soldier on the casualty list presented below except for Sergeant John Lawton, Company D, Fifth Cavalry and Private Walter Peterson, Company F, Fifth Cavalry. On October 21, 1879, the *Cheyenne Daily Leader* documented the arrival at Camp Carlin of some of the wounded from Milk Creek while they were in transit to the post hospital at Fort D. A. Russell. The paper mentions the actual injuries or maladies sustained by each arrival and includes Lawton and Peterson.[5]

Sergeant John Lawton is listed with a crushed foot and Private Walter Peterson as having contracted typho-malarial fever at the front. These soldiers might not have been listed as casualties by Cherry or Payne if their conditions were not inflicted by the Indians. Lawton could have injured his foot during a period outside of combat and Peterson could just have become ill. It is surprising that more soldiers are not described as having a fever, considering that their drinking water was from stagnant pools with scores of dead animals nearby.

The last name in the following list is Robin Sanders, a civilian blacksmith from Camp Carlin who was wounded in the right leg.[6] This blacksmith may be the Rodney mentioned in Cherry's account, but both have been retained on the list because the two names do not totally correspond.

Rankin also mentions three names that are not included here.[7] One is Private J. H. Nicholas, who was wounded in the side. Private Nicholas might be a mistaken translation for Nicholas Heeney, due to the similarity in names, initials, and company assignment. Their wounds, however, are different. Since no J. H. Nicholas appears on the muster rolls, he is not listed as a casualty. The second is a Private Evershell, who was wounded twice at the entrenchment. This soldier is likely Private Eichwurzel, Company E, Third Cavalry, who was already identified by Cherry and Payne. The last is Private Oscar Cass, who was slightly wounded early in the battle, about the time Michael Firestone and Amos D. Miller were killed. Rankin does not mention Cass's company, but he apparently was in Payne's skirmish line, so Company F, Fifth Cavalry seems most likely, even though Cass is not on the muster roll. Since Payne does not mention Cass's injury, the wound, if it occurred at all, probably was superficial. There is no reason to believe that every cut and scratch would be reported on official casualty lists.

The black troops of Company D, Ninth Cavalry arrived at the barricade on the morning of October 2. They exposed themselves to every hot spot on the battlefield from that morning through the end of the siege on the morning of October 5. Miraculously, every one of them survived the encounter with hardly a scratch.[8]

Captain Payne also noted specific details of the casualties in an account written the year after the battle. He said in a footnote, "The losses sustained by the troops in this bloody affair were proportionately greater than those suffered by either Federal or Confederate army in any battle of the late civil war, and embraced more than one-third of the whole number of men engaged."[9] Presumably Payne's "whole number of men engaged" did not include Dodge's company. Adding Company D, Ninth Cavalry to the total would have reduced the percentage of casualties to somewhat less than one-third.

Payne went on to summarize casualties by company. Five enlisted men were killed and thirteen wounded in Company F, Fifth Cavalry. Three enlisted men were killed and four wounded in Company D, Fifth Cavalry. One enlisted man was killed and seventeen wounded in Company E, Third Cavalry. A wagon master, a teamster, and a guide also were killed. Two teamsters and one employee of Mr. John Gordon were wounded. According to Payne, thirty-seven Indians were killed, and many more doubtless were wounded.[10] These figures compare exactly with the list for soldiers in Payne's Company F but are short in the totals for wounded from each of the other companies and for the civilians.

Rankin mentions that thirty-eight men were wounded, most only slightly. He states that some of the most painful, though not serious, injuries were an ankle wound on Sergeant James Montgomery, Company E, Third Cavalry, a thigh wound on Private John Mahoney, Company E, Third Cavalry, an arm wound on Private F. Simmons, Company F, Fifth Cavalry, a heel wound on John C. Davis, who was in charge of sutler supplies for J. W. Hugus, and a skin abrasion over Captain J. Scott Payne's abdomen.[11]

INDIANS

Indian casualties are much more difficult to assess because fewer detailed accounts have been documented. Special Agent Charles Adams provides one of the more reliable counts. He met with all of the chiefs who had engaged in the Milk Creek battle less than a month after the incident. The Indians discussed their casualties, and on October 24, 1879 Adams sent a telegram summarizing these talks to Secretary of the Interior Carl Schurz.[12] Adams said that the Indians acknowledged twenty-three casualties during the first day of the battle. These Indians either were killed outright or died from their wounds. The Utes sustained fourteen additional fatalities in subsequent fighting against the employees at the agency and the various freighters on the road. The combined total killed-in-action is thirty-seven.

On March 20, 1880, Ute Chief Jack testified before the Committee of Indian Affairs of the U.S. House of Representatives. When asked by the committee chairman how many Indians were killed in the fight with the soldiers, Jack talked extensively with Chief Ouray before answering. Then he indicated that nineteen were killed and seven were missing or unaccounted for.[13]

The two Denver correspondents cite the total of twenty-three killed during the battle with the soldiers. They add that two others were severely wounded and an undetermined number slightly wounded.[14] The general of the army reports total Indian losses at thirty-nine, which probably includes casualties from all related battles and slightly errs to excess.[15]

The names of some of the Indians killed in action are available from Indian testimony. The White River Ute Commission gathered evidence concerning the conflict between October 26, 1879 and January 7, 1880. Several Indians testified during these proceedings. Colorow identified seventeen killed in action and two missing as of December 1, 1879. The fatalities include: Tah-titz, Wah-cha-pe-gatz, Chu-ca-watz, Uah-pa-chatz, Ca-tol-seu, Cat-su-atz, Wa-wa-gutz, Tet-putz-sin-iah, Yan-cap, Pager, Wa-pa-qua, Pou-shun-lo, Son-ie-er-atz, Tu-rah, Pah-wintz, Tu-wu-ick, and Poh-neh-atz. Pou-witz and Pat-soock were still missing at the time of his testimony.[16] The two Denver newsmen identify only three fatalities: Ouray's nephew; Wattsconavot, meaning Doctor; and Catolowop, meaning Fat Man.[17]

Livestock

Historical sources are vague about the total number of livestock lost by the White River Expedition. Several authorities mention one figure or another, but it is difficult to determine where they got their information. Some primary records, however, yield a few clues.

Post returns for Fort D. A. Russell indicated that the Fifth Cavalry companies lost 110 horses during the engagement. Company E of the Third Cavalry lost all fifty head of their riding stock. The Ninth Cavalry relief company lost thirty-eight saddle horses, all but four of their original mounts. These figures suggest that the expedition left behind at least 198 dead horses.[18]

Indians killed or drove off all of John Gordon's fifty-six oxen. A total count of mules, however, is a more difficult figure to establish. Documentary evidence suggests that the quartermaster wagons were each pulled by a six-mule team. The sutler wagon and other vehicles may have used six-mule teams too. Thornburgh had gathered twenty-five wagons from Rock Creek, but some authors argue that he actually began the expedition with thirty-three. The major left eight wagons at Fortification Creek and moved on with the remainder. Therefore, he may have entered Milk Creek Valley with anywhere from seventeen to twenty-five wagons. At least two were lost south of the creek when the Indians attacked, so troopers only corralled between fifteen and twenty-three wagons. Most early sources indicate that from fifteen to seventeen wagons were used in the barricade. If all of the mules were killed by October 5, we can assume that there were as many as ninety to 102 carcasses. If twenty-five wagons were used, 150 mules may have died. One source, however, indicates that twelve mules survived past October 3.[19] At a minimum, then, around three hundred animals lay dead near the barricade when Merritt arrived.

Table B.1

Casualties at Milk Creek, September 29, 1879–October 5, 1879

Name	Rank	Co.	Regiment	Remarks
KILLED				
1. Thornburgh, Thomas T.	Maj.		4th Inf.	Buried at Omaha, NE
2. Cuff, Dominick	Pvt.	E	3rd Cav.	Buried at Milk Creek
3. Lynch, Michael	Pvt.	D	5th Cav.	Buried at Milk Creek
4. Mooney, Thomas	Pvt.	D	5th Cav.	Buried at Milk Creek
5. Wright, Charles	Pvt.	D	5th Cav.	Buried at Milk Creek
6. Dolan, John	1 Sgt.	F	5th Cav.	Buried at Milk Creek
7. Burns, John	Pvt.	F	5th Cav.	Buried at Milk Creek
8. Firestone, Michael	Pvt.	F	5th Cav.	Buried at Milk Creek
9. Miller, Amos D.	Wgnr.	F	5th Cav.	Buried at Milk Creek
10. McKee, Samuel	Pvt.	F	5th Cav.	Buried at Milk Creek
11. Lowry, C. Grafton	Guide		Civilian	Buried at Milk Creek
12. McGuire, Thomas	Teamster		Civilian	Buried at Milk Creek
13. McKinstry, William	Wagon mastr		Civilian	Buried at Milk Creek
WOUNDED				
1. Lupton, Allen	Sgt.	E	3rd Cav.	Gunshot, right leg
2. Montgomery, James	Sgt.	E	3rd Cav.	Gunshot, left ankle
3. Eichwurzel, Chas. F.	Cpl.	E	3rd Cav.	Gunshot, right hand, left arm
4. Hunter, Frank	Cpl.	E	3rd Cav.	Gunshot, right foot
5. Budka, Joseph	Pvt.	E	3rd Cav.	Slight gunshot, in neck
6. Clark, William H.	Pvt.	E	3rd Cav.	Wound in left side
7. Conway, James	Pvt.	E	3rd Cav.	Flesh wound, left temple

Appendix B

Name	Rank	Co.	Regiment	Remarks
8. Crowley, John	Pvt.	E	3rd Cav.	Gunshot, left side of head
9. Donovan, John	Pvt.	E	3rd Cav.	Gunshot, left foot
10. Duran, Orlando H.	Pvt.	E	3rd Cav.	Gunshot, right arm
11. Ferguson, Thomas	Pvt.	E	3rd Cav.	Flesh wound, left side
12. Hansen, Marcus	Pvt.	E	3rd Cav.	Wounded
13. Lavelle, Edward	Pvt.	E	3rd Cav.	Gunshot, right side, back
14. Lewis, Thomas	Pvt.	E	3rd Cav.	Gunshot, right foot
15. Mahoney, John	Pvt.	E	3rd Cav.	Gunshot, right leg/thigh
16. Mitchell, Willard W.	Pvt.	E	3rd Cav.	Gunshot, left leg
17. McNamara, Thomas	Pvt.	E	3rd Cav.	Flesh wound, right thigh
18. Patterson, Joseph	Pvt.	E	3rd Cav.	Gunshot, left leg
19. Schubert, William M.	Far.	E	3rd Cav.	Gunshot, left thigh, left arm
20. Paddock, James V.S.	2Lt.	D	5th Cav.	Flesh wound, right hip, right thigh
21. Lawton, John S.	Sgt.	D	5th Cav.	Right foot crushed/sprained
22. Bernhardt, Frederick	Pvt.	D	5th Cav.	Shot through right hand
23. Heeney, Nicholas W.	Pvt.	D	5th Cav.	Shot through left ankle
24. Lynch, Thomas	Pvt.	D	5th Cav.	Shot through right cheek—mouth to ear
25. Muller, Ernest	Pvt.	D	5th Cav.	Slight scalp wound above left ear
26. Payne, John Scott	Capt.	F	5th Cav.	Skin abrasion over abdomen, gunshot left shoulder/arm
27. Merrill, John	Sgt.	F	5th Cav.	Gunshot, left shoulder
28. Esser, William	Pvt.	F	5th Cav.	Gunshot, face and back of neck, mouth, cheek
29. Gibbs, James T.	Pvt.	F	5th Cav.	Wounds in left foot
30. Hoaxey, John	Pvt.	F	5th Cav.	Wounded
31. Kussman, Emil	Pvt.	F	5th Cav.	Gunshot, left arm (fracture) & side
32. Patterson, Eugene	Pvt.	F	5th Cav.	Gunshot, right leg, foot, and ankle

Appendix B

Name	Rank	Co.	Regiment	Remarks
33. Peterson, Walter	Pvt.	F	5th Cav.	Wounded from the front; typho-malarial fever
34. Schickedonz, Eugene	Pvt.	F	5th Cav.	Gunshot, right arm
35. Simmons, Frank E.	Pvt.	F	5th Cav.	Gunshot, left breast/arm, right breast
36. Steiger, Gottleib	Pvt.	F	5th Cav.	Gunshot, right leg
37. McDonald, John	Tpt.	F	5th Cav.	Gunshot, left thigh/hip
38. Sutcliffe, Frederick	Tpt.	F	5th Cav.	Gunshot, right leg
39. Grimes, Robert B.	AAS		Command	Flesh wound, left shoulder
40. Davis, John Chas.	Sutler		Civilian	Heel
41. Kane, Thomas (Cain)	Teamster		Civilian	Left breast
42. Nelson, Fred	Teamster		Civilian	Left shoulder and leg
43. Rodney	Blacksmth		Civilian	Wounded
44. Saunder (Sanders), Robin	Blacksmth		Civilian	Right leg

Appendix C

Citations for Bravery at the Battle of Milk Creek

Throughout history, different cultures have recognized battlefield valor in many ways. Perceived victors, however, generate much more publicity than the vanquished. It is difficult to determine if any Ute warriors were singled out for bravery, because the Utes left Milk Creek in defeat. They probably avoided overt commendation because notoriety might have brought unwanted attention from the federal government.

In contrast, bravery was acknowledged by several means for United States soldiers at Milk Creek in 1879. At least thirty participants were honored, making it one of the most decorated battles of the Indian wars (Table C.1). Eleven soldiers received the Medal of Honor, the nation's highest award for conspicuous gallantry in battle.[1] None of the Medal of Honor recipients were from either of the companies detached from Fort Fred Steele: Company E, Third Cavalry or Company E, Fourth Infantry.

Five soldiers from Company F, Fifth Cavalry were among those who received Medals of Honor: Grimes, Moquin, Poppe, Roach, and Merrill. The first four of these soldiers were issued medals on January 27, 1880, less than four months after the battle. They were the first Milk Creek veterans to receive citations. Merrill's medal was issued on June 7, 1880.

These five soldiers had each performed different acts of courage. Sergeant Edward P. Grimes, born in Dover, New Hampshire, was cited for having voluntarily brought up a supply of ammunition while under heavy fire at nearly point-blank range. The skirmishers he reached were almost out of ammunition at the time and were surrounded on three sides by the enemy. Grimes's actions were on the first day of battle, when Captain

Lawson's Company E, Third Cavalry needed cartridges during their retreat to the wagon circle.

Corporal George Moquin was born in New York, New York. His citation was simply for gallantry in action between September 29–October 5, 1879. Moquin had volunteered as one of the couriers on the night of September 29, and it probably is for this service that he received the medal.[2]

Sergeant John A. Poppe was born in Cincinnati, Ohio. His medal also was awarded for unspecified gallantry in action between September 29–October 5, 1879. During the early afternoon of September 29, Payne had sent Poppe with a ten-man detachment to help Lawson's and Cherry's retreat.[3] Poppe also single-handedly lit the grass around the wagons to set a counter-fire against the Indians blaze.[4]

Corporal Hampton M. Roach was born in Concord, Louisiana. Roach was particularly active at the entrenchment north of the creek. He erected breastworks under enemy fire and kept the command supplied with water on three consecutive nights. Water details were constantly exposed to close-range fire from Indians lying in ambush along the streambanks. Although he was a young junior corporal, Roach was given full charge of the water supply.[5]

Sergeant John Merrill, born in New York, New York, received his medal for remaining on duty and rendering gallant and valuable service in spite of a painful wound. Merrill had been shot in the left shoulder. Most of the wounded were protected in pits dug behind the wagons at the entrenchment, but Merrill apparently elected to help defend the barricade position rather than remain in the makeshift field hospital.

Four Medals of Honor were awarded to soldiers from Company D, Fifth Cavalry. These men were Murphy, Widmer, Lawton, and Philipsen. Their company had been in charge of the wagon train north of Milk Creek at the time of the initial engagement.

Corporal Edward F. Murphy, born in Wayne County, Pennsylvania, was cited for gallantry in action. His medal was awarded on April 23, 1880. Murphy was the second soldier to volunteer as a courier on the evening of September 29.[6]

Widmer and Lawton were honored for volunteering to accompany a small detachment on a very dangerous mission. First Sergeant Jacob

Widmer, born in Germany, was issued his medal on May 4, 1880. Sergeant John S. Lawton, born in Bristol, Rhode Island, was issued his medal on June 7, 1880. Lawton's citation also specified coolness and steadiness under fire. Lawton was awarded his medal for gallantry during the first day of battle, when he took a five-man squad to the rescue of Lawson and Cherry. Perhaps this was part of Poppe's larger detachment or some unrelated reinforcement effort. According to Theo. F. Rodenbough, the detachment was exposed to heavy fire and lost three men before reaching the shelter of the trenches.[7] If there were fatalities during this rescue, it must have been right near the trenches, because none of this detachment was left on the battlefield. Widmer may have been the other survivor of this squad.

Blacksmith Wilhelm O. Philipsen, born in Germany, received his medal for voluntarily joining with nine others to attack and capture a strong position held by the Indians. The medal was issued December 12, 1894. Philipsen's gallantry probably was shown while serving as a member of Poppe's detachment on September 29.

The two remaining Medals of Honor were awarded to soldiers from Company D, Ninth Cavalry. This troop rode to the battle from Twenty-Mile Park and entered the entrenchment on the morning of October 2, 1879.

The first of these to receive a medal was Sergeant Henry Johnson, who was born in Boynton, Virginia. As sergeant of the guard, Johnson voluntarily left fortified shelter while under heavy fire at close range and made the rounds of the pits to instruct the sentries. He also fought his way to Milk Creek and back as part of a skirmish line to bring water to the wounded and the rest of the besieged soldiers. Sergeant Johnson received his medal on September 22, 1890.

Preston Amos includes Johnson's exploits at the battle of Milk Creek with the biographies of black medal recipients from other engagements. Henry was one of eighteen black soldiers to receive the congressional Medal of Honor between 1870 and 1890. He was the third to be cited for bravery in 1879. According to Amos, Henry was a twenty-one-year-old laborer when he enlisted in 1867. Johnson retired thirty-one years later and settled in Washington, D.C. He died in 1904 and was buried in Arlington National Cemetery.[8]

The last Medal of Honor for bravery at Milk Creek was issued on April 2, 1898, almost nineteen years after the battle. It was awarded to Captain Francis S. Dodge, who led Company D, Ninth Cavalry during the campaign. The citation was for commanding a force of forty men who rode all night to the relief of the besieged White River Expedition. Dodge reached the field at daylight on October 2 and joined in the action, fighting for three days.

Captain Dodge was born on September 11, 1842 in Danvers, Massachusetts, and eventually entered military service from there. Dodge had high praise for the performance of his black troops, who accomplished a forced march of seventy miles with little food and no sleep.[9]

Some contemporary observers believed that political influence played a part in determining who received recognition for bravery during the campaign. The absence from the medal roster of any soldier from Company E, Third Cavalry was great cause for concern in Wyoming. Concern was particularly acute in reference to the company commander, Captain Joseph J. Lawson, for his exemplary performance at Milk Creek. Lawson received no federal recognition, even though commanding officer Payne singled Lawson out as the first entry in his official report that lists soldiers who exhibited conspicuous gallantry (Appendix D). It was admittedly difficult for any officer to receive the Medal of Honor during this period following the Civil War, apparently because of a lack of understanding of an amendment to the enabling statute, but other forms of recognition were possible. One territorial newspaper wrote of Lawson:

> His soldierly qualities under fire in the battle field, were not a match for political intrigue and a knowledge of the ways of the lobby, and failing recognition in the official documents of the War department, it remained for both houses of the legislature of Wyoming to attest and promulgate, in unanimous resolutions, a deserved recognition for his coolness and bravery in saving the entire band from annihilation by the Utes.[10]

This resolution supposedly was conferred by Wyoming's Sixth Legislative Assembly during their 1879 session, which began on November 4 and closed sometime after Christmas. However, it is not mentioned in the session books for 1879, which would be the logical source, because the next legislature after 1879 was not elected until November 1880, and these newly elected legislators did not convene until January 1882, eleven months after the newspaper article was written.[11] The session book for this year does not appear to list all of the joint resolutions and memorials that may have passed in the legislature. Some numbers in the sequence seem to be missing, and one of these could have been Lawson's formal recognition. Wyoming's Sixth Legislative Assembly also recognized Captain Payne and Lieutenants Cherry and Paddock with similar joint resolutions of thanks for bravery, heroic conduct, and efficient services during the engagement and subsequent siege.[12]

Albert F. Gleim lists sixteen soldiers who were awarded the Certificate of Merit for gallantry in action against the Utes, although only fifteen are mentioned here because one Company E, Third Cavalry recipient, John Maloney, is considered to be a duplicate of John Mahoney. No soldier by the name of Maloney exists on the Company E, Third Cavalry muster roll for the period in question.[13] Certificate of Merit recipients were members of a fairly elite group, because only fifty-nine such awards were presented from 1874 to 1891.[14]

More Certificates of Merit were issued for bravery at Milk Creek than for any other battle during this period, and even more would have been awarded if Captain Joseph Lawson had had his way. Captain Lawson had submitted the names of twenty-five of the forty-nine Company E, Third Cavalry troopers for this acknowledgment. But General Sherman returned the recommendations, believing that 51 percent of the troop was too large a number. The general asked Lawson to be more discriminating in his assessment and resubmit nominations only for the most worthy. Lawson returned recommendations for four troopers, who were duly approved, and who were issued certificates in December 1881.[15] Additional troopers from the company received later certificates.

Eventually, seven Certificates of Merit went to Company E, Third Cavalry troopers (not counting Maloney); seven went to Company F of the Fifth Cavalry; and one went to a private from Company H, Fourth Infantry.[16]

Company E, Third Cavalry held the right flank and was the last company to retreat, along with Cherry's small detachment. Brennan,

Crowley, Mahoney, McNamara, and Joseph Patterson were honored for their brave fighting and assistance to the wounded during the retreat. All of these men, except Brennan, were wounded themselves. Mahoney's citation was issued on December 13, 1881 and also credited him for "fighting alone unaided for three quarters of an hour over every inch of the ground for nearly a mile, against an enemy force 10 times their number."[17]

Mahoney was born in the village of Kilcrohane, County Cork, Ireland on December 23, 1853.[18] He immigrated to the United States when he was eighteen and later joined the army. His enlistment ended in 1882, and he settled in Rawlins, Wyoming to work as a clerk in the Pacific House. He soon became involved in the sheep industry and entered partnership with A. M. Startzell, another Company E, Third Cavalry veteran of the Milk Creek battle. Mahoney was quite active in public affairs and even served a term as a state senator. He died in Rawlins on June 24, 1931, after complications set in from his old battle wound received at Milk Creek.[19]

The final two Company E, Third Cavalry certificate recipients were Thomas Hogan (whose real name was L'Near Rumsey) and Thomas Lewis. Both of these men were honored for unspecified bravery.

Company F, Fifth Cavalry exploits were a bit more varied. Carpenter had saved Payne's life by bringing him a remount after the captain lost his own horse at the beginning of the charge to the knoll. Clark rescued a wounded comrade from near enemy lines, but the injured man died on route. The fatality must have been Firestone, because Eugene Patterson allegedly went after Miller. Combs, Klingensmith, and McDonald also were recognized for assisting wounded comrades under heavy fire during the retreat. Eakle and Eugene Patterson had been isolated in exposed positions and were being closed off by Indians, but they each fought back to the wagons on foot. Patterson also broke up the carbines that had been abandoned by the wounded so that Indians couldn't use them. His bravery continued during the siege at the barricade.

Private Samuel W. Hagerman was the lone infantryman to receive an award for bravery at Milk Creek. His certificate was given for

> special bravery and good conduct, in action against hostile
> Ute Indians, while driving an ambulance containing two

sick soldiers and cut off from the train by 10 or 12 Indians, he fought his way through, delivering the sick at the train, then volunteered to charge the bluffs with the men of Troop D, 5th Cavalry, doing good fighting, and exhibiting conspicuous coolness in building breastworks and fighting off the fire which started to burn out the troops.[20]

Hagerman had received four endorsements from officers who knew him and his qualifications.[21] Captain William H. Bisbee, Fourth Infantry, who took over command of Fort Fred Steele upon the death of Major Thornburgh, forwarded endorsements for Hagerman from himself and three eyewitnesses from the campaign. Captain Lawson, Company E, Third Cavalry, Acting Assistant Surgeon Robert Grimes, and Second Lieutenant James Paddock, Company D, Fifth Cavalry all supported the recognition. Hagerman not only had preserved the ambulance, the men therein, saved his mule team from capture, and fought the fire, but he also took part in water detail.

An act of Congress approved July 9, 1918 provided for a Distinguished Service Medal to be issued in lieu of the Certificate of Merit.[22] Four Milk Creek veterans who had earned certificates also were issued these medals: Private Kenrick B. Combs, Company F, Fifth Cavalry, born in Stafford County, Virginia; Private Thomas Hogan, Company E, Third Cavalry, born in Wayne County, Michigan; Private Samuel Klingensmith, Company F, Fifth Cavalry, born in West Newton, Pennsylvania but who entered service from Greensburg, Pennsylvania; and Private Thomas Lewis, Company E, Third Cavalry, born in Burlington, Vermont.

M. Wilson Rankin mentions War Department medals awarded to two soldiers for whom no additional references yet substantiate the claim.[23] The first was John Donovan, Company E, Third Cavalry, who allegedly carried ammunition to Lawson's retreating troop and was the first to discover Thornburgh's body. The second soldier mentioned was Private James Hickman (unlisted on muster rolls), who allegedly stripped flaming canvas from one of the wagons outside the corral during the Indians' offensive in the middle of the afternoon on the first day.

The Indian Wars Campaign Medal was authorized in 1905.[24] Thirty-six names on the list of recipients resemble names of Milk Creek veterans and are included below along with their campaign medal number (Table C.2). The tabulated names are spelled as they appear in J. M. Carroll's *The Indian Wars Campaign Medal: Its History And Its Recipients*. These closely match names on the muster rolls for the fall of 1879 (Appendix A). The table includes names that match between the two lists when the middle initial is included, and those whose names include a middle initial on one list but not on the other. Names whose middle initials do not match are not included.

Not all of these are Milk Creek veterans, but some certainly are. Silas A. Wolf, Wilhelm O. Philipsen, and Butler D. Price are examples of good matches. In other cases, some names show up more than once, so only one of the recipients could be from Milk Creek. Also, many veterans are listed from different regiments than those involved at Milk Creek, but transfers subsequent to the battle prevent the use of this information to confirm identities. More biographical information is needed on each recipient before a more accurate accounting can be completed.

Recognition may have been conveyed to other soldiers who fought at Milk Creek, but additional records have not been reviewed, if any exist. Other accounts also offer different totals. For instance, Sprague states that "twelve rank and file heroes at Milk Creek received Medals of Honor or Certificates of Merit soon, but it was not until the 1890s that Captain Payne, Captain Dodge and Major Thornburgh (posthumously) were cited by Congress for gallantry."[25] Records do not indicate that either Thornburgh or Payne ever received either the congressional Medal of Honor or a Certificate of Merit.

Table C.1

Awards for Bravery at the Battle of Milk Creek, Colorado

Name	Company	Award
Brennan, John, Pvt.	E 3rd Cav.	Certificate of Merit
Carpenter, Clarence, Wagoner	F 5th Cav.	Certificate of Merit
Cherry, Samuel A., 2nd Lt.	F 5th Cav.	Legislative Resolut.
Clark, Charles J., Pvt.	F 5th Cav.	Certificate of Merit
Combs, Kenrick B., Pvt.	F 5th Cav.	Disting. Service Medal
Crowley, John, Pvt.	E 3rd Cav.	Certificate of Merit
Dodge, Francis S., Capt.	D 9th Cav.	Medal of Honor
Eakle, Samuel P., Farrier	F 5th Cav.	Certificate of Merit
Grimes, Edward P., Serg.	F 5th Cav.	Medal of Honor
Hagerman, Samuel W., Pvt.	H 4th Inf.	Certificate of Merit
Hogan, Thomas, Pvt. (Rumsey)	E 3rd Cav.	Disting. Service Medal
Johnson, Henry, Serg.	D 9th Cav.	Medal of Honor
Klingensmith, Samuel, Pvt.	F 5th Cav.	Disting. Service Medal
Lawson, Joseph J., Capt.	E 3rd Cav.	Legislative Resolut.
Lawton, John S., Serg.	D 5th Cav.	Medal of Honor
Lewis, Thomas, Pvt.	E 3rd Cav.	Disting. Service Medal
Mahoney, John, Pvt.	E 3rd Cav.	Certificate of Merit
McDonald, John, Trumpeter	F 5th Cav.	Certificate of Merit
McNamara, Thomas, Pvt.	E 3rd Cav.	Certificate of Merit
Merrill, John, Serg.	F 5th Cav.	Medal of Honor
Moquin, George, Corp.	F 5th Cav.	Medal of Honor
Murphy, Edward F., Corp.	D 5th Cav.	Medal of Honor
Paddock, James V. S., 2nd Lt.	D 5th Cav.	Legislative Resolut.

Name	Company	Award
Patterson, Eugene, Pvt.	F 5th Cav.	Certificate of Merit
Patterson, Joseph, Pvt.	E 3rd Cav.	Certificate of Merit
Payne, J. Scott, Capt.	F 5th Cav.	Legislative Resolut.
Philipsen, Wilhelm O., Blksm.	D 5th Cav.	Medal of Honor
Poppe, John A., Serg.	F 5th Cav.	Medal of Honor
Roach, Hampton M., Corp.	F 5th Cav.	Medal of Honor
Widmer, Jacob, 1st Serg.	D 5th Cav.	Medal of Honor

Table C.2

Selected Indian Wars Campaign Medal Recipients

Name	Medal No.	Name	Medal No.
Silas A. Wolf	522	Charles M. Wright	822
William Clark	394	Edward P. Grimes	1095
Marcus H. Hanson	1862	John J. Fitzgerald	1290
Thomas Hogan	1157	Hampton M. Roach	325
Thomas J. Lewis	563	John B. McDonald	1358
Thomas Lewis	1107	John J. Burns	853
William Lewis	1257	John W. Caldwell	963
William H. Miller	299	Robert H. Walker	1799
William H. Miller	1678	Butler D. Price	1189
Frank Morton	1050	John Murphy	434
Charles A. Williams	701	John Murphy	1046
Charles E. Williams	1418	John T. K. Walsh	1715
Charles Williams	1621	Caleb Benson	1485
John Hamilton	199	Thomas H. Jones	821
John Hamilton	1105	William I. Reed	543
Wilhelm O. Philipsen	972	John Shipley	1075
Charles M. Gilbert	1036	John Shipley	1218
John Adam	628/1786 (replaced)	Frank A. Douglas	1266

Appendix D

Official Reports And Selected Correspondence Regarding the Milk Creek Battle

OFFICIAL REPORT OF CAPTAIN J. SCOTT PAYNE[1]

> Headquarters White River Expedition
> Camp on Milk River Col.
> October 5, 1879

To the Assistant Adjutant General
Department of the Platte
Fort Omaha Neb.

Sir:

I have the honor to submit the following report of the operations of this command from the date of its departure from Fort Fred Steele Wyo. to this present time.

The expedition composed of Company "E" 3rd Cavalry (Lawson's), "D" 5th Cavalry (Paddock's), "F" 5th Cavalry (Payne's) and "E" 4th Infantry (Price's) commanded by Major T. T. Thornberg 4th Infantry left Fort Steele on the 21st of September and marched to Fortification Creek Col. upon which stream it encamped on the 25th ult. Here Price with his Company was detached and left for the purpose of establishing a supply camp, and a part of the wagon train sent to Rawlins for rations and forage, the Cavalry battalion proceeding to Bear River where it went into camp on the night of the 26th. During the afternoon of this date several Ute Indians of prominence, among them Jack & Saarwick of the White River Agency and Unque an Uncompahgre, who had a pass from the

Agent at Los Pinos, came into our camp, talked freely with the Commanding Officer Major Thornburgh and departed about nightfall apparently in good humor and well satisfied at what they had learned.

At Williams Fork of Bear River, where we camped on the 27th one Eskridge, an Agency employe since killed as we have been informed by Indians near the Agency, came in accompanied by Colororo, the Indian interpreter "Henry," "Bummer Jim," and other Utes with a dispatch from Mr. Meeker to Major Thornburgh. A reply was sent to Mr. Meeker by the Indian, Eskridge remaining with the command until the next afternoon when he was dispatched to the Agency with a second communication to Mr. Meeker.

Copies of this correspondence were forwarded by Major Thornburgh to your Headquarters and it is only necessary to refer to them here. It was observed that Colorow and the Indians with him in our camp on the 27th, were surly and not disposed to talk, but upon departing they appeared to be better satisfied and slight if any apprehension was entertained of the rapidly approaching trouble.

We camped the 28th on Deer Creek and began our march the morning of the 29th at 6:30 o'clock, reaching Milk river about 10 o'clock.

After watering the cavalry horses at the stream, two companies "E" 3rd and "F" 5th Cavalry under the immediate command of Major Thornburgh turned off the road, taking a trail that bore away to the left, while "D" 5th Cavalry remained with the train which followed at a distance of perhaps a mile. At this time no signs of Indians had been observed by Major Thornburgh, except a freshly started fire in the bottom grass, an incident with which we had grown so familiar that no apprehension were excited by it. Lieut. Cherry, Adjutant of the command accompanied by guide Rankin and a small party of soldiers, was in the advance and upon passing over some high ground intermediate between the road which we had left and the trail, discovered the Indians in heavy force drawn up in line of battle or more correctly speaking, lying in ambush along the high ridges which completely covered and commanded the road. With a quick and soldierly perception of the situation Lieut. Cherry turned back & made signals for the command to retrace its steps, just as the leading company "F" 5th Cavalry was decending [*sic*] a ridge into the valley beyond. "F" Company was immediately conducted to the side of the hill on its' left flank. While "E" 3rd Cavalry was halted on the high ground it occupied and both Companies once dismounted and deployed by Major Thornburgh's orders as skirmishers "E" 3rd Cavalry on the right along the crest of the ridge rt. [?] and "F" Company 5th Cavalry as well up the side of the hill–which constantly ascending, stretched away indefinitely–as the nature of the ground would permit.

Our line at this time resembled the letter "V" the point towards the Indians and that portion of it formed by "F" Company 5th Cavalry projecting considerably beyond the point of junction and being deflected to the left so as to prevent the enemy from turning that flank. At this time attempts were made by Major Thornburgh in person and by Lieut. Cherry to communicate with the Indians but efforts in this direction were met by a shot and at once a hot fire was opened upon us, and the fight began all along our lines.

The Indians had displayed admirable skill in the selection of the ground upon which to give us battle, and it was soon apparent that our position in the face of an enemy superbly armed and greatly our superior in force, was untenable.

With sound judgement and a quick and thorough perception of the situation, Major Thornburgh determined to form a junction with Co. "D" 5th Cavalry which was protecting the wagon train, and with this end in view directed the Companies engaged to fall back slowly.

The Command retired as directed in perfect order, the led horses being kept well protected between the skirmish lines of the two Companies whilst a heavy and effective fire did great execution amongst the savages and prevented any serious attempt on their part to break through our lines. Failing in their efforts in front, the Indians endeavered to cut the command off from the train, which had by Major Thornburgh's order, gone into park on the right bank of Milk river, and to accomplish this purpose passed around our left flank, beyond Carbine range and concentrated in great force upon a knoll to the left of and completely commanding our line of retreat. Major Thornburgh upon discovering this new danger, directed me to charge the knoll with twenty men of my Company, to sweep the Indians off and then at once, without attempting to hold the hill, to fall back upon the train and take measures for its protection. This duty being performed and the way opened for the retirment of the led horses, I repaired to the wagon train and at once took steps looking to the defence.

Major Thornburgh doubtless started for the train shortly after giving me the order refered to, and was shot and instantly killed just after crossing the river and within 500 yards of the wagons.

His gallantry was conspicuous from first to last and grief for his death was general and profound.

In the meantime Captain Lawson with "E" Company 3rd Cavalry and Lieut. Cherry with a detachment from "E" Company 3rd and "F" Company 5th Cavalry gallantly held the Indians in check in front, gradually retiring, Lieut. Cherry with his detachment covering the retreat.

Upon reaching the train I found it parked on the right bank of Milk River about 200 yards from water, the wagons forming the north side of a corral elliptical in shape, its long axis running East and West and the south side exposed to a fierce fire from the Indians, who massing in the ravines along the river and upon commanding heights, were making a determined effort to capture and destroy the train before it could be placed in condition for defence.

The animals were crowded within the area indicated and I at once directed some twenty or more of those wounded to be led out and shot along the open space referred to, thus making continuous our line of defence and affording cover for our sharp shooters. As soon as these arrangements were completed, the men were ordered to unload the wagons, and use bedding, grain and flour sacks for breastworks. I cannot speak too highly of their conduct at this time. Though exposed to a galling fire, by which many men and horses were stricken down they worked with alacrity and courage and in a short time our corral was in as good a state for defence as the means at hand would permit. About this time Lieut. Paddock, who was encouraging the men by the exposure of his person, and intelligently and courageously carrying out my instructions, was wounded in the hip.

As Captain Lawson and Lieut. Cherry whose gallant fight in covering the retreat deserves high commendation, had not yet returned to camp, I became solicitous for their safety and detached Serg't. Poppe of my Company with twelve men to proceed down the road in the direction from which they were approaching. In a short time thereafter I was greatly relieved at seeing Captain Lawson and Lieut. Cherry with their command enter the entrenchments.

A new and critical danger now threatened us. The Indians foiled in their efforts to prevent the concentration of the command at the train or to drive us out of it by a furrious [sic] and concentrated fire, took advantage of a high wind blowing directly towards us, and fired the tall dry grass and sage brush down the river. At the moment this peril was realized I observed that the Indians supply train of Mr. Gordon, was parked within 75 yards of my position and so situated as to command our approach to water. Seeing this and fearing that under cover of the smoke, the Indians might make a lodgment in this train, which in my judgment could have been disastrous to the command, and with the further view of burning the grass on the north side of the corral so as to present as little surface as possible to the Indian fire when it should approach, I directed the grass on that side to be fired and in a few moments was gratified to see Gordon's train in flames.

The fire from down the valley approached with great rapidity -and struck the exposed point of the corral igniting bundles, grain and flour sacks, wagon sheets & c. and for a few moments threatened us with destruction. The officers and men at this critical moment when the Indians made their most furious attack displayed superb gallantry. Several lives were lost, many wounds received, but the fire was extinguished and our greatest danger passed.

From this time about 2:45 P.M. until nightfall, the Indians kept up a furious fire, doing great damage to our stock, fully three fourths of them being killed or so severely wounded that they were killed by my order.

At dark a large body of Indians charged down behind Gordon's burning train, delivering volley after volley. They were repulsed easily and fled after suffering the loss of several warriors, who were distinctly seen to drop from their saddles.

During the night our dead animals were hauled off, a full supply of water for 24 hours was procured, the wounded were cared for, entrenchments were dug, and by daylight the corral was in a good condition for defence.

Couriers were sent out with dispatches at midnight and a general feeling of confidence inspired the entire command. Ammunition and rations were distributed in the several trenches, and I felt that sense of security for my command which sprang from a knowledge of its gallantry and fortitude.

During the next day the Indians kept up an almost incessant fire killing all of our animals but fourteen mules, but doing no other damage. We were uninterrupted on the night of the 30th but after that time the enemy gave us no rest.

During the night of the 1st, our water party was fired upon at short range, and one man of "F" Company 5th Cavalry shot through the face. The guard for the water party returned this fire with effect, killing one Indian.

On the morning of the 2nd, Captain Dodge and Lieut. Hughes with "D" Company 9th Cavalry came into our camp, adding materially to our fighting strength and bringing the welcome news that our Couriers had gone through safely.

I cannot express in too high terms my appreciation of the gallantry of these brave officers and men, and it is peculiarly gratifying to know that they have received that praise which such courage richly deserves.

Colonel Merritt with his command after a march which has no parallel reached us this morning and were received with hearty and prolonged cheers by my gallant men, whose patience, fidelity and courage were thus speedily rewarded by rescue from great and impending peril.

I can find no suitable words in which to express my admiration for the officers and men of my command.

Their conduct was beyond all praise; they were gallant under fire, patient during suspense, and confident through all. It is my greatest pride to have commanded them and to know that one more page in the glorious annals of the American Soldier has been illustrated by their valor.

I forward herewith copy of an order bearing this date of this report congratulating my command upon their conduct and rescue. Therein mention is made of instances of conspicuous gallantry on the part of officers and men to which I respectfully invite attention.

My losses have already been reported and embraced one third of my effective force.

One officer, Major Thornburgh, and nine enlisted men were killed, and three officers Cap't. Payne and Lieutenant Paddock and A. A. Surgeon Grimes and forty-three enlisted men were wounded.

Besides these Wagon Master McKinstry, Guide Lowry and one teamster were killed and two teamsters wounded.

From Mr. Brady who has just come into camp under a flag of truce, I learn that the Indians admit a loss of 37. I am satisfied their losses were heavy as they fought at short range and many were seen by officers and men to fall.

I desire to express my thanks to Mr. John Gordon and guide J. P. Rankin for their gallant conduct in carrying dispatches from our beleagured camp. I trust that in some way their invaluable services may be recognized and suitably rewarded.

All of our wounded men were brought from the field but it was impossible to recover until the arrival of General Merritt's command the bodies of Major Thornburgh and two enlisted men.

The Indians had an abundance of ammunition which they expended freely, and were generally armed with the improved Winchester rifles.

I estimate their strength at from 300 to 350. From their disposition it was apparent that we were expected to approach by the road. Had we done so I am satisfied we would have met with great disaster.

I am Sir
Very Respectfully
Your Obed't. Servant
J. Scott Payne
Captain 5th Cavalry
Commanding

General Orders No. 1 by Captain J. Scott Payne[2]

Headquarters Batt'n 3rd & 5th Cav.
White River Expedition
October 5th, 1879

General Orders
   No. 1
   I. The Commanding Officer desires to extend to the officers and men of this Battalion his congratulations upon their safe deliverance from great

peril, –and to express to them his thanks for their gallant conduct in the fierce battle with an overwhelming force of Indians, on the 29th ult., and the subsequent siege.

II. Much was demanded of you, and your response, in every instance, was prompt, soldierly and courageous. During the terrible siege of six days, when the enemy's fire was almost incessant, and your hardships pressed to the very limit of endurance; when suffering with cold, without shelter or covering, you worked in the trenches, realizing that as you labored you might be digging your own graves, –you coolly calculated the chances of life and death, and preserved through all the vicissitudes of an experience seldom sent to try the souls of men, that morale which is at once the severest and finest test of discipline, efficiency and valor.

III. No instance of misbehavior has been reported, but conspicuous acts of gallantry were frequent. It is with particular pleasure that the Commanding Officer takes this occasion to invite attention to the following:

Captain Lawson, of the Third Cavalry, during the battle of the 29th, displayed that coolness under fire which is so important in moments of great danger, and the high courage that extends to those who are brought under its influence:

2" Lieut. S A. Cherry, 5th Cav'y. bore an honorable and important part in the engagement. Through his sagacity, the intentions and position of the Indians were first discovered, and his personal gallantry under fire was conspicuous:

Lieut. Paddock exposed his person freely, –encouraged his men by his presence at points where the enemy's fire was striking down men and horses all around him, and was painfully wounded while gallantly carrying out the orders of his commanding officer:

Lieut. Wolf, A.A.Q.M. parked his train when the engagement began, and rendered valuable and gallant service during the attack thereon:

A. A. Surg'n. Grimes was unremitting in his attentions to the wounded, both during the engagement and afterwards, notwithstanding a painful wound which he received while gallantly discharging his duties under fire:

The following non-commissioned officers and enlisted men deserve special mention for conspicuous gallantry:

Company "E" 3rd Cavalry:

Sergeants Neurohr, Lupton, Montgomery, McKernin and Nolan;–Corporals Eichwurzel, Secrist and Hunter; –Privates La Parle, Burton, Morton and Donovan:

Company "D" 5th Cavalry:

Serg't. Craig, Corporal Murphy, and Privates Sharpe, Booth, Hart, Marshall and Whitbeck:

Company "F" 5th Cavalry:

Sergeants Grimes and Poppe; –Corporals Moquin and Roach; Trumpeters McDonald and Sutcliffe, and Privates Carpenter, Combs, Clark, Eakle, Gibbs, Fulk, Klingensmith, Patterson, and Schickedonz.

IV. Too much praise cannot be give Captain Dodge and Lieut. Hughes, 9th Cav'y and command for their timely and gallant march to our relief.

V. The memory of our late gallant commander Major Thornburgh, and our heroic comrades who fell with him, will ever be dear to this command. Their lives were not lived in vain for their death was glorious.

VI. Relief has come at last! Your brave comrades, under the command of the gallant and skillful Merritt, have reached you, after the most marvellous march known to military annals, and you can greet them with a conciousness of duty well performed, and heartfelt gratitude for their speedy arrival.

By order of Captain Payne
S. A. Cherry
Lieut. 5th Cavalry
Batt'n Adjutant

Letter of Captain Joseph Lawson Company E, Third Cavalry[3]

In camp on Milk River Colorado
October 9th, 1879

Dear Serg't. Ambrose.

No doubt you have heard of our engagement with the treacherous Utes. A party of them met us on Bear Creek, and another party met us on

Williams Fork. They professed friendship—Amongst the number was old Colorow. On the morning of September 29th about one mile from Milk Creek, and twenty-five miles north of White River Agency we were met by the Utes, secreted amongst the sage brush near the mouth of a bad canyon. Lieut. Cherry discovered them, and was ordered by Major Thornburgh to hail them. He took fifteen men of 'E' Company (my company) and approached them, and hailed them. They replied with bullets. Major Thornburgh, and Captain Payne, were riding at the head of the column—'F' 5th cavalry in advance, my company next—'D' Company Lieut. Paddock; about one and one-half miles to the rear in charge of the wagon train. Captain Payne was ordered to take position on a hill to our left. I to take a hill to our right. I dismounted my company leaving every fourth man to hold horses. Here the fight became general at every point. The Indians appeared on all sides, and on nearly all the bluffs, and in all the ravines. The fifteen men of my company with Lieut. Cherry fought gallantly, and every man of my company fought valiantly. At this time Major Thornburgh approached me and informed me that Captain Payne and his company would fall back to a knoll—then to fall back on him. I sent word to Lieut. Cherry to fall back on me—and we would cover the retreat. As Captain Payne's company were about to start, or had started, his girth broke and he got a fearful fall. One of his men dismounted and assisted him on his horse. The Captain's horse having got away. 'F' Company 5th Cavalry, followed by the Captain, he badly bruised, went to the wagon train—found the train being parked—and Lieut. Paddock fighting the Indians—and the Lieut. wounded. I fell back slowly; with my company dismounted, and fought all the way. Every man doing his duty. One of my men informed me that Major Thornburgh was killed half a mile ahead of us. I tried to reach his remains—here my horse was shot the second time under me—and also Sergeant Neurohr's horse. As all of my men were up, and we had our wounded with us we fell back to the balance of our command, but fought all the way. One stubborn resistance gave time to form temporary breastworks of men's bundles, flour & corn sacks, and wagons, & dead horses. Here we fought and entrenched—our horses being shot down rapidly—as they were all on the high points around us. We entrenched—all we could do was to save our men. On the Second of October, Captain Dodge; 9th Cavalry re-inforced us with thirty-five men.

He got into our entrenchments all right–but in a few hours all his horses except three, or four, were killed. On the morning of October fifth, the gallant General Merritt came to our relief with four companies cavalry, and five of Infantry. Since then Captain Vroom, with his company, and one of the 'Fifth' arrived. This day (9th inst) Major Bryant, with 4 companies of the 14th Infantry joined us. The Indians are not far off, whether they will fight so large a command is uncertain. As 'E' Company 3rd Cavalry, 'D' & 'F' 5th Cavalry and 'D' 9th Cavalry have lost all their horses–will return at once. All the horses of my company that were with the expedition are dead except Magerlein's, and the horse rode by Lieut. Price–they were back at the supply camp. Everything has been quiet since the Fifth. General Merritt is a going to remain and follow up the Indians. The four companies of cavalry that were in the fight, and all dismounted, march tomorrow morning for Rawlins. That is 'E' 3rd. Cav.; 'D' & 'F' 5th Cav; & 'D' 9th Cav. We take Major Thornburgh's remains with us–also all our wounded. Private Cuff is buried on the battle field. None of the wounded of 'E' Company 3rd Cavalry, except Sergeant Montgomery, Sergeant Lupton, and Private Mahoney, are suffering much. Corporal Hunter is all right, all the rest of the wounded are doing well. Mr. Davis, sutler, is going in with us, he is improving, the ball being cut out of his foot. The weather is cold. Snow on the ground. Hope to reach Fort Steele about the 16th inst. We start for the post tomorrow morning at 7 o'clock.

> Very respectfully
> Joseph Lawson
> Captain 3rd
> Cavalry

Lieutenant S. A. Cherry letter[4]

> Headqrs. White River Expedition
> Camp on Milk River, Col.
> October 8, 1879

Lieut. John G. Bourke 3rd Cav'y.
A.D.C.

Sir:

In compliance with your request, I have the honor to furnish herein, a complete list of the killed and wounded in the engagement with hostile Utes, on Milk River Col., Sep't. 29" and 30" and Oct. 1", 2", 3" and 4", 1879:–

Killed

Major T. T. Thornburgh 4th Infantry
First Serg't. John Dolan Co. "F" 5th Cavalry
Wagoner Amos D. Miller Co. "F" 5th Cavalry
Private John Burns Co. "F" 5th Cav'y
   " Samuel McKee Co. "F" 5th Cav'y
   " Michael Lynch Co. "D" 5th Cav'y
   " Thomas Mooney Co. "D" 5th Cav'y
   " Charles Wright Co. "D" 5th Cav'y
   " Dominick Cuff Co. "E" 3rd Cav'y
Wagon Master McKinstry
Teamster McGuire
and Guide Lowrie
Pvt. Michael Firestone Co. "F" 5th Cav'y

Wounded

Cap't. J. Scott Payne 5th Cav'y.–flesh wound in arm and side
2 Lieut. Jas. V. S. Paddock 5th Cav'y:–flesh wound in thigh
A. A. Surg'n Rob't. D. Grimes.–flesh wound in shoulder
Serg't. John Merrill Co. "F" 5th Cav'y
Trumpeter Frederick Sutcliffe Co. "F" 5th Cav'y
   " John McDonald Co. "F" 5th Cav'y
Pvt. William Esser Co. "F" 5th Cav'y
   " James T. Gibbs Co. "F" 5th Cav'y
   " John Hoaxey Co. "F" 5th Cav'y
   " Emil Kussman Co. "F" 5th Cav'y
   " Eugene Patterson Co. "F" 5th Cav'y
   " Eugene Schickedonz Co. "F" 5th Cav'y
   " Frank E. Simmons Co. "F" 5th Cav'y
   " Gottleib Steiger Co. "F" 5th Cav'y

"   Frederick Bernhardt Co. "D" 5th Cav'y
"   Nicholas W. Heeney Co. "D" 5th Cav'y
"   Thomas Lynch Co. "D" 5th Cav'y
"   Ernest Muller Co. "D" 5th Cav'y
Serg't. Allen Lupton Co. "E" 3rd Cav'y
"   James Montgomery Co. "E" 3rd Cav'y
Corp'l. Charles F. Eichwurzul Co. "E" 3rd Cav'y
"   Frank Hunter Co. "E" 3rd Cav'y
Farrier William Schubert Co. "E" 3rd Cav'y
Private James Budka Co. "E" 3rd Cav'y
"   John Crowley Co. "E" 3rd Cav'y
"   William Clark Co. "E" 3rd Cav'y
"   Orlando Duren Co. "E" 3rd Cav'y
"   John Donovan Co. "E" 3rd Cav'y
"   Thomas Ferguson Co. "E" 3rd Cav'y
"   Marcus Hansen Co. "E" 3rd Cav'y
"   Edward Lavelle Co. "E" 3rd Cav'y
"   Thomas Lewis Co. "E" 3rd Cav'y
"   William Mitchell Co. "E" 3rd Cav'y
"   John Mahoney Co. "E" 3rd Cav'y
"   Thomas McNamara Co. "E" 3rd Cav'y
"   Joseph Patterson Co. "E" 3rd Cav'y
Teamster Nelson
"   Cain
Train Blks. Rodney

In addition to the above, a freighter, name unknown, was wounded–To the best of my knowledge, this is a complete list of the killed and wounded–The nature of the severe wounds can be ascertained from the Surgeon's report.

Very Respectfully
Your Obdt. Serv't
S. A. Cherry
Lt. 5th Cav.
Adjutant

Official Report of Captain Dodge, Company D, 9th Cavalry[5]

In the Field
Rawlins Springs Wyo.
October 19th, 1879

To The Adjutant General
District New Mexico

Sir:

My last report was dated Middle Park September 25th. The opperations [sic] of my Company since that date are as follows. Leaving my Supply Camp on Grand River on the 27th ulto. for White River Agency, in compliance with telegrams from Headquarters District N.M. dated September 13th and 18th respectively. I had marched to and camped on a small stream emptying into Bear River 15 miles south of Steamboat Springs by the 30th. I left camp as usual on the 1st inst. (October) at 6:30 A.M. After marching about 10 miles a paper was found in the sage brush by the side of the road on which was written the following — Hurry up, the Troops have been defeated at the Agency and signed E.E.C. Ordering the train to keep closed up with the column I pushed forward to Hayden which I found deserted. While searching the buildings here a party of citizens came up, among them a Mr. Gordon who had left the intrenchments two days before and from whom I learned the exact situation. I then moved down Bear River as rapidly as possible until 4:30 P.M. when I went into camp, causing all ordinary dispositions to be made for a nights rest. Having seen my men were supplied with 225 rounds of ammunition and three days rations per man, I ordered the wagons repacked at half past eight, and with a guard of eight men sent them to Price's Supply Camp on Fortification Creek while I started with the rest of the company for Pain's [sic] command. I took with me one pack mule on which were carried a couple of blankets and a few picks and spades. The force left me consisted of 2 officers, 35 soldiers and 4 citizens—Gordon and a citizen named Lithgow having volunteered to act as guides. I decided to follow a trail in preference to the road. The night was bright and cold, and the march unimpeded. At 4 o'clock we reached the main road about 5 miles from the intrenchments, and shortly afterwards came upon the dead bodies of 3 men, who were lying in a gulch near which a train loaded with annuity goods had been burnt by the Indians. Half an hour later we arrived at Pain's command. Singularly enough the Indians did not molest us in the least and I can only account for it by supposing that they imagined a much stronger force coming in and were unwilling to expose themselves. However, we were scarcely inside the trenches when they commenced a fusilade which was kept up at intervals for the next three days. Of 42 animals taken into the trenches with my Company, but four are left, all of which are wounded.

I made the best disposition for them I could but it was impossible to shelter them on all sides and the Indians completely surrounded us.

General Merritt's command arrived on the morning of the 5th inst. relieving us from our awkward situation and on the 10th I was ordered to take the remnant of Pain's companies with my own, and the wounded back to this point which I reached last night. I am now under orders from Department Headquarters to proceed to Fort Union and expect to leave here the morning of the 21st.

In conclusion I wish to say a word in favor of the enlisted men of my command whose conduct throughout was exemplary. They endured a forced march of 70 miles, loss of sleep, lack of food, and the dispositions attendant on their situation without a murmur and have proven themselves good soldiers and reliable men.

> I am Sir
> Very Respectfully
> Your Obed't. Servant
> F. S. Dodge
> Captain 9th Reg't./Co. D
> Commanding

PARTIAL LETTER OF JOHN C. DAVIS TO HIS WIFE WRITTEN ON LETTERHEAD OF J.W. HUGUS & CO. POST TRADERS, U.S.A., FORT FRED. STEELE, WYO., 18__.

No date given[6]

Command consisted of one Company 3rd U. S. Cavalry and 2 Co's. 5th U. S. Cav. Major Thornburgh commanding.

Sep. 29th 1879 left camp in Deer Canyon at 6:15 a.m. Major Thornburgh with 'E' Co. 3rd Cav. and 'F' Co. 5th Cav. in advance. 'D' Co. 5th Cav. guarding wagon train which consisted of 25 government teams and my team. After travelling about six miles we noticed the grass had lately been set on fire and was still burning in some places, we trotted teams through the fire. On seeing fire Major Thornburgh with his advance guard rode further ahead thinking Indians might be near, seeing none he kept about 2 miles ahead of wagon train, when within sight of Milk River (12 miles from our camp in Deer Canyon) a courier arrived from Thornburgh with orders for us to corral wagon train as he had found Indians & was fighting them. We still advanced wishing to reach Milk River so we could get water, which was a mile from where courier met us. On arriving at Milk River we went into corral, from our corral we could plainly see Indians & soldiers fighting, & hear the yells of both parties. We had been in corral some 20 minutes when Cap't. Payne with his company (F Co. 5th cav.) charged from a bluff about 500 yards distant and came into corral. Indians followed him closely & only from the fire we kept up on Indians from corral would have succeeded in surrounding Payne & cutting him off from wagon train. Payne gave orders to unload wagons and make breastworks of contents, also to shoot horses & mules for breastworks, but before orders could be obeyed the Indians who had followed Payne up had taken the bluffs on 3 sides of us & commenced fighting. Under the fire of probably 100 Indians we went to work & succeeded in unloading 10 wagons. Much anxiety was expressed for Cap't. Lawson with his company ('E' Co. 3rd Cav.) who were still fighting the Indians on the bluffs (where they were first seen). At last Cap't. Lawson succeeded in cutting his way through the Indians and was greeted with many cheers on arriving at the corral. After Cap't. Lawson's arrival, fighting commenced in real earnest. The Indians having no opposition on the bluffs, all came on bluffs surrounding corral & kept up a murderous fire. Our corral was circular about 100 yards across and into this corral were crowded over 200 men, 153 mules & 186 horses. Some 400 Indians were on the bluff, all armed with Winchester repeating rifles, from 1 p.m. until dark at 5:30 p.m. these 400 Indians kept up a continuous fire killing during that time 12 men, 127 mules, 183 horses & wounding 46 men. At about 3 p.m. Indians seeing they could not drive us from corral though [*sic*] to burn us out by setting fire to grass & sage brush in the bottom which favored by strong west wind would come sweeping up the bottom followed by about 150 Indians who kept firing through the flame & smoke. The fire caught the first wagon and much fear was expressed by all that we should be burned up & then we would have been at the entire mercy of the Indians. But thanks to Cap't. Lawson who regardless of all danger called up his men to assist him went to the fire & succeeded in putting it out, not however before he saw 16 men fall around him. Out of these 16, six died or were shot dead, it was the most critical time of the besiegment & there was not a man present who did not thank God for the deliverance from a burning death. Cap't. Lawson was given no praise in papers here, but he is entitled to all praise for his heroic conduct in putting. . . .

Notes

Preface
1. Buys, "Accounts of the Battle at Milk Creek: Implications for Historical Accuracy," p. 71.
2. Ibid., p. 63.
3. Ibid., p. 79.
4. Payne, "Incidents of the Recent Campaign Against the Utes," p. 114.
5. Knight, *Following the Indian Wars: the Story of the Newspaper Correspondents Among the Indian Campaigners*, p. 302; "Report of General George Crook," in Secretary of War, *Report of the Secretary of War for the Year 1880*, p. 79.
6. Knight, pp. 300–302.
7. In recent years archaeologists have made major contributions to the interpretation of Indian wars battlefields. Perhaps the best example is research at the site of the Little Bighorn battle in Montana which generated several publications. Two good references are: Scott et. al., *Archaeological Perspectives on the Battle of the Little Bighorn*; Fox, *Archaeology, History, and Custer's Last Battle*.
8. Thornburgh Monument (5RB982), Battle of Milk River site, Rio Blanco County, Colorado, For a general sense of the archaeological research potential see: Werner, *Meeker—the Story of the Meeker Massacre and Thornburgh Battle September 29, 1879*; Eugene A. Patterson interview in Meschter, unpublished notes and correspondence.

Chapter One: Seeds of Discord
1. Nathan C. Meeker to Commissioner of Indian Affairs, August 11, 1879. Adjutant General, U.S. Army, "The Ute Uprising, 1879."
2. Utley, *Frontier Regulars: the United States Army and the Indian 1866–1891*, pp. 332–333; Dunn, *Massacres of the Mountains: A History of the Indian Wars of the Far West, 1815–1875*, p. 582.
3. Utley, p. 333.
4. "Report of the General of the Army," in Secretary of War, *Report of the Secretary of War for the Year 1879*, p. 12; Josephine Meeker testimony, U.S. House, *Testimony in Relation to the Ute Indian Outbreak, Taken by the Committee on Indian Affairs*, p. 90. Josephine Meeker testified that there were no more than 200 or 250 White River Warriors and that there were only a half dozen more Ute warriors who were not from White River who may have taken part in the incidents.
5. Smith, *Ouray: Chief of the Utes*, pp. 91–117.
6. McCartney, *Crisis of 1873*, p. 64.
7. Ibid., p. 50; Yeoman, *A Guide Book of United States Coins*, p. 167; Van Allen and

Mallis, *Comprehensive Catalog and Encyclopedia of Morgan & Peace Dollars*, pp. 23–24.
8. Yeoman, pp. 167–168.
9. Utley, p. 333.
10. Ibid., p. 333.
11. U.S. Department of the Interior, *Annual Report of Commissioner of Indian Affairs to the Secretary of the Interior for the Year 1879*, p. 23.
12. Ibid., p. 25.
13. Huseas, "Thornburgh and Fort Steele," p. 21; N. C. Meeker to E. A. Hayt, Commissioner of Indian Affairs, July 7, 1879, Letters received by the Office of the Adjutant General (Main Series), 1871–1880.
14. Nathan C. Meeker to Commissioner of Indian Affairs, August 11, 1879, Adjutant General.
15. Brigadier General George Crook endorsement, August 4, 1879, Adjutant General.
16. Nathan C. Meeker to Commissioner of Indian Affairs, August 11, 1879, Adjutant General.
17. U.S. Department of the Interior, p. 27.
18. Sprague, *Massacre: The Tragedy at White River*, p. 133; Hayt testimony, U.S. House, *Testimony in Relation to the Ute Indian Outbreak*, p. 32; Frye, *Atlas of Wyoming Outlaws at the Territorial Penitentiary*, pp. 50, 74, 78.
19. Smith, pp. 157–158; Sprague, pp. 175–177. The dates of the letter and telegram concerning Johnson's assault on Meeker are found in National Archives Microfilm, Record Group 94, Copy 666, Roll 513.
20. See correspondence in Dodge, Main Series. Also see Sprague, pp. 179–180.

CHAPTER 2: THE WHITE RIVER EXPEDITION

1. General Crook to Commanding Officer, Fort Fred Steele, Wyo., September 16, 1879. Adjutant General, U.S. Army, "The Ute Uprising, 1879," Roll 513.
2. Sprague, *Massacre: The Tragedy at White River*, pp. 181–182; War Department, *War of the Rebellion: Official Records of the Union and Confederate Armies*, p. 178.
3. U.S. Army, *Official Army Register for January 1879*; *Cheyenne Daily Leader*, October 3, 1879, Coe Library, University of Wyoming, Laramie.
4. U.S. Army, *Official Army Register for January 1879*; *Cheyenne Daily Leader*, Oct. 3, 1879.
5. Sandoz, *Cheyenne Autumn*, p. 157.
6. Sprague, p. 336.
7. Miller and Wedel, *Archaeological Survey and Test Excavations at Fort Fred Steele State Historic Site*, p. 100.
8. General Crook to Commanding Officer, Fort Fred Steele, Wyoming, September 16, 1879. Adjutant General.
9. Captain Wm. H. Bisbee, Inspection Report of Fort Fred Steele, Wyo. September 1, 1879, Fort Fred Steele, Wyo., Historical Documents Collection, Document Box 50.
10. Miller and Wedel, p. 100.
11. Shockley, *The Trap-Door Springfield in the Service*, p. 18; Mangum, *Battle of the Rosebud: Prelude to the Little Bighorn*.

12. Inspection Report of Fort Fred Steele, Wyo., September 1, 1879.
13. Thornburgh to Adjutant General, Department of the Platte, September 16, 1879. Fort Fred Steele, Wyo., Historical Documents Collection.
14. Thornburgh to Col. Bronson, September 16, 1879, Fort Fred Steele, Wyo., Historical Documents Collection.
15. Thornburgh to Adjutant General, Department of the Platte, September 16, 1879, Fort Fred Steele, Wyo., Historical Documents Collection.
16. Telegram sent from Fort Omaha, Neb., September 17, 1879, Letters Received by the Office of the Adjutant General (Main Series), 1871–1880.
17. Special Orders No. 81, Department of the Platte, September 18, 1879, Post Returns, Fort D. A. Russell, Wyoming, August–October 1879.
18. *Cheyenne Daily Leader*, Vol. XII, No. 311, September 18, 1879, p. 1.
19. Telegrams sent from Fort Fred Steele, September 17, 1879. Fort Fred Steele, Wyo., Historical Documents Collection.
20. McClellan, *This is Our Land*, Vol. 1, p. 9.
21. U.S. Army, *Official Army Register for January 1880*, pp. 25, 121.
22. Vaughn, *The Reynolds Campaign on Powder River*, p. 183; Hedren, *Fort Laramie in 1876*, pp. 216–217.
23. Green, *Slim Buttes, 1876: an Episode of the Great Sioux War*, p. 125.
24. *Cheyenne Daily Leader*, October 12, 1879.
25. Telegrams sent from Fort Fred Steele, September 17, 1879, Fort Fred Steele, Wyo., Historical Documents Collection.
26. Sprague, p. 192; "Certificate of Capt. J. Scott Payne 5th U.S. Cavalry Concerning Loss and Destruction of Train and Supplies at Battle on Milk River (Colo.) September 29th, 1879," *Annals of Wyoming*, pp. 137–140; *Cheyenne Daily Leader*, October 26, 1879; Tallent, *Black Hills, or, the Last Hunting Ground of the Dakotas*.
27. Thornburgh to Adjutant General, Department of the Platte, September 19, 1879, Fort Fred Steele, Wyo., Historical Documents Collection.
28. Spooner, "The Outbreak of September, 1879," p. 1124; Regular Army Muster Rolls: Company D, Fifth Cavalry, August 31–October 31, 1879.
29. *Sentinel*, V. 11, No. 22, September 27, 1879, cited in Meschter, *A Carbon County Chronology 1867–1879*.
30. United States Continental Command Records, No. 245 (3868) Special Orders No. 72, Fort Fred Steele, September 20, 1879.
31. Ibid.; Fort D. A. Russell, Wyo., Post Returns, September 1879; U.S. Army, *Official Army Register for January 1880*, p. 133.
32. Telegrams sent from Fort Fred Steele, September 20, 1879, Adj. Gen., Main Series.
33. Fort Laramie, Wyo., correspondence.
34. McClellan, *This is Our Land*, Vol. 2, pp. 3–9.
35. Fort Fred Steele, Wyo., Post Returns, September 1879.
36. *Cheyenne Daily Leader*, February 5, 1881, p. 4.
37. Meschter, unpublished notes and correspondence; *Carbon County Journal*, Sat., Nov. 29, 1879, information from Butler D. Price; *Carbon County Journal*, Sat., Dec. 27, 1879; information from McCauley, *Report on White River Agency, Colo.*, in U.S. Senate, pp. 12–36; Meeker, Colo. Chamber of Commerce, "Historical Episodes of

Meeker"; Regular Army Muster Rolls. Price calculates the distance from Rawlins to Baggs Ranch/Snake River as fifty-seven miles in the *Carbon County Journal*, but it is closer to sixty-six miles in his company's muster rolls. McCauley calculates the distance to Snake River Crossing as sixty-four miles. Since the map distance between Baggs's Ranch and the river crossing is less than a mile (see Map 3.2), and McCauley's measurements were odometer readings, a figure around sixty-four to sixty-six seems the best. Consequently, the distances traveled between September 22–24 in Table 2.1 are based on comparing McCauley's figures with Price's company muster rolls. Price's information is included here because McCauley did not mention as many spots believed to have been used for camps by the White River Expedition. McCauley's total distance from Rawlins to Milk Creek calculates to 143.14 miles.

38. U.S. Army, *Official Army Register for January 1880*, p. 196; McClellan, Vol. 2, pp. 90–107.
39. Telegrams from Fort Fred Steele, September 21, 1879, Fort Fred Steele, Wyo., Historical Documents Collection.
40. "Report of the General of the Army," in Secretary of War, *Report of the Secretary of War for the Year 1879*, p. 9; Burkey, "The Thornburgh Battle with the Utes on Milk Creek," p. 91; Rankin, "The Meeker Massacre from Reminiscences of Frontier Days," p. 91. Rankin claims that the expedition had twenty-eight wagons and one ambulance. Sprague, p. 193. Sprague argues that the column included thirty-three six-mule wagons and the sutler wagon, 220 mules and 150 horses.
41. Rodenbough, *Uncle Sam's Medal of Honor*, p. 349.
42. Ibid.; Sprague, p. 193.
43. Payne, "Incidents of the Recent Campaign Against the Utes," p. 114.
44. "Report of the General of the Army," in Secretary of War, *Report of the Secretary of War for the Year 1879*, p. 9; Sheridan, *Record of Engagements with Hostile Indians Within the Military Division of the Missouri from 1868–1882*, p. 88; *Cheyenne Daily Leader*, October 7, 1879.
45. Spooner, p. 1124; Dawson and Skiff, *The Ute War: A History of the White River Massacre*, p. 20.
46. Sprague, pp. 193–194.
47. Fort D. A. Russell Post Returns, September 1879.
48. *Meeker Herald*, September 27, 1929; Meschter, unpublished.
49. "Report of the General of the Army," in Secretary of War, *Report of the Secretary of War for the Year 1879*, p. 9.
50. Medical History File, Fort Fred Steele (partial), October 1879, Fort Fred Steele, Wyo. Historical Documents Collection.
51. *Sentinel*, Vol. 11, No. 22, September 27, 1879, in Meschter, p. 615; Regular Army Muster Roll.

CHAPTER 3: MARCH TO MILK CREEK

1. White River Expedition letter, to Commissioner of Indian Affairs, September 26, 1879, U.S. Department of the Interior, *Annual Report of the Commissioner of Indian Affairs to the Secretary of the Interior for the Year 1879*, p. xxxi.
2. Sprague, *Massacre: The Tragedy at White River*, p. 191; Conniss, "Recollections of

Taylor Pennock," p. 209; U.S. Senate, McCauley, *Report on White River Agency, Colo.*
3. Payne, "Incidents of the Recent Campaign Against the Utes," pp. 114–115.
4. Meschter, unpublished notes and correspondence; S. A. Cherry to Mrs. Thornburgh, October 23, 1879, photocopy of letter in *Meeker Herald*, Davis, Collection; Regular Army Muster Rolls, Company E, Third Cavalry, August 31–October 31, 1879.
5. Meschter, unpublished.
6. Ibid.; Wyoming Nineteenth Century General Land Office Township Maps; Startzell, "Thornberg [sic] Massacre at Meeker"; Meschter, unpublished. The manuscript was written before July 27, 1931; the citation date of 1931 is only an estimate.
7. U.S. Senate, McCauley, pp. 20–21; Payne, p. 116. This leg of the journey introduces one of the main discrepancies in the literature: that is, where exactly was Lieutenant Price's supply camp? Sprague (194–195) and others indicate that the supply camp was at the junction of Little Bear Creek and Fortification Creek. But this location is scarcely eight miles from the Yampa River via the agency road. In contrast, Payne (116) describes what sounds like the northern reaches of Fortification Creek where it issues out from the rugged country to the east, and says that Price's camp was established here, concluding that the expedition followed down or near Fortification Creek eighteen miles before they went into their next camp at the Yampa River. Payne's description requires that Price's camp be farther up Fortification Creek than its junction with Little Bear Creek for this distance to fit, perhaps at a spot near the eastern end of Fortification Rocks, which are about three miles south of the first creek crossing on the agency road. This latter position is the supply camp location depicted in Map 3.2. Price's company muster rolls for August 31–October 31, 1879 identify the camping area used as Fortification Spring. Only careful archaeological investigation at these localities is likely to resolve the dispute.
8. U.S. Senate, McCauley.
9. U.S. Department of the Interior, p. XIX.
10. U.S. Senate, McCauley, pp. 21–23.
11. Sprague, pp. 194–196; see also endnote number 7.
12. White River Expedition letter to Commissioner of Indian Affairs, September 25, 1879, U.S. Department of the Interior, p. xxxi.
13. Sprague, p. 196; U.S. House, Payne testimony, *Testimony in Relation to the Ute Indian Outbreak, Taken by the Committee on Indian Affairs*, pp. 170–171; Ibid., Cherry testimony, pp. 62–63.
14. Payne, p. 116.
15. Rennicke, "The Rivers of Colorado," *Colorado Geographic Series*, No. 1, p. 88.
16. Sprague, pp. 196–197; U.S. House, Jack testimony, *White River Ute Commission Investigation*, pp. 69–71; Payne, p. 116.
17. Jack testimony, *Committee on Indian Affairs*, p. 194.
18. Payne, p. 117; Jack testimony, p. 194.
19. Payne testimony, p. 171.
20. Jack testimony, p. 194; Sprague, p. 197.
21. Jack testimony, pp. 194–195. An Indian named Bennett is usually mentioned in connection with Chinaman. Bennett and Glasseye, however, may be the same person.
22. Payne testimony, p. 171.

23. Jack testimony, *Ute Commission Investigation*, p. 71.
24. Payne, p. 117.
25. Jack testimony, *Committee on Indian Affairs*, p. 195.
26. Cherry testimony, p. 63.
27. White River Expedition letter, September 26, 1879, U.S. Department of the Interior, p. xxxi.
28. Cherry testimony, p. 64.
29. U.S. Senate, McCauley, p. 23.
30. Sprague, p. 199.
31. U.S. Senate, McCauley, p. 24.
32. Ibid., p. 25.
33. Sprague, pp. 198–199. Beaver Creek springs is interpreted here as the same area as the lakes at the head of Beaver Creek, near present day Aldrich Lakes. This is also the Beaver Springs area in the expedition's narrative.
34. Ibid., p. 199; Payne, p. 118.
35. Payne testimony, p. 172; U.S. House, *Testimony in Relation to the Ute Indian Outbreak*, Henry James testimony, p. 203.
36. Payne, p. 119.
37. Ibid., p. 127.
38. Sprague, pp. 199–200. Some researchers consider Meeker's note to be a reply to the major's letter of September 25, 1879, but others don't believe Lowry had yet reached the agency, and I agree with the latter scenario.
39. Meeker to Thornburgh, September 27, 1879, U.S. Department of the Interior, p. xxxi.
40. Sprague, p. 201; U.S. House, *White River Ute Commission Investigation*, Colorado (Colorow) testimony, p. 63.
41 Sprague, p. 201; Colorado (Colorow) testimony, p. 62.
42. Colorado (Colorow) testimony, pp. 62–63.
43. Ibid., p. 62.
44. Sprague, p. 201.
45. White River Expedition letter, September 27, 1879, Secretary of War, *Report of the Secretary of War for the Year 1879*, pp. 9–10.
46. Payne testimony, p. 172.
47. James testimony, p. 204.
48. Rankin, "The Meeker Massacre from Reminiscences of Frontier Days," pp. 100–101.
49. Sprague, p. 202. This reference is accurate with respect to the camp, but Sprague describes the command as traveling up Deer Creek from Williams Fork.
50. Payne, p. 119.
51. Sprague, pp. 202–203; U.S. House, *Testimony in Relation to the Ute Indian Outbreak*, pp. 115–117.
52. McClellan, *This is Our Land*, Vol. 2, p. 149.
53. Burkey, "The Thornburgh Battle with the Utes on Milk Creek," p. 96.
54. Sprague, pp. 203–204.
55. Payne testimony, p. 172.
56. *Cheyenne Daily Leader*, October 23, 1879.

57. Cherry testimony, p. 64; Payne testimony, p. 172.
58. Payne testimony, p. 172; Sprague, pp. 203–204.
59. White River Expedition letter, September 28, 1879, Secretary of War, *Report of the Secretary of War for the Year 1879*, p. 10. For a slightly different version see U.S. Deptartment of the Interior, p. xxxii.
60. Dunn, *Massacres of the Mountains: a History of the Indian Wars of the Far West, 1815–1875*, p. 605.

Chapter 4: September 29, 1879

1. Captain J. Scott Payne to General Crook, October 1, 1879, United States Continental Command Records, Department of the Platte, Related to the White River Expedition.
2. Payne, "Incidents of the Recent Campaign Against the Utes," p. 119.
3. Patterson, interview with *Meeker Herald*, February 11, 1937, Meschter unpublished notes and correspondence. Captain Dodge issued 225 rounds of ammunition per trooper as he prepared to ride to the relief of Captain Payne and the White River Expedition. See his official report in Appendix D.
4. John C. Davis to Mrs. J. C. Davis, Davis, Collection; Rankin, "The Meeker Massacre from Reminiscences of Frontier Days," p. 99.
5. John C. Davis letter, Davis, Collection.
6. Smith, *Ouray: Chief of the Utes*, p. 77.
7. Owens, "Jo Rankin's Great Ride," W. O. Owens Collection, pp. 6–10.
8. Payne, pp. 119–120. Accounts differ as to the time of this descent. Sprague, *Massacre: the Tragedy at White River*, p. 205, states that it was about 8:00 A.M., but this interval would have given the expedition only an hour and a half to cover the ground between Deer Creek camp and Milk Creek, a minimum of six miles across drainages and up inclines. Thornburgh's command was not a forced march, but rather a cautious advance toward the reservation. They were in no particular hurry and still anticipated meeting with an Indian contingent that would accompany Thornburgh to the agency. I consider Payne's recollection as the most accurate because he was a participant and responsible for an official report of the engagement.
At least two stories account for the name Milk Creek. According to M. Wilson Rankin, Joe's cousin, the name derives from an incident in 1872 when a freighter dropped two cases of Gail Borden Eagle Brand condensed milk near the stream, see Sprague, p. 337, Rankin, p. 93. In contrast, First Lieutenant C.A.H. McCauley reported in 1878 that the stream was so called from "the whitish appearance of its waters, due to matter in solution acquired in its flow over the Cretaceous deposits at its headwaters." U.S. Senate, McCauley, *Report on White River Agency, Colo.*, p. 28.
9. Payne, pp. 119–120.
10. U.S. House, *Testimony in Relation to the Ute Indian Outbreak*, Payne testimony, p. 173.
11. Merritt, "Marching Cavalry," p. 74.
12. Payne, p. 120.
13. Payne testimony, p. 173.

218 Notes

14. Startzell, "Thornberg [sic] Massacre at Meeker"; also in Meschter, unpublished. The manuscript was written before July 27, 1931; the citation date of 1931 is only an estimate. Also, see Rankin, p. 102; Sprague, p. 206.
15. Rankin, p. 102; Payne testimony, p. 173. Payne does not acknowledge Rankin with the foresight to use the cutoff trail on September 29. Detours like this were common because old Indian trails crossed the agency road repeatedly. The cavalry often would take a cutoff trail while the wagons would follow the road.
16. Sprague, p. 206. The reference to a private accompanying the ambulance may refer to Samuel W. Hagerman of Company H, Fourth Infantry rather than to an O'Malley who does not show up on the company muster roll. That Thornburgh's ambulance accompanied him rather than stayed with the rest of the wagons may indicate that he still planned to take a small party in the wagon to the agency for talks with the Utes, even though the entire command continued to advance.
17. S. A. Cherry to Mrs. Thornburgh, October 23, 1879, photocopy of letter in *Meeker Herald*, Davis, Collection.
18. Sprague, p. 207.
19. *Cheyenne Daily Leader*, October 23, 1879. The baggage wagons and two-wheeled forge were abandoned in the fight.
20. Emmitt, *The Last War Trail: The Utes and the Settlement of Colorado*, pp. 195–196.
21. Ibid., p. 196. Much of Emmitt's information comes from interviews with Saponise, a Ute Indian who had been a fifteen-year old participant in the battle.
22. Sprague, *Colorado: a Bicentennial History*, p. 96.
23. U.S. House, *Testimony in Relation to the Ute Indian Outbreak*, Cherry testimony, p. 65.
24. Rankin, p. 103; Startzell.
25. Cherry testimony, p. 65.
26. Rankin, p. 103. Rankin indicates that the time was about 10:30 A.M., but 11:00 A.M. seems more reasonable since they crossed the creek about 10:30 and the fight broke out between 11:30 and noon.
27. S. A. Cherry to Mrs. Thornburgh, October 23, 1879, Davis, Collection.
28. Payne, p. 120; Upton, *Cavalry Tactics: United States Army*, p. 271; Fox, *Archaeology, History, and Custer's Last Battle*, pp. 140–141.
29. McChristian, *An Army of Marksmen*, p. 8. Discusses spacing between soldiers in skirmish line. For similar spacing in skirmish lines, see Upton (243); Cherry testimony, p. 65.
30. Payne testimony, p. 174.
31. Cherry testimony, pp. 65, 70; U.S. House, *White River Ute Commission Investigation*, Jack testimony, p. 192; U.S. House, *White River Ute Commission Investigation*, Yanco (an Uncompaghre Ute) testimony, pp. 34–35.
32. Jack testimony, p. 196; U.S. House, *White River Ute Commission Investigation*, Colorado (Colorow) testimony, p. 64.
33. Jack testimony, pp. 195–198.
34. Rankin, p. 100.
35. Jack testimony, p. 196.
36. Chief Jack, quoted in Colorado (Colorow) testimony, p. 64.

37. Chief Jack, quoted in Post Office Department special agent Charles Adams's testimony, U.S. House, *Testimony in Relation to the Ute Indian Outbreak,* p. 14.
38. Jack testimony, p. 196; Yanco testimony, pp. 34–35. Yanco, an Uncompaghre Ute, testified that he had advanced very near the soldiers when the soldiers fired the first shot. He may have been either with Jack near Payne's company or over to the west with Colorow's group in front of Cherry. He remembered seeing a soldier make signs with either a handkerchief or a hat. If he saw a handkerchief he must have been near Payne and Thornburgh, but if he saw a hat he probably was farther downstream, near Cherry. His proximity to the soldiers makes it more likely that his position was with Jack whose Indians had been maneuvering closer to the skirmish line. He also testified, however, that troops were deployed above and below him which suggests that he was near Cherry and below Lawson's position.
39. Jack testimony, p. 197. Jack estimated fifty Indians were involved in the battle early on; U.S. Department of the Interior, p. 33, says that there were at least 100 Indians at this time. One hundred or more Indians must have been present because, even with an advantage of terrain, they were divided between two skirmish lines and were facing at least 100 troopers.
40. Rankin, pp. 102–121.
41. Payne.
42. Emmitt, p. 200.
43. Cherry testimony, p. 65; McClellan, *This is Our Land*, Vol. 2, p. 170.
44. Rankin, pp. 104–121; Payne testimony, pp. 170–181; McClellan, p. 171. McClellan claims that Private John Burns, rather than Private Amos Miller, was killed with Firestone. However, recollections by Eugene A. Patterson (Miller's bunkmate) suggest that it probably was Miller who was killed at this time. Patterson's recollections were published in the *Meeker Herald,* February 11, 1937 (photocopy). Private Oscar Cass does not appear on muster rolls (see Appendix A).
45. Rankin, pp. 101–121.
46. Payne testimony, p. 174.
47. Spooner, "The Outbreak of September, 1879," p. 1125.
48. Payne, p. 121.
49. Cherry testimony, p. 66.
50. Rankin, p. 104. Rankin identifies Sergeant Thomas Nolan as one of the horse holders, but misclassifies him as a private.
51. Letter sent by Joseph Lawson, October 9, 1879, United States Continental Commands Records. Sergeant James Montgomery was wounded in the left ankle while fighting with Lawson's company at the end of the ridge near Milk Creek.
52. Payne, p. 121.
53. Payne testimony, pp. 170–181.
54. Rankin, pp. 104–105.
55. Dawson and Skiff, *The Ute War: A History of the White River Massacre,* p. 25.
56. Werner, *Meeker—the Story of the Meeker Massacre and Thornburgh Battle September 29, 1879,* p. 136; Rankin, p. 103; Sprague, p. 209; Huseas, "Thornburgh and Fort Steele," p. 23; Dan Davidson, Director, Moffat County Museum, Craig, Colo., 1994, Personal Communication.

57. Emmitt, p. 200; Jack testimony, pp. 196–197.
58. Emmitt, p. 200.
59. Rankin, p. 105; John C. Davis letter, Davis, Collection.
60. Rankin, pp. 101–121.
61. Payne testimony, p. 175.
62. *Cheyenne Daily Leader,* October 23, 1879 (This reference claims that there were fifteen wagons in the corral); Brandes, *Military Posts of Colorado,* p. 50 (Mentions that the wagons were overturned, but it is more likely that the wagons were parked with the beds still fastened to running gear); Dawson and Skiff, p. 26. According to the Denver correspondents, at least eight wagons were positioned in the breastworks on the north and east sides of the oval and eight others were drawn up inside for corralling the livestock, while trenches were needed to the south and west to reinforce the position.
63. Payne, p. 122.
64. Rankin.
65. Rodenbough, *Uncle Sam's Medal of Honor,* p. 359.
66. Ibid., p. 360. Many details pertaining to the trooper(s) sent to the wagons for cartridges to resupply Cherry and Lawson's men are ambiguous. Lieutenant Cherry's small detachment probably had fallen back close to Lawson's company by the time they were one thousand yards southwest of the wagons, and cartridge resupply may have been almost simultaneous for both detachments and not the actions of two different volunteers. If Private Donovan was sent from Lawson's company for ammunition, then he would have been the first to see Thornburgh's body and report it to his superiors. Lawson does not mention Donovan specifically, but he does confirm that "one of my men informed me that Major Thornburgh was killed half a mile ahead of us." Letter sent by Joseph Lawson, October 9, 1879, United States Continental Commands Records. Sergeant Grimes was not one of Lawson's men but Private Donovan was, and the information about Thornburgh would have reached Lawson about the same time as a resupply of ammunition.
67. Dawson and Skiff, p. 24.
68. Fox.
69. Sharp and Dunnigan, *The Congressional Medal of Honor: The Names, The Deeds,* p. 665.
70. Rodenbough, p. 362. Sergeant James Montgomery was wounded in his left ankle and had to be mounted on his horse to make it back to the wagons.
71. Cherry testimony, p. 66; Rankin, pp. 105–106.
72. Rankin, p. 106.
73. Emmitt, pp. 202–203; Johnson testimony, U.S. House, *White River Ute Commission Investigation,* p. 8.
74. Rankin, p. 107.
75. Ibid., p. 107.
76. Telegram received at Fort Fred Steele, September 29, 1879, Medical History File, Fort Fred Steele, Wyo., Historical Documents Collection. Photocopy on file at the Office of the Wyoming State Archaeologist, Laramie. Document Box 50.
77. Meeker to Commissioner of Indian Affairs, September 29, 1879, U.S. Department of the Interior, p. xxxii.

78. Meeker letter, September 29, 1879, U.S. House, *White River Ute Commission Investigation,* pp. 39–40. For a slightly different version see: Secretary of War, *Report of the Secretary of War for the Year 1879,* Vol. I, p. 10. In the original letter, Meeker wrote "If you have trouble in getting through the canyon to-day let me know in force." General William T. Sherman interpreted this to mean "in what force," hence the parenthetical (what) in some versions.
79. Rankin.
80. John C. Davis letter, Davis, Collection. Davis's letter provides the numbers used here for mules and horses, but he says that there were more than 200 men in the corral.
81. Cherry testimony, p. 66; Werner, p. 39.
82. Rankin, p. 106.
83. Rodenbough, pp. 357–359.
84. Dawson and Skiff, p. 32. One study mentions that trowel bayonets were useful digging tools: Scott, "A Sharp Little Affair: the Archaeology of the Big Hole Battlefield." Troopers at Milk Creek presumably didn't have the benefit of trowel bayonets that had been so useful at the 1877 battle of the Big Hole, but picks and shovels were in the wagons. Also see *Cheyenne Daily Leader,* October 23, 1879.
85. *Cheyenne Daily Leader,* October 23, 1879; Ibid., October 21, 1879.
86. Emmitt, p. 203.
87. John C. Davis letter, Davis, Collection; Sprague, p. 213.
88. Ibid.
89. Rankin, p. 106.
90. Ibid.
91. Payne, "Certificate of Capt. J. Scott Payne 5th U.S. Cavalry Concerning Loss and Destruction of Train and Supplies at Battle on Milk River (Colo.) September 29, 1879," pp. 137-140.
92. Emmitt, p. 204.
93. Burkey, "The Thornburgh Battle with the Utes on Milk Creek," p. 106; Letter sent by Joseph Lawson, October 9, 1879, United States Continental Commands Records; Startzell.
94. Rankin, p. 107.
95. Ibid.
96. Emmitt, p. 204.
97. *Cheyenne Daily Leader,* October 4, 1879.
98. John C. Davis letter, Davis, Collection.
99. McClellan, Vol. 2, p. 171, says that Private John Burns was killed during the early skirmishing before the cavalry retreat to the wagons. However Eugene Patterson gives an account of Private Amos Miller's death on the battlefield. See *Meeker Herald,* February 11, 1937, photocopy in Meschter, unpublished. Patterson was Miller's bunkmate so I accept his story. By process of elimination, this means that Burns must have been killed at the breastworks on the afternoon of September 29.
100. Payne testimony, p. 175; John C. Davis letter, Davis, Collection.
101. John C. Davis letter, Davis, Collection.
102. Sprague, pp. 213–315.
103. Dawson and Skiff, p. 27.
104. Captain J. Scott Payne telegram, October 1, 1879, United States Continental Commands Records. The parenthetical [killing of] does not appear in the original,

but adding it makes Payne's message more clear. The casualties had occurred by the time the captain wrote his dispatch.
105. Payne, p. 124; Sprague, p. 214.
106. *Farmer's Almanac* No. 87 1879, William Ware & Co.; Meschter, unpublished.
107. Joseph Lawson, October 9, 1879, U.S. Continental Commands Records. Lawson wrote that all of his company horses were dead, except one ridden by trooper Magerlein. He mentioned that Lieutenant Price's horse had survived which suggests that horses with Price's command had been sent ahead from Fortification Creek to accompany the expediton. Magerlein's horse and Price's were at the Supply Camp, (presumably Price's camp on Fortification Creek) when Lawson wrote his letter on October 9. The reason these two mounts survived the fight at the entrenchment may have been because they were selected by couriers on the evening of September 29. This also might explain how they got to Fortification Creek before the cavalry left Milk Creek for home.
108. Emmitt, pp. 204–205.
109. Meschter, unpublished.
110. Rodenbough, p. 366.

CHAPTER 5: ENTRENCHMENT AT MILK CREEK
1. Emmitt, *The Last War Trail: The Utes and the Settlement of Colorado,* p. 218.
2. Dawson and Skiff, *The Ute War: A History of the White River Massacre,* p. 32.
3. Ibid.; *Cheyenne Daily Leader,* October 28, 1879 mentions sixteen pits sixty feet long, three feet wide, and four feet deep. It further states that the elliptical corral was 75 feet by 125 feet in extent, which calculates to 9,375 square feet.
4. Dawson and Skiff, p. 34.
5. *Cheyenne Daily Leader,* October 26, 1879.
6. Sheridan, *Record of Engagements with Hostile Indians Within the Military Division of the Missouri from 1868–1882,* p. 90; Payne, "Incidents of the Recent Campaign Against the Utes," p. 123; *Cheyenne Daily Leader,* October 23, 1879.
7. *Cheyenne Daily Leader,* October 26, 1879.
8. Payne, pp. 114–129.
9. Rankin, "The Meeker Massacre from Reminiscences of Frontier Days," pp. 112–113.
10. Ibid.; Sheridan, p. 90. Payne (123) also states that a recruit was shot in the face on this night. He probably was talking about Esser, since other troopers didn't receive the same type of wound. Dawson and Skiff (41) say this happened on the sixth night, but an eyewitness account in the *Cheyenne Daily Leader,* October 9, 1879, specifically places the incident on the night of October 1.
11. Emmitt, p. 216.
12. Ibid., p. 218.
13. S. A. Cherry to Mrs. Thornburgh, October 23, 1879, photocopy of letter in *Meeker Herald,* Davis Collection.
14. Ibid.; Dawson and Skiff, p. 39.
15. Payne, p. 125.
16. Ibid., p. 126.
17. Dawson and Skiff, p. 34.
18. Payne, p. 125.

19. Owens, "Jo Rankin's Great Ride," p. 12.
20. Meschter, unpublished notes and correspondence.
21. *Cheyenne Daily Leader*, October 2, 1879.
22. Rankin, p. 108.
23. The Prugh papers, quoted in Meschter, unpublished.
24. Owens, pp. 16–17; Telegram sent from Rawlins, Wyo., October 1, 1879, United States Army Continental Commands Records, Department of the Platte, Related to the White River Expedition.
25. Meschter, unpublished. Meschter calculates the travel of 136 miles in about 24 hours.
26. Brown, *The Fetterman Massacre*, pp. 205–206.
27. *Cheyenne Daily Leader*, October 2, 1879. This reference publishes the message to Bisbee as being sent from Milk River, Colorado, but Price was not at the battlefield until October 5 when he arrived with the relief force led by Colonel Merritt. Rankin, p. 119, mentions that Price went with Merritt.
28. Rankin, p. 107.
29. *Cheyenne Daily Leader*, October 14, 1879.
30. Rankin, p. 108; Dodge, "Official report to the Adjutant General, District of New Mexico."
31. Rankin.
32. Ibid., p. 110; Dodge, October 19, 1879.
33. Rankin, p. 110.; Dodge, October 19, 1879. Dodge mentions a slightly different version of the E.E.C. note.
34. Dodge, October 19, 1879.
35. Ibid.; Rankin, p. 110.
36. Payne, p. 125.
37. Emmitt, p. 220.
38. Ibid., p. 221.

Chapter 6: The Whitest Black Men in the Cavalry

1. Dodge, "Official Report to the Adjutant General, District of New Mexico."
2. *Cheyenne Daily Leader*, October 26, 1879.
3. Dawson and Skiff, *The Ute War: A History of the White River Massacre*, p. 40.
4. Ibid., p. 34.
5. Ibid., p. 35.
6. Ibid., p. 36.
7. Ibid., p. 36.
8. Dodge, "Official report"; Rankin, p. 110.
9. Sprague, *Massacre: The Tragedy at White River*, p. 221.
10. Dawson and Skiff, p. 40.
11. Ibid., pp. 38–39.
12. Rankin, pp. 111–112.
13. *Cheyenne Daily Leader*, October 26, 1879.
14. Payne, "Incidents of the Recent Campaign Against the Utes," p. 119; Sprague, p. 64.
15. Dawson and Skiff, p. 39; McClellan, *This is Our Land*, Vol. 2, p. 229.
16. Rankin, p. 112.

17. *Cheyenne Daily Leader,* October 26, 1879.
18. Rankin, p. 112.
19. Ibid.
20. Emmitt, *The Last War Trail: The Utes and the Settlement of Colorado,* pp. 222–224.
21. *Cheyenne Daily Leader,* October 26, 1879; Dawson and Skiff, pp. 37–38.
22. Leckie, *The Buffalo Soldiers: a Narrative of the Negro Cavalry in the West,* p. 208. According to Leckie, Sergeant Johnson went on water detail on the evening of the fifth day of battle.
23. Emmitt. Discusses the weather conditions during the battle.
24. Rankin, p. 112.
25. Dawson and Skiff, p. 37.
26. Rankin, p. 111.
27. Dawson and Skiff, p. 38.
28. Ibid., p. 39.; McClellan, p. 231.
29. Dawson and Skiff, pp. 39–40.
30. *Cheyenne Daily Leader,* October 26, 1879; Emmitt, p. 312.
31. Bisbee, *Through Four American Wars: the Impressions and Experiences of Brigadier General William Henry Bisbee,* p. 213.
32. *Cheyenne Daily Leader,* October 3, 1879.
33. Telegram received at Fort Fred Steele, October 2, 1879, Fort Fred Steele, Wyo., Historical Documents Collection.
34. *Cheyenne Daily Leader,* October 8, 1879.

Chapter 7: Merritt's Lightening March

1. Merritt, "Marching Cavalry," p. 78.
2. Finerty, *War-Path and Bivouac: the Big Horn and Yellowstone Expedition,* p. 277.
3. Merritt, "Marching Cavalry," p. 78.
4. Ibid.
5. Ibid., p. 74.
6. Ibid., p. 78.
7. Merritt, "Three Indian Campaigns." See pages 732–737 for Milk Creek incident. This article is also in Merritt, *Merritt and the Indian Wars,* pp. 24–29; Kimball, *A Soldier-Doctor of Our Army: James P. Kimball Late Colonel and Assistant Surgeon-General, U.S. Army,* pp. 92–109.
8. Rankin, "The Meeker Massacre from Reminiscences of Frontier Days," p. 117.
9. Merritt, "Three Indian Campaigns," p. 732.
10. Post Returns, Fort D. A. Russell, August–October 1879.
11. Rankin, p. 118.
12. Post Returns, Fort D. A. Russell, August–October 1879.
13. Rankin, p. 118.
14. Ibid.
15. Ibid., p. 117; Merritt, "Three Indian Campaigns," p. 733.
16. Merritt, "Three Indian Campaigns," p. 733; Kimball, p. 98. Rankin (117) says the first train left Cheyenne at 2:00 P.M. and the second followed at 5:00 P.M.
17. Kimball, p. 98. Kimball mentions four companies, but only three are indicated on Fort Sanders, Wyoming Post Returns, October 1879.

18. Ibid.
19. Post Returns, Fort Sanders, October 1879.
20. Merritt, "Three Indian Campaigns," p. 733.
21. Rankin, p. 118.
22. Ibid.
23. Ibid.; Sprague, *Massacre: The Tragedy at White River*, p. 222. Sprague indicates that more than one correspondent accompanied the relief force.
24. Merritt, "Three Indian Campaigns," p. 733 map, and p. 734; McClellan, *This is Our Land*, Vol. 2, p. 336.
25. Rankin, pp. 118–119.
26. Merritt, "Marching Cavalry," pp. 73–75.
27. Merritt, "Three Indian Campaigns," p. 734; Kimball, p. 99.
28. Ibid.
29. Ibid.
30. Merritt, "Three Indian Campaigns," p. 736.
31. Rankin, p. 119.
32. Merritt, "Three Indian Campaigns," p. 736; Kimball, p. 99.
33. Rankin, p. 119.
34. Kimball, pp. 99–100; Merritt, "Three Indian Campaigns," p. 736.
35. Kimball, p. 100.
36. Ibid.
37. Merritt, "Three Indian Campaigns," pp. 736–737.
38. Ibid., p. 737.
39. Rankin, p. 119.
40. Merritt, "Three Indian Campaigns," p. 737.
41. Kimball, p. 101.
42. Merritt, "Three Indian Campaigns," p. 737.
43. Payne, "Incidents of the Recent Campaign Against the Utes," p. 128.
44. Kimball, p. 101.
45. Payne, p. 128.
46. Dawson and Skiff, *The Ute War: A History of the White River Massacre*, p. 42.
47. Kimball, pp. 101–102.
48. Ibid., p. 102.
49. Rankin, p. 122.
50. Startzell, "Thornberg [sic] Massacre at Meeker"; Hauser, "Meeker Massacre and Colonel Merritt's Record Ride to the Relief of Captain Payne's Beleagered [sic] Troops on Milk River, Colorado," p. 3.
51. Kimball, p. 102.
52. Ibid., p. 103.; Rankin, p. 120.
53. Rankin, pp. 119–120.
54. Emmitt, *The Last War Trail: The Utes and the Settlement of Colorado*, p.226; McChristian, *An Army of Marksmen*, p. 66.
55. Rankin, p. 120.
56. Ouray message, October 2, 1879, U.S. Department of the Interior, *Annual Report of the Commisioner of Indian Affairs to the Secretary of the Interior for the Year 1879*, pp. xxxiii–xxxiv.

57. Letter sent by W. M. Stanley, October 2, 1879, U.S. House, *White River Ute Commission Investigation*, pp. 28–29.
58. Kimball, p. 103; Sprague, pp. 225–226.
59. Sprague, p. 222; John G. Bourke, *On the Border with Crook*, pp. 426–427. Bourke also mentions the incident, but does not name Lowry.
60. Rankin, p. 119; Dawson and Skiff, p. 43; Dunn, *Massacres of the Mountains: a History of the Indian Wars of the Far West, 1815–1875*, p. 612.
61. S. A. Cherry to Mrs. Thornburgh, October 23, 1879, photocopy of letter in *Meeker Herald*, Davis, Collection.
62. Kimball, p. 103; Werner, *Meeker—the Story of the Meeker Massacre and Thornburgh Battle September 29, 1879*, p. 126. Contains a letter written by Robert B. Grimes to Surgeon General Jos. K. Raines on September 30, 1879, obviously before Grimes had seen Thornburgh's body. Grimes must have drawn this conclusion based on information from Private Donovan or some other trooper who had seen the body on the way back to the barricade on September 29.
63. Sprague, p. 209.
64. *Cheyenne Daily Leader*, October 23, 1879.
65. Kimball, p. 103.
66. Rankin, p. 121; Kimball, p. 103.
67. Kimball, p. 103.
68. Rankin, p. 121.
69. Kimball, p. 104, for quote; also see Rankin, p. 120 for mention of Merritt moving camp.
70. Shields, "Army Life on the Wyoming Frontier," p. 342.
71. Letter sent by Joseph Lawson, October 9, 1879, United States Continental Commands Records, Department of the Platte, Related to the White River Expedition; Kimball, p. 103; Rankin, p. 121; Miller and Wedel, eds. *Archaeological Survey and Test Excavations at Fort Fred Steele State Historic Site*, pp. 99–100. Fort Fred Steele interment records do not include burials of soldiers killed at Milk Creek. It is still unknown, however, whether or not the soldiers and civilians buried near the breastworks on the battlefield ever were disinterred and reburied elsewhere. They apparently were not reburied in a national cemetery according to written communication to the author from William Jayne, Department of Veterans Affairs, National Cemetery System, Washington, D.C., December 16, 1992.
72. *Cheyenne Daily Leader*, October 26, 1879.
73. Dawson and Skiff, p. 43.
74. *Cheyenne Daily Leader*, October 26, 1879.
75. Dawson and Skiff, p. 40.
76. Letter sent by Joseph Lawson, October 9, 1879, United States Continental Commands Records; Dodge, "Official Report to the Adjutant General, District of New Mexico"; Rankin (121) says they left on October 7, but he is mistaken.
77. Rankin, p. 121.
78. Brandes, *Military Posts of Colorado*, p. 51; Sprague, pp. 226–228.

Chapter 8: Aftermath
1. Letter sent by Joseph Lawson, October 9, 1879, United States Continental Commands Records, Department of the Platte, Related to the White River Expedition.
2. Marshall, *Crimsoned Prairie: the Indian Wars*, p. 2.
3. Marsh, *The Utes of Colorado: People of the Shining Mountains*, pp. 143–145; Jan Pettit, *Utes: the Mountain People*, pp. 35–39.
4. U.S. Army, *Official Army Register for January 1881*, p. 268.
5. Dawson and Skiff, *The Ute War: A History of the White River Massacre*, p. 44; *Cheyenne Daily Leader*, October 19, 1879.
6. Census Records for 1880, Fort Fred Steele.
7. Sprague, *Massacre: The Tragedy at White River*, p. 323.
8. Ibid.
9. *Cheyenne Daily Leader*, February 1, 1881.
10. Mangum, *Battle of the Rosebud: Prelude to the Little Bighorn*; Greene, *Slim Buttes, 1876: an Episode of the Great Sioux War*.
11. Hedren, *With Crook in the Black Hills*, pp. 32, 57–58.
12. Finerty, *War-Path and Bivouac: The Big Horn and Yellowstone Expedition*, p. 221.
13. Vaughn, *Indian Fights: New Facts on Seven Encounters*, p. 194.
14. Ibid.; *Cheyenne Daily Leader*, February 1 and February 5, 1881.
15. *Army and Navy Journal*, February 5, 1881, pp. 542–543; *Cheyenne Daily Leader*, February 5, 1881; Miller and Wedel, eds., *Archaeological Survey and Test Excavations at Fort Fred Steele State Historic Site*; Jayne, Department of Veterans Affairs National Cemetery System, written communication to author, December 16, 1992.
16. Vaughn, p. 195.
17. U.S. House, *White River Ute Commission Investigation*, p. 80.
18. Miller and Wedel; Sprague, p. 323.
19. Ibid.; McClellan, *This is Our Land*, Vol. 2, pp. 717–719.
20. S. A. Cherry to Mrs. Thornburgh, October 23, 1879, photocopy of letter from *Meeker Herald*, Davis, Collection; U.S. Army, *Official Army Register for 1882*, p. 362; Sprague, p. 323.
21. Meschter, "Sixty days to and in Yellowstone Park by Henry A. Kirk," p. 7; Miller, Family Genealogy Records; Wentworth, *America's Sheep Trails*, p. 316.
22. Startzell, "Thornberg [sic] Massacre at Meeker"; Peterson, *Men of Wyoming*, p. 237; Erwin, *Historical Blue Book*, pp. 720–721.
23. Joan Page, personal communication 1992–1993; Gleim, *The Certificate of Merit. U.S. Army Distinguished Service Award 1847–1918*, p. 9.
24. Meschter, unpublished notes and correspondence.
25. Ibid.; *Meeker Herald*, September 27, 1929.
26. Meschter, unpublished; *Meeker Herald*, February 11, 1937.
27. Ibid.
28. Ibid.
29. Ibid.
30. Ibid.

31. Ibid.
32. Rankin, "The Meeker Massacre from Reminiscences of Frontier Days," p. 144.
33. Sprague, p. 323; Meschter, unpublished, contains a reference to the *Meeker Herald*, January 1, 1919 regarding Sherrod.
34. Garrett, "Some Recollections of an Old Freighter," p. 90.
35. U.S. House, *White River Ute Commission Investigation*.
36. Ibid., p. 76.
37. U.S. House, *Testimony in Relation to the Ute Indian Outbreak, Taken by the Committee on Indian Affairs*.
38. Smith, *Ouray: Chief of the Utes*, p. 175.
39. U.S. House, *Testimony in Relation to the Ute Indian Outbreak*.
40. Bourke, *On the Border with Crook*, p. 349; Emmitt, *The Last War Trail: The Utes and the Settlement of Colorado*, p. 331.
41. DeBarthe, *Life and Adventures of Frank Grouard*, p. 120.
42. *Cheyenne Daily Leader*, October 3 and 7, 1879.
43. Rankin, p. 144.
44. Smith, p. 176.
45. Ibid., p. 182.
46. Ibid., p. 193.
47. Marsh, p. 167.
48. Pettit, p. 135; Marsh, p. 111.

Appendix A
1. Rankin, "The Meeker Massacre from Reminiscences of Frontier Days," p. 118.

Appendix B
1. S. A. Cherry to Lieutenant John G. Bourke, October 8, 1879, United States Continental Commands Records, Department of the Platte, Related to the White River Expedition.
2. Letter sent by J. S. Payne October 25, 1879, United States Continental Commands Records.
3. *Omaha Daily Bee* (Date not visible), American Heritage Center, University of Wyoming, Acc. No. 801 (In 2-bat-me); Sprague, p. 322.
4. Dawson and Skiff, *The Ute War: A History of the White River Massacre*, pp. 27–29, 178.
5. *Cheyenne Daily Leader*, October 21, 1879.
6. Ibid.
7. Rankin, "The Meeker Massacre from Reminiscences of Frontier Days," pp. 104–106, 121.
8. *Cheyenne Daily Leader*, October 26, 1879.
9. Payne, "Incidents of the Recent Campaign Against the Utes," pp. 128–129.
10. Ibid., p. 129.
11. Rankin, p. 121.
12. Charles Adams to Secretary Schurz, October 24, 1879, *Senate Executive Document* No. 31, 46th Congress, 2nd Session, 1879–80, Vol. I, pp. 13–14.

13. Jack testimony, U.S. House, *Testimony in Relation to the Ute Indian Outbreak, Taken by the Committee on Indian Affairs*, p. 202.
14. Dawson and Skiff, p. 29.
15. "Report of the General of the Army," in Secretary of War, *Report of the Secretary of War for the Year 1879*, p. 13.
16. Colorado (Colorow) testimony, U.S. House, *White River Ute Commission Investigation*, p. 64.
17. Dawson and Skiff, p. 29.
18. Fort Fred Steele and Fort D. A. Russell Post Returns.
19. *Cheyenne Daily Leader*, October 9, 1879. An article in *Capper's Weekly* from March 5, 1921 and reprinted in *Winners of the West*, entitled "The Meeker Massacre and Ute Jack's Death: an Old Indian Fighter's Reminiscences," states that there were 276 horses and mules dead in one place.

Appendix C

1. Sharp and Dunnigan, *The Congressional Medal of Honor: The Names, the Deeds*.
2. Payne, "Incidents of the Recent Campaign Against the Utes," p. 124.
3. Rodenbough, *Uncle Sam's Medal of Honor*, p. 362.
4. Ibid.
5. Ibid., p. 364.
6. Payne, p. 124.
7. Rodenbough, p. 363.
8. Amos, "Above and Beyond in the West: Black Medal of Honor Winners, 1870–1890," pp. 14–17.
9. Ibid., p. 17.
10. Young, *The General's General: the Life and Times of Arthur MacArthur*, pp. 160–161. This reference deals with officers getting the Medal of Honor. *Cheyenne Daily Leader*, February 5, 1881, for the quote.
11. Larson, *History of Wyoming*, p. 136.
12. *Session Laws of Wyoming Territory Passed by the Sixth Legislative Assembly, Convened at Cheyenne, Wyo., November 4, 1879*, Wyoming Territorial Legislative Assembly; Price, *Across the Continent with the Fifth Cavalry*, pp. 451, 573, and 576.
13. Gleim, *The Certificate of Merit: U.S. Army Distinguished Service Award 1847–1918*; Regular Army Muster Rolls.
14. Rickey, *Forty Miles a Day on Beans and Hay*, p. 310.
15. Gleim, p. 9.
16. Ibid., pp. 42–43.
17. *Reflections: a Pictorial History of Carbon County-1990*, p. 135.
18. Ibid.
19. Ibid., Supplement section.
20. Gleim, p. 43.
21. Endorsements from Fort Fred Steele, October–November 1879 recommending Certificate of Merit to Private Samuel W. Hagerman, Fort Fred Steele, Wyo., Historical Documents Collection.
22. U.S. Army, Office of the Adjutant General, *American Decorations*, pp. 835–845.

23. Rankin, "The Meeker Massacre from Reminiscences of Frontier Days," pp. 105–106.
24. Carroll, *Indian Wars Campaign Medal: Its History and its Recipients.*
25. Sprague, *Massacre: The Tragedy at White River,* p. 322.

Appendix D

1. Official report of Captain J. Scott Payne, October 5, 1879, United States Continental Commands Records, Department of the Platte, Related to the White River Expedition.
2. General Orders No. 1, White River Expedition, October 5, 1879, United States Continental Commands Records.
3. Captain Joseph Lawson to Sergeant Ambrose, October 9, 1879, United States Continental Commands Records.
4. Lieutenant S. A. Cherry, October 8, 1879, United States Continental Commands Records.
5. Dodge, "Official Report to the Adjutant General, District of New Mexico."
6. J. C. Davis to Mrs. J. C. Davis, no date, On letterhead of J. W. Hugus & Co. Post Traders, U.S.A., Fort Fred. Steele, Wyo., Davis, Collection.

Bibliography

Manuscripts

Adjutant General, U.S. Army, (main series). Letters received relating to the Ute Uprising, 1879. National Archives. Record Group 94, microfilm copy 666, Roll 513 (April to October 1879); Roll 514 (October to December 1879).

Bisbee, Wm. H., "Inspection Report of Fort Fred Steele, Wyo., September 1879." National Archives. Record Group 92.

Davis, John Charles. Collection, American Heritage Center 801, University of Wyoming, Laramie, Wyo.

Dodge, F. S. "Official Report to the Adjutant General, District of New Mexico, October 19, 1879." Office of the Adjutant General (Main Series) Letters Received relating to the Ute uprising, Oct. (part) to Dec. 1879. National Archives, Record Group 94, Microfilm copy 666, Roll 514.

Fort D. A. Russell, Wyoming, Post Returns, September–October 1879. National Archives. Microfilm 617, Roll 1051.

Fort Fred Steele census records for 1880. Session Laws of Wyoming 1927 (microfilm). State Archives, Division of Cultural Resources, Wyoming Department of Commerce, Cheyenne, Wyo.

Fort Fred Steele, Wyoming, Historical Documents Collection. University of Wyoming Archaeological Repository, Document Box 50. Typed transcripts by Robert A. Murray of documents from National Archives Record Groups 98 and 159.

———. Post Returns, September–October 1879. National Archives. Microfilm copy 617, Roll 380.

Fort Laramie, Wyo., correspondence, 1870–1881. Microfilm F 769 .F6 F58, 1960Z, Reel 1, Coe Library, University of Wyoming, Laramie, Wyo.

Fort Sanders, Wyo., Post Returns, October 1879. National Archives. Microfilm 617, Roll No. 1094.

Meeker (Colorado) Chamber of Commerce, "Historical Episodes of Meeker," brochure.
Meschter, Daniel Y., Unpublished notes and correspondence. Mark Miller, Laramie, Wyo.
Miller, Isaac C., Family Genealogy Records. Mark Miller, Laramie, Wyo.
Owens, W. O. "Jo Rankin's Great Ride", 1937. W. O. Owens Collection. American Heritage Center, University of Wyoming, Laramie, Wyo.
Regular Army Muster Rolls: Company E Fourth Infantry, Company E Third Cavalry, Companies D & F Fifth Cavalry, Company D Ninth Cavalry. National Archives. Record Group 94.
Startzell, A. M. "Thornberg [sic] Massacre at Meeker," 1931. Colorado Historical Society, Denver, Colo.
Thornburgh Monument (5RB982), Battle of Milk River site, Rio Blanco County, Colorado, National Register of Historic Places inventory. Nomination form by Don Rickey, Steve Wing and Mary Shipman, 1973. Colorado Historical Society, Denver, Colo.
United States Continental Commands Records, Department of the Platte, Related to the White River Expedition. National Archives. Record Group 393. Microfilm copy 770, Roll 245.

GOVERNMENT PUBLICATIONS

Sheridan, P. H. (Lieutenant-General). *Record of Engagements with Hostile Indians Within the Military Division of the Missouri from 1868 to 1882.* Government Printing Office, Washington, D.C., 1882. (Facsimile edition by the Old Army Press, Bellevue, Nebr., 1969).
U.S. Army, Office of the Adjutant General. *American Decorations*: a List of Awards of the Congressional Medal of Honor, the Distinguished-Service Cross, and the Distinguished-Service Medal Awarded Under Authority of the Congress of the United States 1862–1926. Government Printing Office, Washington, D.C., 1927.
──────. *Official Army Register for January 1879.* Washington, Janury 1, 1879.
──────. *Official Army Register for January 1880.* Washington, January 1, 1880.
──────. *Official Army Register for January 1881.* Washington, January 1, 1881.

———. *Official Army Register for January 1882*. Washington, January 1, 1882.

U.S. Department of the Interior. Commission of Indian Affairs. *Annual Report of the Commissioner of Indian Affairs to the Secretary of the Interior for the Year 1879*. Government Printing Office, Washington, D. C., 1879.

U.S. House. *Report of the Indian Commission*. 45th Congress, 3d sess. H. Exec. Doc., no.84, serial 1858. Government Printing Office, Washington, D.C., 1879.

———. *Testimony in Relation to the Ute Indian Outbreak, Taken by the Committee on Indian Affairs*. 46th Congress, 2d sess. H. Mis. Doc., no. 38, serial 1931. Government Printing Office, Washington, D.C., 1880.

———. *White River Ute Commission Investigation*. 46th Congress, 2d sess., 1880 H. Exec. Doc, no. 83, serial 1925, Government Printing Office, Washington, D.C., 1880.

U.S. Senate. *Report on White River Agency, Colorado, Including Wagon Roads Thereto, Indian Agency, the Valley, Etc., Etc., with Map*, by C.A.H. McCauley. In message from the President of the United States communicating the report of the Special Ute Commission, pp. 12–36. 45th Congress, 3rd sess., 1879, S. Exec. Doc., no. 62, serial 1831. Government Printing Office, Washington, D. C., 1879.

———. *Letter from the Secretary of the Interior Transmitting Correspondence Concerning the Ute Indians in Colorado*. 46th Congress, 2d sess. Senate Ex. Doc., no. 31, serial 1882. Government Printing Office, Washington, D.C., 1880.

War Department. *War of the Rebellion: Official Record of the Union and Confederate Armies*. Series 1, Vol. XX. Operations in Kentucky, Middle and East Tennessee, North Alabama, and Southwest Virginia, Nov. 1, 1862–Jan. 20, 1863; Stone's River or Murfreesborough; Part I of II; Reports. Government Printing Office, Washington, D.C., 1887.

———. Secretary of War. *Report of the Secretary of War for the Year 1879*, Volume I. U.S. House Executive Documents, no. 1, pt 2. 46th Congress, 2d session, Vol. 2, pp. 1–188, serial 1903. Government Printing Office, Washington, D. C., 1879.

———. *Report of the Secretary of War for the year 1880.* U.S. House Executive Documents, no. 1, pt. 2. 46th Congress, 3d sess., Vol. 2, pp. 1–242, serial 1952. Government Printing Office, Washington, D. C., 1881.

Wyoming Territorial Legislative Assembly. *Session Laws Passed by the Sixth Legislative Assembly*, Cheyenne, Wyoming, November 4, 1879. Leader Steam Book & Job Print, Cheyenne, Wyo., 1879.

Articles

Annals of Wyoming, Vol. 3, No. 2, 1925, pp. 137–140. [Certificate of Captain J. Scott Payne, Fifth U. S. Cavalry, Concerning Loss and Destruction of Train and Supplies at Battle on Milk River (Colo.) September 29, 1879].

Burkey, Elmer R. "The Thornburgh Battle with the Utes on Milk Creek." *The Colorado Magazine* 13(3) (1936), pp. 90–110.

Buys, Christian J. "Accounts of the Battle at Milk Creek: Implications for Historical Accuracy." Colorado Historical Society Essays in Colorado History, *Essays & Monographs*, Number 4 (1986), pp. 59–80.

Conniss, I. R. "Recollections of Taylor Pennock." *Annals of Wyoming* 6 (1&2) (1929), pp. 199–212.

Fleek, Sherman L. "Race Against Deadly Odds." *Wild West*, October (1989), pp. 40–48.

Garrett, T. S. "Some Recollections of an Old Freighter." *Annals of Wyoming* 3(1) (1925), pp. 86–93.

Hauser, C. R. "Meeker Massacre and Colonel Merritt's Record Ride to the Relief of Captain Payne's Beleagered [*sic*] Troops on Milk River, Colorado." *Winners of the West* 11(2), p. 3, January 30, 1934.

Hebard, G. R. "Data on Battle at Milk River." *Annals of Wyoming* 3(2) (1925), pp. 137–144.

Huseas, Marion M. "Thornburgh and Fort Steele." *Council on Abandoned Military Posts–U.S.A. Periodical* 5(4)(1973), pp. 17–24.

"Meeker Massacre and Ute Jack's Death: An Old Indian Fighter's Reminiscences, The." *Winners of the West* 13(9), p. 3 August 30, 1936.

Merritt, W. (Brigadier General). "Marching Cavalry." *Journal of the United States Cavalry Association* 1(1) (1888), pp. 71–78, March.

Merritt, Wesley (General). "Three Indian Campaigns." *Harper's New Monthly Magazine* 80(479) (1890) pp. 720–737, April.
Meschter, Daniel Y. (editor). "Sixty Days to and in Yellowstone Park by Henry A. Kirk." *Annals of Wyoming* 44(1) (1972), pp. 5–23.
Patterson, Eugene A., interview, in "Great Fun Says Survivor of Thornburg [sic] Massacre," *Meeker Herald,* February 11, 1937.
Payne, J. S. "Incidents of the Recent Campaign Against the Utes." *The United Service* 2(1) (1880), pp. 114–129, January.
Rankin, M. Wilson. "The Meeker Massacre from Reminiscences of Frontier Days." *Annals of Wyoming* 16(2) (1944), pp. 87–145.
Riddle, Jack P. "Besieged on Milk Creek." *Great Western Indian Fights*, pp. 281–291. The Potomac Corral of the Westerners. University of Nebraska Press, Lincoln, 1960.
Shields, Alice Mathews. "Army Life on the Wyoming Frontier." *Annals of Wyoming* 13(4) (1941), pp. 331–346.
Spooner, H. W. "The Outbreak of September, 1879." *Journal of the United States Cavalry Association* (1910), pp. 1124–1128, May.

Newspapers

Army and Navy Journal
Carbon County Journal
Cheyenne Daily Leader
Harper's Weekly
Meeker Herald
Omaha Daily Bee
Sentinel (Laramie)

Maps

Colorado Nineteenth Century General Land Office Township Maps. Surveyor General's Office, Denver, Colo. 1875–1908.
Craig, Colorado; Wyoming 1954 (revised 1974). USGS Map 1:250,000 (Series V502, Edition 3, NK 13–10).
Rawlins, Wyoming; Colorado 1954 (limited revision 1962). USGS Map 1:250,000 (Series V502, Edition 2, NK 13–7).

Thornburgh Quadrangle Colorado, 7.5 Min. Series, Topographic. USGS, Denver, Colorado, 1966, photorevised 1987.

Wyoming Nineteenth Century General Land Office Township Maps. Surveyor General's Office, Cheyenne, Wyo., 1873–1888.

Books

Alberts, Don E. *Brandy Station to Manila Bay: A Biography of General Wesley Merritt.* Presidial Press, Austin, Texas, 1980.

Alcorn, Gay Day. *Tough Country: The History of the Saratoga & Encampment Valley 1825–1895.* Legacy Press, Saratoga, Wyoming, 1984.

Amos, Preston E. *Above and Beyond in the West: Black Medal of Honor Winners, 1870–1890.* Potomac Corral, the Westerners, Washington, D.C., 1974.

Bancroft, Hubert Howe. *The Works of Hubert Howe Bancroft,* Vol. 25, History of Nevada, Colorado and Wyoming 1540–1888. The History Company, San Francisco, California, 1890.

Bisbee, William Haymond. *Through Four American Wars: The Impressions and Experiences of Brigadier General William Henry Bisbee as Told to His Grandson William Haymond Bisbee.* Meador Publishing Company, Boston, Massachusetts, 1931.

Bourke, John G. *On the Border with Crook.* Charles Scribner's Sons, New York, 1891. First Bison Book Printing, University of Nebraska Press, Lincoln, 1971.

Brandes, T. Donald. *Military Posts of Colorado.* The Old Army Press, Fort Collins, Colorado, 1973.

Brown, Dee. *The Fetterman Massacre.* Originally published: *Fort Phil Kearny, an American Saga.* Putnam, New York, 1962. First Bison Book Printing, University of Nebraska Press, Lincoln, 1971.

Carroll, J. M. *Indian Wars Campaign Medal Its History and Its Recipients.* J. M. Carroll Company, 1979, Bryan, Texas.

Crook, George. *General George Crook: His Autobiography.* Edited by Martin F. Schmitt. University of Oklahoma Press, Norman, 1960.

Dawson, Thomas F. and F.J.V. Skiff. *The Ute War: A History of the White River Massacre.* Tribune Publishing House, Denver, Colorado, 1879.

(Reprinted by Johnson Publishing Company, Boulder, Colorado, 1980).

DeBarthe, Joe. *Life and Adventures of Frank Grouard*. University of Oklahoma Press, Norman, 1958.

Dunn, J. P., Jr. *Massacres of the Mountains: a History of the Indian Wars of the Far West 1815–1875*. Archer House, Inc., New York, 1958.

Emmitt, Robert. *The Last War Trail: The Utes and the Settlement of Colorado*. University of Oklahoma Press, Norman, 1954.

Erwin, Marie H. *Historical Blue Book*. Bradford–Robinson Printing Co., Denver, Colorado, 1946.

Farmer's Almanac No. 87. William Ware & Co. Boston, 1879.

Finerty, John F. *War-Path and Bivouac: The Big Horn and Yellowstone Expedition*. University of Nebraska Press, Lincoln, 1966.

Fox, Richard Allen, Jr. *Archaeology, History, and Custer's Last Battle*. University of Oklahoma Press, Norman, 1993.

Frye, Elnora L. *Atlas of Wyoming Outlaws at the Territorial Penitentiary*. Jelm Mountain Publications, Laramie, Wyoming, 1990.

Gleim, Albert F., LTC, USA. *The Certificate of Merit: US Army Distinguished Service Award 1847–1918*. Arlington, Virginia, 1979.

Greene, Jerome A. *Slim Buttes, 1876: an Episode of the Great Sioux War*. University of Oklahoma Press, Norman, 1982.

Hammer, Kenneth M. *The Springfield Carbine on the Western Frontier*. The Old Army Press, Bellevue, Nebraska, 1970.

Hedren, Paul L. *With Crook in the Black Hills: Stanley J. Morrow's 1876 Photographic Legacy*. Pruett Publishing Company, Boulder, Colorado, 1985.

———. *Fort Laramie in 1876*. University of Nebraska Press, Lincoln, 1988.

Joint Centennial Committee of Saratoga and Encampment, Wyoming. *Saratoga & Encampment, Wyoming: an Album of Family Histories*. Portfolio Publishing Company, The Woodlands, Texas, 1989.

Kimball, Maria Brace. *A Soldier-Doctor of Our Army: James P. Kimball, Late Colonel and Assistant Surgeon-General U.S. Army*. Houghton Mifflin Company, Boston and New York, 1917.

Knight, Oliver. *Following the Indian Wars: the Story of the Newspaper Correspondents Among the Indian Campaigners*. University of

Oklahoma Press, Norman, 1960.

Larson, T. A. *History of Wyoming.* University of Nebraska Press, Lincoln, 1965.

Leckie, William H. *The Buffalo Soldiers: A Narrative of the Negro Cavalry in the West.* University of Oklahoma Press, Norman, 1967.

Mangum, Neil C. *Battle of the Rosebud: Prelude to the Little Bighorn.* Upton & Sons, El Segundo, California, 1987.

Marsh, Charles S. *The Utes of Colorado: People of the Shining Mountains.* Pruett Publishing Company, Boulder, Colorado, 1982.

Marshall, S.L.A. *Crimsoned Prairie: the Indian wars.* Da Capo Press, Inc., New York, 1972.

McCartney, E. Ray. *Crisis of 1873.* Burgess Publishing Company, Minneapolis, Minnesota, 1935.

McChristian, Douglas C. *An Army of Marksmen.* The Old Army Press, Fort Collins, Colorado, 1981.

McClellan, Val J. *This is Our Land,* Volume 1. Vantage Press, New York, 1977.

———. *This is Our Land,* Volume 2. Western Publishers, Jamestown, Ohio, 1979.

Merritt, Wesley (General). "Three Indian Campaigns." *Merritt and the Indian Wars,* with a biographical essay by Barry C. Johnson. The Johnson-Taunton Military Press, London, England, 1972.

Meschter, Daniel Y. (compiler). *A Carbon County Chronology 1867–1879.* Cheyenne, Wyoming, 1970. (In Coe Library, University of Wyoming, Laramie).

Miller, Mark E. and Dale L. Wedel (editors). *Archaeological Survey and Test Excavations at Fort Fred Steele State Historic Site.* Report by the State Archaeologist's Office, on file at Wyoming Department of Commerce, Cheyenne, 1992.

Peterson, Clarence Stewart. *Men of Wyoming.* C. S. Peterson, Denver, Colorado, 1915.

Pettit, Jan. *Utes: the Mountain People.* Johnson Books, Boulder, Colorado, 1990.

Price, George F. *Across the Continent with the Fifth Cavalry.* Antiquarian Press, Ltd., New York, 1959.

Reflections: A Pictorial History of Carbon County—1990. Carbon County Museum, Rawlins, Wyoming, 1990.

Rennicke, Jeff. "The Rivers of Colorado," *Colorado Geographic Series*, No. 1. Falcon Press Publishing Co., Inc., Billings and Helena, Montana, 1985.

Rickey, Don, Jr. *Forty Miles a Day on Beans and Hay.* University of Oklahoma Press, Norman, 1963.

Rodenbough, Theo. F. (collector and editor). *Uncle Sam's Medal of Honor: Some of the Noble Deeds for Which the Medal has been Awarded, Described by Those Who Have Won It 1861–1886.* G. P. Putnam's Sons, New York, 1886.

Sandoz, Mari. *Cheyenne Autumn.* Avon Books, New York, 1953.

Scott, Douglas D., Richard A. Fox, Jr., Melissa Connor, and Dick Harmon. *Archaeological Perspectives on the Battle of the Little Bighorn.* University of Oklahoma Press, Norman, 1989.

Scott, Douglas D. "A Sharp Little Affair," *Reprints in Anthropology*, Vol. 45, J & L Reprint Company, Lincoln, Nebraska, 1994.

Sharp and Dunnigan. *The Congressional Medal of Honor: The Names, The Deeds.* Sharp and Dunnigan Publications, Forest Ranch, California, 1984.

Shockley, Philip M. *The Trap-Door Springfield in the Service.* Eleventh edition. World-Wide Gun Report, Inc., Aledo, Illinois, 1958.

Smith, P. David. *Ouray: Chief of the Utes.* Wayfinder Press, Ouray, Colorado, 1990.

Sprague, Marshall. *Massacre: the Tragedy at White River.* University of Nebraska Press, Lincoln, 1957.

———. *Colorado: a Bicentennial History.* W. W. Norton & Company, Inc., New York, 1976.

Tallent, Annie D. *Black Hills, or, the Last Hunting Ground of the Dakotas.* A complete history of the Black Hills of Dakota, from their first invasion in 1874 to the present by Annie D. Tallent. Nixon Jones Printing Co., St. Louis, 1899.

Upton, Emory. *Cavalry Tactics: United States Army.* D. Appleton and Company, New York, 1874.

Utley, Robert M. *Frontier Regulars: The United States Army and the Indian 1866–1891.* Macmillan Publishing Co., Inc., New York, 1973.

———. *The Indian Frontier of the American West 1846–1890.* University of New Mexico Press, Albuquerque, 1984.

Van Allen, Leroy C. and A. George Mallis. *Comprehensive Catalog and Encyclopedia of Morgan & Peace Dollars*, 3d ed., DLRC Press, Virginia Beach, Virginia, 1991.

Vaughn, J. W. *With Crook at the Rosebud.* The Stackpole Company, Harrisburg, Pennsylvania, 1956.

———. *The Reynolds Campaign on Powder River.* University of Oklahoma Press, Norman, 1961.

———. *Indian Fights: New Facts on Seven Encounters.* University of Oklahoma Press, Norman, 1966.

Wentworth, Edward Norris. *America's Sheep Trails.* Iowa State College Press, Ames, Iowa, 1948.

Werner, Fred H. *Meeker—The Story of the Meeker Massacre and Thornburgh Battle September 29, 1879.* Werner Publications, Greeley, Colorado, 1985.

Yeoman, R. S. *A Guidebook of United States Coins*, 43rd Edition, 1990. Western Publishing Company, Inc., Racine, Wisconsin, 1989.

Young, Kenneth Ray. *The General's General: the Life and Times of Arthur MacArthur.* Westview Press, Boulder, Colorado, 1994.

Index

Pages with photos appear in italics

Acari, 69, 87
Adams, Charles, 156, 175
Ahu-u-tu-pu-wit, 156
Alamosa Gulch, 28
Aldrich Lakes, 95
Ammunition, 15, 36, 46, 47, 67–68
Amos, Preston, 183
Annuity goods, 9
Archaeology, xii–xiii
Augisley, John, 43
Augur, Jacob, 141

Bagg's crossing, 132
Bailey, Edward L., 128
Baker, Jim, *116(fig.18), 124(fig.26)*, 129–30, 132
"The Barricade Constructed Between the Two Bluffs Occupied by the Indians," *120(fig. 22)*
Bear River, 7, 132, 193
Beaver Creek, 42
Beaver Springs, 56, 95
Beecher Island, x, 10
"Behind the Breastworks" (Remington), *121(fig. 23)*
Big Horn and Yellowstone Expedition, x, 17, 21, 125, 157
Bisbee, William H., 13, 14, 15, 25, 90, 102, 187
Black Hills, 19
Blake, F. E., 53
Bland-Allison Act, 4
Boardman, W. P., xii
Booth, Joseph, 201
Bourke, John G., 16, 171
Brackett, Albert G., 21

Brady, Joseph W., 137, 138, 139, 156, 199
Breastworks, 85, 95, 220(n62)
Brennan, John, 185
Brigham, J. H., 141
Brock, Solomon, 128
Bronson, Colonel, 16, 19
Browne, Edward H., 129
Brunot Treaty, 3
Brush Creek, 8
Bryant, Major, 203
Buffalo Soldiers. *See* Company D, Ninth Cavalry; Ninth Cavalry
Bullwhacker Jack, 72
Bummer Jim, 42, 43, 194
Burials, 141, 226(n71)
Burns, John, 76, 153, 219(n44), 221(n99)
Burton, Henry, 201

Camp Carlin, 128, 173
Camp Sheridan, 12
Canalla; Canavish. *See* Johnson
"Captain Dodge's Troopers to the Rescue" (Remington), *122(fig. 24)*
Carpenter, Clarence, 64, 66, 186, 201
Carroll, J. M.: *The Indian Wars Campaign Medal: Its History And Its Recipients*, 188
Cass, Oscar, 62, 174
Casualties, 154; army and civilian, 62, 64, 75, 76, 171–75, 178–80, 203–5, 221–22(n104); livestock, 76, 78, 97–99, 100–101, 176–77; Ute, 69, 78, 87, 175–76
Catolowop, 176

Ca-tol-seu, 176
Cat-su-atz, 176
Certificates of Merit, 185–87
Charlie (Charley), 101, 156
Cherry, Samuel A., 17, 18, 24, 33, 36, 38, 40, 43, 45, 46, 48, 55, 56, 157, 171, 182, 185, 200; casualty list of, 203–5; death of, 151–52; at Milk Creek, 57–60, 61–62, 67, 68, 80–81, 88, 139–40, 142, 147, 153, 194, 195, 196, 197, 202
Cheyenne Daily Leader (newspaper), 24, 140, 173
Chicago Times (newspaper), xii
Chicago Tribune (newspaper), xii, 130, 172
"Chief Who Shoots The Stars." *See* Thornburgh, Thomas Tipton
Chinaman, 37
Chipeta, 156–57
Chu-ca-watz, 176
Citations for bravery, 189–91; Certificates of Merit, 185–87; Medals of Honor, 181–84; War Department, 187–88
Civilians, 19, 166, 167, 171, 172, 174, 175
Clark, Charles, 186, 201
Clark, Ed, 91
Coal Creek, Coal Creek Canyon, 42, 48, 49
Cojo, 101
Colby, Fred A., 18
Collum, Joe, 46
Colorado, 2–3, 4, 158
Colorow, 2, 5, 42, 47, 57, *108(fig. 6)*, 156, 158–59, 176; meeting with, 43, 44–45, 194, 202; at Milk Creek, 60, 61, 68–69, 81, 85, 87–88, 100, 102
Combs, Kendrick B., 186, 187, 201
Commerce, 19
Commission of inquiry, 156
Committee on Indian Affairs hearing, 156–57, 159
Company A, Fifth Cavalry, 127
Company B, Fifth Cavalry, 127

Company B, Fourth Infantry, 128
Company C, Fourth Infantry, 128
Company D, Fifth Cavalry, 17, 20, 24, 25, 78, 127, 163, 175, 182–83, 193; at Milk Creek, 75, 76, 80(map), 100, 195, 203
Company D, Ninth Cavalry, 91, 92, 97, 99, 167, 174, 183–184, 198, 203
Company E, Fourth Infantry, 13, 14, 21, 33, 89, 165, 193
Company E, Third Cavalry, 13, 14, 21, 24, 30, 53, 56, 57, 149, 162, 175, 176, 184, 185–86, 193; at Milk Creek, 59, 63, 75, 80(map), 195, 196, 202, 203
Company F, Fifth Cavalry, 17, 20, 24, 53, 57, 58, 78, 127, 164, 175, 181, 185, 186, 193; at Milk Creek, 62, 63, 66, 68, 76, 80(map), 82(map), 87, 153, 154, 194–95, 198, 202, 203
Company F, Fourth Infantry, 129
Company H, Fourth Infantry, 13, 14, 24, 185
Company I, Fifth Cavalry, 127
Company I, Fourth Infantry, 127, 128
Company I, Third Cavalry, 142
Company K, Third Cavalry, 14
Company M, Fifth Cavalry, 127
Company M, Third Cavalry, 14
Compton, Charles E., 130, 132
Conway, James, 172
Cooke, Philip St. George, 127
Cooper, Joseph A., 11
Correspondents, x, xii, 85, 130
Costigan, John, 25, 152, 153
Couriers, 78–79, 88–92, 182, 197
Cow Creek, 130
Craig, William, 201
Cre-pah, 156
Crook, George, xi, xii, 6, 8, 10, 11, 12, 13, 15, 16, 17, 21, 77, 148; and Chief Jack, 37, 61, 157
Crowley, John, 186
Cuff, Dominick, 75, 203

Danforth, E. H., 4
Davis, John C., 53, 61, 66, 95, *116 (fig. 17)*, 155, 172, 175, 203, 208–9
Dawson, Thomas F., 85, 142, 143
"Death of Major Thornburgh While Leading a Charge to Secure the Wagon Train," *118(fig. 20)*
Deer Creek, 46–47, 53, 194
Denver Tribune (newspaper), xii, 172
Department of the Interior, ix, 5
Department of the Missouri, 5–6, 148
Department of the Platte, 6, 148
Dillon, Malachi W., 141
Distinguished Service Medals, 187
Dodge, Francis S., 70, 77, 91, 92, 95, 136, 143, 149, 184, 188, 201; and relief expedition, 96–97, 99, 198, 202–3, 206–7
Dogs, 88
Dolan, John, 64, 65, 73
Donovan, John (James), 67, 68, 173, 187, 201, 220(n66)
Douglas (Quinkent), 2, 5, 57, 71, 87, 99, *106(fig. 3)*, 156, 157
Dresser, Frank, 143
Dresser, Harry, 143
Dry Cow Creek, 30
Duffy, Tom, 132
Dyer, John C., xii, 130
Dunn, Jimmy, 91

Eakle, Samuel P., 186, 201
Eaton, George, 143
Ebenezer, 156
Economy, 3–4
Edison, Thomas, 100
Eichwurzel (Evershell), Charles F., 74, 75, 174, 201
Elk Head Creek, 35
Emmitt, Robert, 102; *The Last War Trail*, 69, 136
Equipage, 14–15
Eskridge, Wilmer, 42, 43, 46, 49, 72, 143, 194

Esser, William, 87, 95, 222(n10)
Eyewitness accounts, x–xi

Fairfield, Sam, 155
Farming, 5
Fetterman massacre, 90
Fifth Cavalry, 16, 17, 18, 25, 127–28, 163, 164, 176; citations for bravery in, 181–83, 185–86. *See also by company*
Fifth Cavalry Field Staff and Band, 128
"Fighting for Water" (Zogbaum), *123 (fig. 25)*
Finerty, John F., xii, 150
Fires, 6, 8, 53, 74–75, 84, 194
Firestone, Michael, 62, 68, 141, 153, 186, 219(n44)
Forced march, 127; of relief expedition, 130–36
Fort D. A. Russell, 17, 20, 25, 125, 127, 168
Fort Fred Steele, ix, 6, 11, 90, 102, 151; expedition preparations at, 20–22; men and equipment at, 13–15, 25
Fortification Creek, xiii, 25, 30, 32, 103, 193; relief expedition on, 132, 133, 206; supply camp on, 33, 34, 89, 215(n7)
Fort Leavenworth, 6, 157
Fort Lewis, 91
Fort McKinney, 14
Fort Sanders, 128–29, 168–69
Fort Washakie, 158
Fourth Infantry Regiment, 11, 25, 127, 128–29, 136, 165, 185–86. *See also by Company*
France, James, 9, 19
Freiscatte, 42
French Creek, 8
Fulk, Henry, 201

Galbraith, Robert M., 90
Gibbs, James T., 173, 201
Glasseye, 37
Gleim, Albert F., 185

Goldstein, Carl, 19, 143
Gordon, George, 19, 40, 91, 134, 141
Gordon, John, 19, 55, 61, 71, 75, 78, 80, 83, 88, 91, 92, 96, 175, 197, 198, 206, 207
Grand River band, 2, 9
Grant, Ulysses S., 17
Greeley, Horace, 5
Grimes, Edward P., 67, 68, *113(fig. 11)*, 181–82, 201
Grimes, Robert, 21, 24, 66, 73, 98, 139, 140, 142, 187, 198, 200, 226(n62)
Guard camp, Ute, 42
Guides, 27–28

Hagerman, Samuel W., 24, 186–87, 218(n16)
Hamilton, Mr., 72
Hansen, Marcus, 172
Harrah ranch, 90
Hart, Jesse B., 201
Hart Gulch, 46
Hatch, Edward, 156
Hayden Valley, 91
Hayt, E. A., 8, 9, 10, 12, 157
Headquarters party, 30
Hearings: congressional, 156–57
Heeney, Nicholas W., 173, 174
Henry, Columbus, 47
Henry, Guy V., 157
Henry Jim, 42, 43, 46, 101, 156, 194
Hewitt's (Hulett's) ranch, 39(map), 40, 89
Hickman, James, 74, 187–88
Hogan, Michael, 100
Hogan, Thomas (L'Near Rumsey), 186, 187
Hornbeck, Mr., 72
Horse races, 5
Horses, 75; care for, 126, 131; as casualties, 76, 97–99, 101–2, 176, 203, 222(n106)
Howband, Carver, 128
Hughes, Lieutenant, 198, 201
Hugus, J. W., 8, 53, 155, 175

Hugus, W. B., 8
Humme, Paul, 128
Hunter, Frank, 201, 203
Ignacio, 2
Iles, Thomas, 35, 92
Iles ranch, 91, 92, 133
Indian Territory, 4, 12
Indian Wars Campaign Medals, 188, 191
Indian Wars Campaign Medal: Its History And Its Recipients, The (Carroll), 188
Innayuirque, 42

Jack, Chief, Captain (Nicaagat; Ute John), 2, 5, 34, 35, 40, 42, 57, 65, 101, *107(fig. 5)*, 137, 138, 149, 156–58, 193, 219(n39); on casualties, 175–76; meeting with Thornburgh, 36–38, 193–94; at Milk Creek, 60–61, 87, 99, 100, 147
Jeffway Gulch, 40, 42
Johnny, 156
Johnson (Canalla; Canavish), 10, 37, 57, 69, 98, 101, *106(fig. 3)*, 145, 156
Johnson, Henry, 100, *114(fig. 13)*, 183
Johnson, Tim, 156

Keon, William, 14
Kimball, James P., 127, 129, 131–32, 133, 136, 139, 140, 141, 143; *A Soldier-Doctor of Our Army*, 141
Klingensmith, Samuel, 186, 187, 201
Kussman, Emil, 73

LaParle, William, 24, 201
Laramie, 20
Last War Trail, The (Emmitt), 69, 136
Lawson, Joseph J., 21, 45, 56–57, 97, *112(fig. 10)*, *121(fig. 23)*, 136, 145, 149, 182, 184, 185, 187, 193, 200; career of, 150–51; at Milk Creek battle, 59, 62, 63, 67–68, 69, 74, 75, 81, 82, 88, 102, 153, 196, 197, 208–9; report of, 201–3, 222(n106)
Lawton, John S., *113(fig. 12)*, 173, 182, 183

Index

Lewis, Thomas, 186, 187
Lewis, William, 56
Lindneux, Robert: "The Thornburgh Battle With the Utes on Milk Creek," *119(fig. 21)*
Lisco, Bill, 133
Lithgow, Mr., 92, 207
Little Beaver Creek, 60
Livestock: care for, 126, 131; as casualties, 76, 78, 97–99, 100–101, 176–77
Locke, Thomas, 152
Los Piños Agency, 2, 156
Lovering, Leonard A., 128
Lowry, Charles Grafton, 33, 34, 47, 50–51, 56, 75, 76, 139, 153, 171–72, 199
Lupton, Allen, 201, 203
Lynch, Michael, 76
Lynch, Thomas, 173

McAndrews, John, 130
McCann, D. J., 9
McCarger, Al, 19, 40, 86, 91
McCauley, C.A.H., 28, 30, 32, 39, 40, 214(n40)
MacClellan, Val: *This Is Our Land*, 130
McCrary, George, 10
McDonald, John, 56, 186, 201
McGuire, Thomas, 75
McKee, Samuel, 75
MacKenzie, Ranald, 158
McKernin, Sergeant, 201
McKinstry, William, 40, 66, 199
McNamara, Thomas, 186
Madsen, Chris, 134, 141
Mahoney (Maloney), John, *115(fig. 13)*, 152, 175, 185, 186, 203
Marshall, S.L.A., 145
Marshall, William J., 201
Massacre: The Tragedy at White River (Sprague), 24–25, 34, 45, 140, 188, 213–14(n39)
Matthews, Edward A., 142
Medals of Honor, 68, 100, 181–84
Meeker, A.D., 156

Meeker, Josephine, 156, 211(n4)
Meeker, Nathan C., x, 1, 4, 27, 38, 40, 70, *107(fig. 4)*, 145–46; and Chief Jack, 36–37; and correspondence with Thornburgh, 33–34, 43–44, 45–46, 47, 49–51, 71–72, 194, 216(n38), 221(n78); death of, 74, 87, 143; requests to army by, 5, 6, 7, 8, 9, 10, 13
Meeker Herald (newspaper), 152, 154
Mellen, Sandy, 92, 96, 139
Merrill, John, 181, 182
Merritt, Wesley, x, 17, *124(fig. 26)*, 136, 139, 142, 143, 146, 154, 155–56; relief expedition under, 125–35, 148, 168–69, 198, 201, 203, 207
Military Division of the Missouri, 5
Military presence: Meeker's request for, 5, 6, 7, 8, 9, 10, 13; Ute opposition to, 35, 40, 43–44, 47, 48, 60, 71, 146
Milk Creek, ix, x, xii, xii–xiii, 37, 41(map), 47, 48, 49; battle at, 59–80, 146–48, 194–99, 208–9; illustrations of, *117–20(figs. 19–22)*; maps of battle at, 80–84; new campground at, 141–42; parleying at, 138–39; relief columns at, 96–99, 135–37; siege at, 85–88, 92–93, 95, 100, 125, 222(n3); visits to, 152–55; White River Expedition at, 54–58
Milk Creek Valley, 42, *105(figs. 1–2)*
Miller, Amos D., 62, 68, 141, 153, 219(n44), 221(n99)
Mining, 3, 4, 6
Mitchell, Willard W., 61
Moffat County, 54
Montgomery, James, 175, 201, 203
Monument, 154, 155
Moody Creek, 46
Mooney, Thomas, 75
Moore, Alexander, 17
Moore, Julius, 19, 143
Moore, Tom, 128, 129
Moquin, George, 78, 88, 91, 181, 182, 201

246 Index

Morapos Creek, 53, 89
Morapos Trail, 89, 91, 92
Morgan, Mr., 103
Morgan, George T., 4
Morrow, Stanley J., *112(fig. 10)*, 149
Morton, Private, 201
Muddy Creek, 28, 30
Murphy, Mr., 25, 26
Murphy, Edward F., 78, 88, 91, 182, 201
Nebraska, 11–12
Neurohr, Joseph, 67, 68, 201, 202
New York Herald (newspaper), xii, 172
New York World (newspaper), xii, 130
Nicaagat. *See* Jack, Chief
Nicholas, J. H., 174
Ninth Cavalry, 91, 92, 97, 98, 100, 154, 167, 174, 176, 183–84
Nolan, Tom, 65, 66, 201

Official reports, 149; Dodge's, 206–7; Payne's, 193–99
Omaha, 172
Omaha Barracks, 90
O'Malley, Private, 24, 56
Ouray, 2, *110(fig. 8)*, 137, 156–57, 158, 175

Paddock, James V. S., 17, 20–21, 61, 151, 185, 187, 193, 200; at Milk Creek, 64, 66, 83, 198, 202
Pa-ger, 176
Pah-wintz, 176
Paruitz, 156
Pasone (Big Belly), 156
Pat-soock, 176
Patterson, Eugene A., 186; visit to Milk Creek by, 152–55
Patterson, Joseph (James), 98–99, 173, 186, 201
Pauvit'z, 99
Payne, J. Scott, xii, 17, 25, 43, 45, 53, 58, 101, *111(fig. 9), 120(fig. 22)*, 129, 149, 157, 185, 188, 217(n8); on casualties, 171–72, 174–75, 198; in command, 68, 69, 73, 76–78; on Deer Creek, 46–47; General Orders from, 199–201; at Milk Creek, 54–55, 57, 59, 62, 63–64, 66–67, 68, 75, 81, 82, 83, 84, 88, 135, 143, 147, 148, 186, 202, 208; official report of, 193–99; strategy of, 48–49, 56, 59; *The United Service,* xi
Peck's store, 35–36, 38, 39(map), 40
Pennock, Taylor, 8, 28
Perkins, Henry, 98–99
Perkin's Store, 46
Peterson, Walter, 173
Philipsen, Wilhelm O., 182, 183, 188
Phillips, John "Portugee," 90
Piah, 100, 101
Pitkin, F. W., 10, 157
Platte River, 12
Poh-neh-atz, 176
Polchow, Mr., 20, 26
Pope, John, 148
Poppe, John A., 68, 74–75, 181, 182, 196, 201
Post, William, H., 143
Pourtave, 42
Pou-shun-lo, 176
Pou-witz, 176
Powder River, 17
Powell Valley, 5, 37
Price, Butler D., xiii, 21–22, 33, 77, 92, 103, 132, 188, 193, 206, 214(n40); messages from, 89, 90, 223(n27)
Price, Shadrack A., 143
Price, Mrs. S. F, 156

Quinkent. *See* Douglas
Quinn, Thomas F., 128

Rankin, Joe P., 36, 45, 55, 56, 58, *115(fig. 16)*, 146, 155, 173, 175, 198, 213–214(n39); as courier, 88–90; as guide, 27–28, 218(n15); at Milk Creek, 65, 66, 74, 78, 143, 194; and relief expedition, 129, 130, 132, 134
Rankin, M. Wilson, 132–133, 136, 187

Index 247

Rawlins, John A., 27
Rawlins, xii, 25–26, 27, 90, 103, 128, 129, 148
Red Cloud, 12
Relief expeditions, xii, 90, 92, 198, 201, 202–3; Dodge's, 96–99, 206–7; Merritt's, 125–36, 148
"Relief of Payne's Command–The Trumpet Signal, The" (Zogbaum), *124(fig. 26)*
Remington, Frederic: "Behind the Breastworks," *121(fig. 23)*; "Captain Dodge's Troopers to the Rescue," *122(fig. 24)*
Reservation system, 9
Retreat: army, 67–69
Reynolds Campaign, 17, 21
Richardson, S. W., 129
Rio Blanco County, 54
Roach, Hampton, 76–77, 181, 182, 201
Road: to White River Agency, 28, 30, 35, 39(map), 40, 42, 55
Robinson, Henry E., 129
Rock Creek, 15, 16, 19, 151
Rodenbough, Theodore, 183; *Uncle Sam's Medal of Honor Winners*, 73
Rodney, Mr., 172
Rosebud, battle of, 21
Royall, William B., 151
Ryan, B. T., 8

Sanders, Robin, 174
San Juan Mountains, 3
Sapavanero, 137
Saponise, 102
Sarvisberry Draw, 56
Schickedonz, Eugene, 102, 173, 201
Schurz, Carl, 12–13, 156, 175
Secrist, Frank P., 56, 58, 201
Semig, Dr., 102
Separation Creek, 28, 29(map)
Serio, 156
Servick, 71
Sharpe, Private, 201
Shepard, Fred, 143
Sheridan, Philip, 10, 24
Sherman, William Tecumseh, 2, 10, 24, 38, 45
Sherrod, William "Dad," 155
Siege: actions during, 85–88, 95, 100, 125, 222(n3)
Silver, 3, 4
Sioux war, x, 19, 21
Skiff, F.J.V., 85, 142, 143
Skirmish lines, 58–59, 61–63, 67, 147, 195
Slim Buttes battle, 17, 21, *112*, 149–50
Snake River, 7, 103, 130, 148
Snake River Crossing, 30, 89
Snipers, 97–98
Soldier-Doctor of Our Army, A (Kimball), 141
Soldier Wells, 28, 30
Son-ie-er-atz, 176
Sowawick (Sowerick; Saarwick), 34, 35, 36, 40, 99, 100, 156–57, 193
Spencer, James H., 11
Sprague, Marshall: *Massacre: The Tragedy at White River*, 24–25, 34, 36, 45, 140, 188, 213–14(n39)
Spring Gulch, 46
Stampede, 75
Stanley, W. M., 138
Startzell, Alta Evelyn Kirk Holt, 152
Startzell, Amandes M., 30, 56, 58, 62, 63, *114(fig. 14)*, 152, 186
Steiger, Gottleib, 173
Stickney, W. S., 30
Stillson, Jerome B., xii
Stinking Gulch, 91, 134, 141
Stones River campaign, 11
Sugar Creek, 28
Sulphur Springs ranch, 90
Sulphur Springs Stage Station, 28
Summers, John E., 69–70
Supplies, 14, 77, 125, 129; medical, 69–70; Ute capture of, 142–43; White River Agency, 40, 86–87
Supply camp, 33, 34, 132, 215(n7)
Sutcliffe, Trumpeter, 201

Tatit'z (Tah-tiz), 69, 176
Taylor, Eugene, 47
Telegraph message, 89, 90
Tet-putz-sin-iah, 176
Third Cavalry, 13, 162, 185. *See also by Company*
This Is Our Land (MacClellan), 130
Thomas, 156
Thomas, Henry G., 11
Thompson, Arthur L., 143
Thornburgh, George W., 12, 171
Thornburgh, J. M., 11
Thornburgh, Lida, 12, 102
Thornburgh, Thomas T., ix, xii, 24, 27, 55, 56–57, 70, 71, *109(fig. 7), 118(fig. 20)*, 143, 146, 188, 193, 198, 201, 203; career of, 11–12; and Colorow, 44–45; and correspondence with Meeker, 33–34, 43–44, 45–46, 49–51, 71; death of, 64–65, 67, 68, 72, 82, 102, 139–40, 171, 196, 198, 202, 220(n66); expedition preparations, 15–17, 18–20, 21; at Milk Creek, 61, 62, 63, 81, 194, 195, 208; meeting with Utes, 36–38, 202; strategies, 47–49, 58, 59; on Ute movements, 6–8
"Thornburgh Battle With the Utes on Milk Creek, The" (Lindneux), *119(fig. 21)*
Tonwah, 42
Topography: of western Colorado, 2–3
Transportation, 15–16, 18
Treaty of Fort Laramie, 19
Treaty of 1880, 158
Troops, 13–14, 17, 153; action of, 59–84, 85–86, 87, 88, 92–93, 95–99, 100, 101–2, 146–48; casualties among, 171–75; roster of, 161–65, 167–69; strength of, 24–25
Tu-rah, 176
Tu-wu-ick, 176
Twenty-Mile Park, 91, 92

Uah-pa-chatz, 176
Uncle Sam's Medal of Honor Winners (Rodenbough), 73
Unco, 61
Union Pacific Railroad, 1, 8, 11, 27, 128
United Service, The (Payne), xi
U.S. House of Representatives, 156–57, 158
U.S. Military Academy, 11, 17, 18, 21, 24
Unque, 35, 36, 40, 193
Utah, x, 158
Ute John. *See* Jack, Chief
"Ute War–Major Thornburgh's Last Charge, The" (Viele), *117(fig. 19)*
Utes, Ute Nation, ix, 129, 133, 145, 158; casualties, 69, 78, 87, 175–76; leaving reservation, 6–8; at Milk Creek, 57–61, 62, 63, 64, 67, 68, 72–74, 75–76, 78, 81–84(maps), 86–88, 92–93, 95, 97–98, 99–100, 101–2, 136–38, 146–48, 154; white contact with, 1–2
Ute Reservation, x, 1, 2, 146, 158; white desires for, 4–5; White River Expedition on, 54–57

Valois, Gustavos, 156
Vaughn, J. W., 150, 151
Vehicles, 15–16
Viele, J.: "The Ute War–Major Thornburgh's Last Charge," *117(fig. 19)*
Volkmar, William J., 17, 20
Von Herrmann, John, 22

Waddel Creek, 46
Wagons, 15–16, 18, 33, 176–77; freight, 40, 55, 72, 74–75, 86–87, 141; at Milk Creek, 61, 63, 64, 66–67, 68–69, 80–84(maps), 148, 197, 220(n62)
Wah-cha-pe-gatz, 176
Wa-pa-qua, 176
War Department, ix, 5–6; medals awarded by, 187–88

Wash, 156
Water detail, 76–77, 87, 100, 182
Wattsconavot, 176
Wausitz (Antelope), 156
Wa-wa-gutz, 176
Weapons, 15, 72, 137, 147, 155
Weber, Emil, 54
Webster, George O., 128
Weit, William B., 128
Western expansion, 3–4
West Point, 11, 17, 18, 21, 24
Whitbeck, Lut, 201
White River Agency, ix, 1, 2, 9, 38, 47, 143; destruction of, 74, 156, 211(n4); Indians from, 6, 7; representatives from, 42–43
White River Expedition, ix, x–xii, xii, 143; movements of, 22–24, 26, 28–35, 40–42, 46–47, 48–49, 53–57; organization of, 13–22; return of, 148–49; strength of, 24–25; troops of, 161–65
White River Ute Commission, 151

Widmer, Jacob, 182–83
Williams Fork Valley, 40, 42, 44–45, 46, 133, 194, 202
Wilson, Black, 46, 60
Wind River Reservation, 157–58
Wolf, Silas A., 24, 53, 61, 66, 151, 188, 200
Wright, Charles, 76

Yaminatz, 87
Yampa band, 2, 9
Yampa River Valley, 35, 39(map), 40, 89, 91–92, 133
Yan-cap, 176
Yanco, 156, 219(n38)
Yellowjacket Pass, 56
Young Man Afraid of His Horse, 12

Zogbaum, R. F.: "Fighting for Water," *123(fig. 25)*; "The Relief of Payne's Command–The Trumpet Signal," *124(fig. 26)*